Legal Theory Today

Legal Norms and Normativity

Legal Theory Today

Founding Editor
John Gardner, Professor of Jurisprudence,
University College, Oxford

TITLES IN THIS SERIES

Law in its Own Right by Henrik Palmer Olsen and Stuart
Toddington
Law and Aesthetics by Adam Gearey
Law as a Social Institution by Hamish Ross
Evaluation and Legal Theory by Julie Dickson
Risks and Legal Theory by Jenny Steele
A Sociology of Jurisprudence by Richard Nobles and David Schiff
Costs and Cautionary Tales: Economic Insights for the Law by
Anthony Ogus

Forthcoming titles:

Law after Modernity by Sionaidh Douglas-Scott
Law and Ethics by John Tasioulas
Law and Human Need by John Stanton-Ife

Legal Norms and Normativity

An Essay in Genealogy

Sylvie Delacroix

·HART·
PUBLISHING

OXFORD AND PORTLAND, OREGON
2006

Published in North America (US and Canada) by
Hart Publishing
c/o International Specialized Book Services
920 NE 58th Avenue, Suite 300
Portland, OR 97213-3786
USA
Tel: +1 503 287 3093 or toll-free: (1) 800 944 6190
Fax: +1 503 280 8832
Email: orders@isbs.com
Website: www.isbs.com

Hart Publishing, 16C Worcester Place, Oxford, OX1 2JW
Telephone: +44 (0)1865 517530 Fax: +44 (0) 1865 510710
Email: mail@hartpub.co.uk
Website: http://www.hartpub.co.uk

British Library Cataloguing in Publication Data
Data Available

ISBN-13: 978-1-84113-455-0 (hardback)
ISBN-10: 1-84113-455-4 (hardback)

Typeset by Compuscript, Shannon
Printed and bound in Great Britain by
TJ International Ltd, Padstow, Cornwall

Acknowledgements

Among all the people who had to put up with the string of end-less questions which this book is made of, Nigel Simmonds had to be particularly patient: when I first started working on these ideas, I was a young PhD student heavily influenced by all sorts of 'Francophile non-sense', fascinated by the impossible 'foundation' of law etc. While I happily take full responsibility for remaining traces of such 'non-sense', I am grateful to him for introducing me to the world of Anglo-Saxon jurisprudence. This early, PhD phase of my work was notably made possible by a Knox scholarship from Trinity College, as well as continuing support from the PFPB.

My later, 'genealogical' move was triggered by a suggestion made in passing by Simon Blackburn during some pre-dinner drinks at Trinity (my dislike for such 'drinks' has since had to be moderated), which supported my work through a one year 'Rouse Ball' post-doctoral award. Certain people deserve special mention at this stage: while Thomas Berns sparked off my interest in Montaigne, Stanley L Paulson's careful reading of my analysis of Kelsen allowed me to clarify my views.

Many friends also played a crucial part in keeping me 'awake', restoring my enthusiasm when it was fading. From this perspective, the incredible year I spent at the Radcliffe Institute for Advanced Study in 2004-05 was the key ingredient to the successful completion of this book. The warmth of the fellowship and the quality of the friendships I found there have transformed my work and the way I work. While Mary Lum and Tarik O'Regan provided late night 'conversation windows', more serious day-time discussions with Sari Nusseibeh about the concept of State, action, identity, Palestine, normativity and the value of life in general (including trees) taught me a lot. I am particularly indebted to Kelly Heuer and Nomnso Kalu for the quality of their research assistance.

There is also one person — Chris Pickard — whose help cannot be summarised in a pretty formula. So I will leave it just like that.

Some sections of chapters 1 and 2 appeared previously in 'Montaigne's inquiry into the sources of normativity' (2003) 16 *The Canadian Journal of Law and Jurisprudence*, 271-286 and in 'Hart's and Kelsen's conceptions of normativity contrasted' (2004) 17 *Ratio Iuris*, 501-520 (© [2004] [copyright owner as specified in the journal]). I thank *The Canadian Journal of Law and Jurisprudence* and *Ratio Iuris* for permission to use this material.

Contents

Introduction

The question which drives the story I am about to tell is not one that lawyers like to think about: how are we able to give ourselves laws? This story could be a boring one. Laws are made by men and women, and the fact that we have had them for so long proves that we are able to create them. There is, however, something about law that makes this answer less straightforward than it seems: as a social artefact, law is also meant to *bind* us. The association of these two features is at the root of a pervasive concern for those endeavouring to account for law's nature: how can law bind us, if it is contingent upon the changing wills and desires of whoever happens to hold political power? Underlying this concern is the idea that law's claim to bindingness is only viable if some form of necessity can commend law as a desirable framework for the organisation of our society. And where would we find such 'commending necessity' if men and women are the exclusive authors, without any other guarantor, of their own laws? What kind of authority would these laws have, which would be at the mercy of a change of will from their subjects (and authors)?[1]

In the Middle Ages, the dominant natural law model provided a convenient answer to this question. However random they may have seemed, our lawmaking practices were claimed to be driven by a higher order of necessity (whether God's or Nature's) reflected in natural laws. As an order independent from and given to us, natural laws allowed lawmakers to overcome the apparent arbitrariness of their practices, and place them under the 'guarantee' of God's will or Nature. When

[1] See GA Cohen 1996, 167.

Introduction

Montaigne began to question our knowledge of natural laws, however, the contingency of lawmaking practices was exposed in a new, more worrisome light. In the 16th century, Montaigne became the first modern figure to voice a question that still haunts contemporary philosophers: how can law have the authority it claims to have, and bind us, if it emerges from social practices whose sole necessity is to address the contingent needs and desires of a certain group of people, more or less representative of the rest of the population?

Montaigne was not only the first modern exponent of this question, he also inaugurated a way of ultimately circumventing it. The contingency characterising lawmaking practices was deemed too shameful, too disproportionate, in relation to law's 'grand' authority: its purported bindingness. So Montaigne invited us to proceed *as if* any inquiry into the context of social interaction giving rise to law were irrelevant to accounting for its normative dimension.[2] This separation, rather than combination, of law's normative and social aspects into two distinct explanatory targets is one of the central characteristics of 20th-century legal positivism. It allowed both Kelsen and Hart to provide an account of law's normative dimension that remained free from the difficulties many philosophers encounter today when reflecting on the concept of normativity. But what exactly is meant by 'normativity'? As a concept that is pervasively used by philosophers in disparate fields, it is deceptively difficult to define, yet much depends on how one defines it.

Broadly speaking, 'normativity' is a convenient word to use whenever one wants to refer to that part of our experience which is not the immediate result of what lies *in* the world, but, on the contrary, somehow makes claims on how the world *ought* to be. Referring to Christine Korsgaard's evocative formulation, one can maintain that the world of normativity covers all those ideas 'that outstrip the world we experience and seem to call it

---

[2] For a full elaboration of Montaigne's strategy in relation to law's normativity, see chapter 1.

into question, to render judgment on it, to say that it does not measure up, that it is not what it ought to be'.[3] From a concept such as equality (leading me to deem these two sticks I hold in my hand to be unequal) to the rules of a game I have just invented, or to the most complex tax laws, all these ideas or rules can be said to be normative in that they are not part of the *actual* world, the world of matter, but instead claim to influence or dictate how certain things or certain matters should be.[4]

From this general perspective, the term 'normative' can be applied to a vast range of statements making some kind of claim on our conduct or judgement. Now, most of these statements formulated in terms of 'ought' do not normally require much philosophical attention. The instructions of a culinary recipe may puzzle you, but deep philosophical reflection about the normative nature of these instructions is not likely to be helpful and may leave you even more puzzled. The obligation to care for one's elderly parents, on the other hand, or the injunction to pay one's taxes, differ from the instructions of a culinary recipe in that they both belong to a system of rules which, in order to exist as a system, needs to be minimally successful in the claims it makes. If none of the rules constituting a legal system were ever respected, we would not talk of law anymore. The same applies to morality: if none of its rules ever *had* a claim on our conduct, we would not be speaking of morality. An essential part of our understanding of law or morality consists in their being *normative* in a sense that differs from the mere grammatical formulation in terms of 'ought'. Legal and moral rules indeed have, or at least seek to have, a *vindicated* claim on our conduct or judgement. When Christine Korsgaard argues that 'the problems of philosophy always or at least very

[3] See CM Korsgaard 1996, 1.

[4] In order, for instance, for the sticks to be equal, they should fit my concept of equality. In order for your behaviour to be part of the game I have invented, it should abide by the rules I have set.

often take the form of trying to understand why some purported normative claim really is normative',[5] she may be pointing towards precisely that distinction between grammatical 'oughts' or 'purported normative claims' on one hand, and successful, vindicated normative claims on the other hand.[6]

In legal theory, this distinction is worth keeping in mind as the same word 'normative' is alternatively (and often indiscriminately) used to either describe the fact that law must be 'capable of being used for guidance'[7] or to refer to the fact that law's requirements must be deemed obligatory by at least part of the population. In the former use of the term 'normative', law's normative dimension is just a feature inherent to its prescriptive character: the advert enjoining one to wear the latest design of pink hats does not differ in any fundamental way from the legal requirement to pay one's taxes: they are both capable of being used for guidance. Defining law's normative dimension by reference to its *obligatory* character, in contrast, restricts the domain of the normative to only those ought statements that have somehow succeeded in being considered binding. This domain restriction requires developing some story, explaining what may or does condition the success of law's purported normative claim.

At a systemic level, this story is often associated with the concept of *authority*. Among the set of standards claiming to dictate

[5] CM Korsgaard 2003a, 51.

[6] According to Korsgaard, an essential task in accounting for the normative status of morality hence consists in explaining what makes a purported moral claim successfully normative. Among those possible explanations, the realist model holds that 'moral claims are normative if they are true, and true if there are intrinsically normative entities or facts which they correctly describe'. According to some Neo-Kantians, by contrast, 'the capacity for self-conscious reflection about our own actions confers on us a kind of authority over ourselves, and it is this authority which gives normativity to moral claims' (CM Korsgaard 1996, 19–20).

[7] This use of the term 'normative' is notably supported by John Gardner, who argues: 'to show that the law is normative, it is only necessary to show that it is capable of being used for guidance. If some people use it for guidance, then obviously it is capable of being used for guidance, and it is normative' (J Gardner, correspondence).

how we should live, law singles out a certain number of them as endowed with a special status requiring us to grant them *a priori* authority. This claim to *a priori* authority is only likely to succeed if law is perceived as generally promoting a certain set of interests, whether they be prudential or moral.[8]

At an individual level (considering the person confronted daily with a set of conflicting standards among which some are legal) the story is often told in terms of *reasons for action*. If the reasons law provides are 'strong enough',[9] then one may hold that the law obligates us to act in a certain way. Now, a growing number of philosophers have expressed scepticism as to the fruitfulness of an account of normativity that relies exclusively[10] on the concept of reason: 'Nobody denies that the notion of a reason is central to that of normativity. The question is whether we need more than that — whether the whole story of the normative can be told in terms of this one notion'.[11] As it emerges from the story I am about to develop, the concept of legal normativity does need more than 'reasons' to be accounted for.

The key to explaining law's normative dimension lies in articulating the gap between the two 'levels' at which one may pitch one's definition of normativity: guidance or obligation. When

---

[8] The perception of the set of interests that law is deemed to promote may vary among the population without necessarily hindering law's claim to authority: a law against littering may to one person promote environmental friendliness, while to another it seems primarily concerned with aesthetic value. On a global scale, this divergent understanding of law's purposes may be deemed the feeding ground of a democratic legal system, contributing to the maintenance of an ongoing assessment of law's alleged purposes.

[9] Unsurprisingly, accounts diverge widely when it comes to defining what is to be counted as 'strong enough'. Some authors, like Raz, insist that the reasons law provides need not be conclusive — i.e. acted upon — in order to be characterised as giving rise to an obligation: as long as those reasons are content-independent and preemptive, they are 'strong enough'.

[10] 'The normativity of all that is normative consists in the way it is, or provides, or is otherwise related to reasons' (J Raz 1999, 67).

[11] J Dancy 2000, at 1. See also: 'Reasons are undoubtedly important, but normativity has other important features, and our preoccupation with reasons distracts us from them' (J Broome 2004, 28).

are the reasons that law provides by virtue of its capacity to guide conduct 'strong enough' to be deemed obligatory? If one is to give any weight to the ideal of civic responsibility, the answer has to be framed in terms of legitimacy: the reasons provided by law are conclusive, and thus gain obligatory force, if law is deemed to promote a set of moral and prudential concerns essential to a 'good' way of living together. Once confronted with the demands of morality or prudence, the reasons provided by law may, for a particular individual at a particular time, fail to give rise to an obligation. This need not rob law of its normative force.

While there is a minimum extent to which law has to succeed in the claims it makes,[12] this need not entail that law always and necessarily has to 'successfully' give rise to an obligation in order to remain normative. Defining legal normativity by merely pointing at law's capacity to guide behaviour will not do. Equating the concepts of obligation and normativity, on the other hand, is equally problematic, as it ignores the way in which the punctual questioning of law's normative force may actually contribute to its renewed vigour. Law's power to bind us is concomitant to a *project* aiming to foster a certain way of living together. This project is in turn bound to change, evolving along the shifting and often conflicting values characterising a pluralist society. Defeating law's normative claim in the name of some moral or prudential concern may, from this perspective, contribute to the ongoing reflection and debate necessary to keep legal normativity 'alive', in touch with the material that first triggered its emergence: the changing demands of morality and prudence.

Note that this story is biased already. Accounting for the success of law's purported normative claim in terms of the capacity we all share to confront law with the aims or values we want it to promote places practical deliberation at the root of law's normativity. For some, such 'subjectification' of legal normativity is

---

[12] If law were to systematically fail to give rise to an obligation, there would indeed be a sense of unease in still considering it to be normative.

akin to crude reductivism: law's capacity to bind us, to impose an obligation upon us, cannot possibly be brought back to subjective value choices. Instead, it has to be explained by reference to some pre-existing natural order whose 'intrinsic' normativity informs and directs our practical deliberation, thus conveniently rescuing it from its apparent arbitrariness. According to the natural law model, the values calling for the emergence and maintenance of a legal system are themselves the instantiation of a higher order eluding human ascendancy.

In the 16th century, Montaigne's challenging our access to such 'higher order' put the *status* of these values in question: instead of getting us closer to the way things are 'meant to be', law's point may be to get us closer to the way *we* want things to be. This fundamental revolution in turn brings up a pervasive difficulty. If law's job is not to approximate a 'natural order of things' independent from and given to us, are we meant to think that we are to be bound by the arbitrary preferences of whoever happens to make the law? The modern revolution[13] asks us to introduce value into the world rather than discovering it there ready-made. Does it hence require us to shake off the enduring 'illusion' that we may rationally solve our disagreements about the values law is meant to promote (and the concomitant illusion that this process of rational argumentation contributes to the 'construction' of law's normativity)? Are we supposed to give up on the possibility of ethical objectivity? My answer to this question is negative; it will be argued for in the process of emphasising the centrality of meta-ethics to jurisprudence.

So my story will be partly historical. It has an underlying agenda: its objective is to defend the possibility of accounting for law's normativity on the basis of a constructivist[14] understanding of moral values. It also has a name: in calling my story a

---

[13] In my story, this 'modern revolution' as it applies to law is associated with a turning point in history: the 28 June 1593 decision by the Paris Parliament to uphold the devolution law which designated Henri de Bourbon as the legitimate heir to the throne. Find out why in section 5.1.3.

[14] For a definition of the 'constructivist' position, see pp 11–12 and pp 83–84.

'genealogy', I connect it to a method whose confused meaning and history exposes one's reader to all sorts of misunderstandings. In my effort to explain what enables law's normative dimension, my allegiance to such a murky methodology has proven its worth. Let me briefly show you why.

To come back to the theme I suggested initially, this book breaks away from the tradition Montaigne inaugurated, and endeavours to account for law's nature in a way that *integrates* in one story the social and normative aspects of law. It would be foolish to claim exclusivity, or even originality, in that endeavour. If anything distinguishes this book, it is the attempt to import into the theory of legal normativity a method which Williams has brilliantly developed in relation to the concept of truthfulness. In *Truth and Truthfulness*, Williams constructs a narrative explaining how truthfulness, as a cultural phenomenon, came about. The method he uses in doing so, which he calls a 'genealogy', 'is a descendant of one of Nietzsche's own methods, but only one kind of descendant among others'.[15] The narrative of this book seeks to explain how law, as a normative phenomenon, comes about. Likewise, it relies on what Williams calls a 'genealogy'. Among the many issues raised by this methodological choice, two of them need to be mentioned at the outset.

The first issue pertains to the very aim or ambition of a genealogical project. In its Greek root, the verb *'genealogein'* means 'telling the origins'. Because of the dual meaning of the term 'origins', this idea can be fundamentally misunderstood. On one hand, the term 'origin' can be defined as 'beginning'.

---

[15] '[. . .] in the end he [Nietzsche] not only defends the idea of there being truths but also gives every sign of thinking that he has uttered some. The name 'genealogy' can be appropriated to styles of writing which also descend from Nietzsche, but which, in contrast to him, try to avoid that commitment [. . .] I do not have the problem that some deniers have, of pecking into dust the only tree that will support them, because my genealogical story aims to give a decent pedigree to truth and truthfulness' (B Williams 2002, 18–19).

In this sense, 'to speak of the origin of a phenomenon requires being capable of assigning it a determinate point in a chronology, or an initial stage in an abstract genesis'.[16] On the other hand, the term 'origin' can also be used to point to what causes or enables the existence of a given phenomenon. This is, roughly put,[17] the sense in which a genealogy consists in 'telling the origins'.[18] A genealogical account of legal normativity does not seek to reach some illusory starting point or 'degree zero' of legal norms. The point of a genealogical perspective is actually to overcome the temptation to assign a fixed and determinate grounding to legal normativity. For some people though, this commitment to a non-foundationalist approach to normativity is necessarily associated with a seditious understanding of law and ethics, which brings in the second issue raised by this genealogical undertaking.

A genealogical account of legal normativity need not be, and in this case is not meant to be, subversive. While Williams has already made clear that the nihilistic undertones often associated with the concept of genealogy due to its Nietzschean roots are unwarranted,[19] this genealogical project is still likely to face incrimination on two counts. On one hand, some people simply do not like to see the normative dimension of law traced back to some contingent social practices that nothing seems to be able to raise above their unacceptable arbitrariness. Like Montaigne, it bothers them. At a certain stage, to keep asking questions, to insist on tracking the genesis of some well-established phenomenon — like law — is simply inappropriate. On that count of 'impertinence', I will not be able to provide much of an answer,

---

[16] S Auroux 1990, 1833 (my translation).

[17] This distinction, and the exact sense in which a genealogy consists in 'telling the origins', will be developed in chapter 4.

[18] To reflect this important terminological distinction, the term 'origin' will be used in its historical sense throughout this book, while the term 'source' will be used to cover the logical/causal aspect of the concept of origins.

[19] These nihilistic undertones are the result of a particular, and unnecessary, interpretation of Nietzsche's works. See B Williams 2002, 18–19.

apart from showing that the apparent arbitrariness of lawmaking practices need not be so very threatening for law's grand authority.

There is also another, more serious objection to providing a genealogical account of legal normativity. That objection arises out of the belief in the existence of some values, entities or 'state of affairs' whose normative dimension is claimed to be 'intrinsic':[20] it is not conditional upon human practices and judgements, and cannot be reduced to anything else. These 'intrinsically normative entities' are claimed to exist independently of us and our beliefs, and are meant to be *discovered* rather than constructed by us. While we may, on this view, elaborate various standards or rules in an attempt to implement some of the intrinsic values we have come to acknowledge, normativity is not a phenomenon which we may explain by reference to the way in which it 'comes about':[21] normativity does not 'come about'.

From this realist perspective, the genealogical endeavour to draw legal normativity *from within* human activity is pointless. In focusing all our attention on the unavoidable contingency characterising lawmaking practices, we may be tempted to think that law's normative dimension owes its possibility to the context of social interaction that brings (and keeps) law into being. Wary of such a dire conclusion, Finnis has vehemently expressed his aversion for the genealogical genre, referring to 'Nietzsche or [. . .] others who like him reduce ethics and nor-

---

[20] The metaphysical position this belief embodies — moral realism — has been defined in many ways. In 1971, Simon Blackburn was the first to introduce — and criticise — the specific term 'moral realism', according to which 'the truth of moral utterances is to consist in their correspondence with some fact or state of affairs' (S Blackburn 1993, 111). Recently, in an article devoted to spelling out the contrast between moral constructivism and moral realism, Korsgaard defines moral realism as: 'the view that propositions employing moral concepts may have truth values because moral concepts describe or refer to normative entities or facts that exist independently of those concepts themselves' (CM Korsgaard 2003b, 100).

[21] 'A genealogy is a narrative that tries to explain a cultural phenomenon by describing a way in which it came about, or could have come about, or might be imagined to have come about' (B Williams 2002, 20).

mative political or legal theory to a search for the genealogy, the immediate and deeper historical (perhaps partly or wholly physiological) sources, of ethical, political, or legal standards. These standards have their immediate sources in exercises of the will of charismatic individuals or power-seeking groups, and their deeper sources in the supposedly will-like sub-rational drives and compulsions of domination, submission, resentment, and so forth'.[22] For Finnis, the source of legal standards lies in 'pre-existing, non-posited principles, binding (on legislator and subject alike) independently of any act of legislation'.[23] Without acknowledging those pre-existing principles, all one is left with, according to Finnis, is the sad picture of a lawmaking process characterised by 'sub-rational drives' and 'compulsive' behaviour.

I have chosen to emphasise the rather dramatic terms Finnis employs when considering the possibility of a genealogical outlook to highlight the excessive dualism in which the moral realism/constructivism debate is often framed. While constructivists may sometimes err on the side of caricature in referring only to the most extreme forms of realism as their target,[24] the reverse is also true of the realists themselves. To refer back to Finnis' formulation, the 'sheer acts of will' constituting the law-creating practices do not have to be informed solely by 'sub-rational drives'. They may for instance flow from moral and political concerns that themselves instantiate moral and ethical values. Crucially (for our story), these ethical values do not have to be derived from pre-existing, intrinsically normative entities *à la* Finnis, and may instead be understood as a kind of cultural 'habitation', to borrow Williams' image.[25] Developing as various

[22] J Finnis 2002, 8.

[23] J Finnis 1985, 80.

[24] As a 'milder' alternative to Platonic versions of moral realism, Stélios Virvidakis for instance isolates what he calls an 'anthropocentric realism', according to which 'moral values and properties are real and independent from us, but at the same time invented and produced by us' (S Virvidakis 1996, at 22, my translation). For more developments see section 4.3.

[25] '[. . .] we shall see their judgments as part of their way of living, a cultural artifact they have come to inhabit (though they have not consciously built it)' (B Williams 1985, 147).

social and cultural practices go along, this 'habitation' is not one that is 'consciously built', thus avoiding the *aporia* associated with a voluntarist constructivism, which presents values as emerging out of the *fiat* of human will. Nor does it share any of the traits classically associated with moral realism's heavy metaphysical presuppositions: in Williams' view, the values a society inhabits are not conceived as 'their best approximation of the truth about right and wrong',[26] and are certainly not deemed to be 'independent' of that society's socio-cultural practices.

This is my answer to the second 'issue' raised by the choice of a genealogical method to account for law's normativity: if there is any trace of 'subversion' in my story, it is not in its content or aim, but in the assumption it seeks to denounce. This assumption consists of thinking that the only alternative to a realist understanding of normativity amounts, at best, to some radical voluntarism *à la* Sartre, and, at worst, to some subversive emphasis on all the base aspects of humanity.

This assumption is an old one. It is central to the emphasis on the ineptitude of human judgement when it comes to value commitments. In its Christian formulation, this assumption underlies the doctrine of the Fall: if it weren't for God inspiring excellence within us and the world around us, we would be hopeless. We would have lost the capacity to see the way in which the world, and we in it, can be made better. Particularly prevalent in the Middle Ages, this doctrine contributed to the success of the natural law model. Seen as a body of rules trying to improve the way we live within this world, the job of human, positive law was to try to get us closer to the 'natural' order of things. Of course we would never really get there, but at least we could try, and this aspiration legitimated law's authority. As fallible, short-sighted beings, we had better comply with the demands of positive law if we ever wanted to live a 'good' life, a life closer to the way it is meant to be.

---

[26] CM Korsgaard 2003b, 109.

While this model still has its proponents today, the 'modern revolution' has opened up a way of thinking of values which traces their source to our own social practices, to the capacity we all share to envision a better way of living together, and to commit ourselves to it. My concept of law relies on this constructivist understanding of values, and argues that law's capacity to serve moral ideals is a central property of law, not just a role that law can play or a function that some communities happen to assign to law. Does this make me a 'constructivist natural lawyer'? Considered alongside the distinction between moral constructivism and moral realism, the traditional natural law/positivism dividing line becomes rather unhelpful. If, as Coleman argues, 'what troubles positivists is not the claim that law has some necessary moral property, but the stronger claim that the moral property law necessarily has (or is said to have) is sufficiently strong to warrant an inference from legality to legitimacy',[27] then my account of law should not, from that perspective, 'trouble' any positivist, as I definitely reject such inference from legality to legitimacy.

In other respects, however, my story is meant to ruffle positivists and natural lawyers alike. Legal positivists have traditionally been rather skimpy in accounting for the way in which their model of the context of social interaction giving rise to law may contribute to their explanation of legal normativity.

Montaigne was the first positivist to set aside the challenge raised by the questioning of the natural law model: if our law-making practices cannot call on any other authority than the contingent preferences of our foolish lawmakers, we had better dismiss them as irrelevant to law's normative dimension. My story begins, in the first chapter, by considering how Montaigne rescued law's normativity from the mess of human affairs by postulating a 'law of pure obedience', enjoining man to obey

[27] J Coleman 2001b, 190.

the law 'because it is the law' without asking any further question. In the second and third chapters, I continue with this theme: in very different ways and for different reasons, the two champions of 20th-century legal positivism — Kelsen and Hart — also endeavoured to account for law's normative dimension independently of the context of social interaction giving rise to it.

Kelsen's project was shaped by a heavy methodological dualism, barring him from referring to any factual proposition in his account of legal normativity. He thus set out to account for law's normativity *from within* (as his moral scepticism also prevented him from referring to any moral proposition): the key to a 'pure', autonomous normative sphere lies, according to Kelsen, in the 'Basic Norm'. Formulated as a transcendental presupposition of Kantian inspiration, it conditions the normative interpretation of the 'material that presents itself as law'.

Hart is not, by contrast, overburdened with any such methodological presuppositions. His affinity for JL Austin's method, aimed at elucidating even the most complex concepts by reference to 'the things people do with words', disposes him to thinking that he can account for law's normativity by referring to the 'critical reflective attitude' typically associated with expressions such as 'it is the law that', 'I have an obligation to . . .' etc. The merit of such a method, for Hart, lies in its deflationary effect on any remnant of foundationalism, any temptation to look for the *grounds* of legal normativity. This method also allows him to 'evade' a philosophical difficulty[28] (which has actually resurfaced in more recent debates) concerning the *status* of morality and its relation to human knowledge.

Now one may, certainly, devise a picture of the web of social practices giving rise to law that is absolutely free of any moral element, concentrating strictly on the instrumental functionality of law. It may even be ventured that such a picture 'realistically' describes the process giving rise to law in bleak, marginal cases.

---

[28] HLA Hart 1994, 168.

One cannot, however, understand law's capacity to bind us independently of the project it is meant to serve.[29] While this project can, strictly speaking, be conceived in purely prudential terms, it will typically also involve moral values. In this context, Hart's scepticism about ethical objectivity presents him with the following choice: he may either strip his description of the social practices giving rise to law of any reference to moral elements, or he may resign himself to depicting these practices as driven by values which are actually nothing but the personal preferences of whoever happens to make the law. While this latter scenario would be consistent with his scepticism, Hart prefers to evade the issue of ethical objectivity altogether, opting for the first scenario instead.

It is this attempt to dismiss the possibility of ethical objectivity as irrelevant which has driven 20th-century legal positivists to separate, rather than combine, the social and normative aspects of law into two distinct explanatory targets.[30] Montaigne may have been the only one candid enough to openly admit it. Separated from the natural order traditionally grounding their normative status, the values presiding over the elaboration of law look awfully like the contingent preferences of our foolish lawgivers; hence Montaigne's relegation of law's empirical sources to the domain of the 'mystical': a 'non-discursive' field that stands beyond what can be expressed or inquired about.[31] Kelsen's Neo-Kantian methodological arguments and Hart's mere 'lack of interest' in the practices giving rise to law may all sound very reasonable in comparison to Montaigne's 'mystical' move. Yet in the end they all lead to the same result, for the same reason: safeguarding law's normativity from the contingency of

---

[29] For further development of this see section 5.2.1.

[30] Traditionally, the existence of law is explained by reference to some kind of convention (see section 5.2.1), while its normative dimension is explained in terms of the difference it makes in one's practical deliberation. This explanation of legal normativity, I argue, can only cope with its 'downstream' side, considering the effect it has on people etc., but not what conditions its possibility.

[31] See section 1.2.3.

lawmaking practices, for fear of not being able to find any trace of objectivity within these practices.

Chapters 1, 2 and 3 tackle the various ways in which Montaigne, Kelsen and Hart respectively endeavoured to account for law's normativity *independently* of the context of social interaction giving rise to law. These chapters can be technical at times, and if you'd rather get straight to my story rather than read about all the sad reasons that stopped these authors from developing theirs, ignore the first part of this book and go to the second one, chapters 4 and 5, in which I set forth my 'genealogy' of legal normativity. Its aim is to challenge the axiomatic status of law's normative dimension. My ambition in explaining how legal normativity *comes about* is to renew the understanding of a phenomenon whose possibility is traditionally taken for granted. While the resulting story is nowhere near as caustic as Nietzsche's account of morality, it does criticise legal theory's scant concern for meta-ethics, and rejects the pervasive assumption that the only alternative to a realist understanding of value amounts, at best, to some crude voluntarism, and, at worst, to some subversive emphasis on all the base aspects of humanity. Whether they are lucky enough to believe in the existence of 'intrinsically normative entities' hanging out there or whether they opt for the constructivist route instead, legal positivists and natural lawyers alike need to take a stand:[32] they cannot account for law's normative dimension without delving into the status of morality.

---

[32] Once they have taken such a meta-ethical stand, they may see little point in still calling themselves 'natural lawyers' or 'legal positivists'.

Part I
Recoiling Strategies

1
Montaigne

Montaigne delighted in telling stories. With a particular predilection for those stories taken from ancient authors, Montaigne's *Essays* sketch the intellectual journey of an inquisitive mind. To the many questions that concern him, any dogmatic answer is treated with suspicion. How do we relate to death? What constitutes a love relationship? How can we be bound by laws? Meant to perturb common understandings, often based on misleading appearances, the questions raised by Montaigne aim at unveiling the true nature of things and, maybe more importantly, *our* true nature.

The story that concerns us, whereby Montaigne seeks to shed light on what grounds law's authority, did not have much currency in the 16th century, as the classical natural law model left it little room. Whether they derive from divine will or from an 'intrinsically normative' concept of nature, natural laws are 'obviously normative', self-evidently grounding the authority of positive laws. So there's not much story to tell, except if one begins to question the existence of Natural Laws: 'Philosophers can hardly be serious when they try to introduce certainty into Law by asserting that there are so-called Natural Laws, perpetual and immutable, whose essential characteristic consists in their being imprinted upon the human race. There are said to be three such laws; or four; some say less, some say more: a sign that the mark they bear is as dubious as all the rest'.[1] Brilliantly impertinent, this passage opens the way for a renewed understanding of

---

[1] M de Montaigne 1991, II 12, 653–654.

law's normativity. If it is not rooted in the 'supernatural order' which natural laws are meant to embody, what, if anything, makes law normative? This question takes Montaigne on a perilous path. Before analysing the nature of that 'peril', I will first consider the motives that led Montaigne to distance himself from the classical natural law theories of his time.

1.1 The Turning Point: A Renaissant Interest in the Historicity of Law

One can sketch two fundamentally different ways of tackling the problem of legal normativity. Between the solution that consists in locating the source of legal normativity in a transcendent concept of the Good, and that which essentially relies on human activity in order to account for the emergence and the possibility of binding law, there is a major conceptual gap that cannot be bridged by a single author or over a single period of time. One can nevertheless isolate some elements that would have allowed or facilitated the passage from one conceptual model to the other. From this perspective, the growing interest in the historicity of law[2] that characterised the work of many 16th-century theorists has often been pinned down as a factor that contributed to the break with medieval theological thought. Against the traditional medieval gloss, some authors (commonly referred to as 'legal humanists') denounced the glossators' lack of respect for the original text of the *Corpus Iuris Civile*, which they covered with commentaries upon commentaries.[3] By contrast, the legal humanists emphasised the human character of law, its substance being essentially historical and residing in the words of

[2] Emphasising the historicity of law essentially amounts to underlining the importance of the contingent relationship that exists between any law and a particular epoch, State or regime.

[3] On this subject, see A Tournon 2000 (particularly interesting for the understanding of the link between Montaigne and Alciati, the main figure of the humanist movement).

the text, which had to be preserved and studied as such. Without entering into details of the debate as to whether or not the idea of the historicity of law would truly have been elaborated by legal humanism,[4] the aim of this section is to understand the role played by this emphasis on the historical value of the law and the way it differed from common awareness of the workings of legal history that already characterised ancient jurisprudence.

Reflecting upon the historical dimension of law and the mutability of legal rules may be deemed an essential component of jurisprudence that as such would always have at least minimally influenced the works of legal theorists. DR Kelley for instance emphasises that, behind the rhetoric of the *Digest* aiming at establishing its meta-historical dimension — Justinian wanting his work to 'prevail for all time' — one can find 'a very substantial awareness of the destructiveness of time, the mutability of laws, and the untrustworthiness of posterity'.[5] In this sense, Justinian — against his will as a legislator — admitted that 'it is characteristic of human jurisprudence to be always indefinitely extending, and there is nothing in it which can endure forever, for nature is constantly hastening to bring forth new forms'.[6] What differentiates this statement from the discourse put forward by a theory such as legal humanism consists in the *consequences* drawn from the historical value of law. Indeed, while most legal theorists have always recognised the historicity of law, this historicity was classically perceived as a *burden*, at odds with the primary vocation

---

[4] There exist two essentially contradictory theses on this issue. While some authors (notably M Gilmore 1941) defend the thesis according to which the legal humanist school initiated an awareness of the historicity of law, others underline that the impact of the humanist movement has to be relativised, especially as its philological methods kept it distanced from the practical concerns of the legal profession (see especially DR Kelley 1984, 229–279, who retreated from his previous defence of the first thesis, establishing a direct link between legal humanism and the awareness of the historicity of law). For more complete references on this debate, see T Berns 2000, 226–227.

[5] DR Kelley 1984, 29.

[6] Quoted by DR Kelley 1984, 29.

of the law: its being eternal and immutable (in the image of the concept of the good from which it was supposed to be derived). By contrast, the trend set forth by the legal humanist movement was to consider this historical value of the law as its primary and inescapable characteristic.

New techniques generally based on an empirical method, such as the comparative study of law, were thus developed, leading to an emphasis on the diversity of national traditions and customs.[7] At the end of the 16th century, Montaigne was deeply influenced by these recent developments and made the historicity of law the essential basis of his theory, leading him to reject as vain any search for natural laws. For Montaigne, there is indeed no point in trying to overcome the historical diversity of law by looking for more fundamental (and enduring) natural laws. 'Nothing is just *per se*, justice being a creation of custom and law'.[8] The laws follow the customs that follow the hazards of the moment's necessities; they can thus only have a fortuitous character.

> What kind of Good can it be, which was honoured yesterday but not today and which becomes a crime when you cross a river! What kind of truth can be limited by a range of mountains, becoming a lie for the world on the other side! Philosophers can hardly be serious when they try to introduce certainty into Law by asserting that there are so-called Natural Laws, perpetual and immutable, whose essential characteristic consists in their being imprinted upon the human race. There are said to be three such laws; or four; some say less, some say more: a sign that the mark they bear is as dubious as all the rest.[9]

---

[7] DR Kelley emphasises that these empirical methods actually developed before the 16th century, but only bore scholarly fruit in the 16th century: 'the point was that while laws were in theory universal in application, in fact they varied according to the diversity of national traditions (*gentes*), of which the Roman itself (as canonists in particular were pleased to point out) was one [. . .] In the legal tradition of the fourteenth century, as in philosophy, there was what may be called a nominalist school that inclined to an empirical approach. So Andrea de Isernia (1316) objected to the common practice of identifying feudal with ancient Roman institutions, and he argued that feudal terms were unprecedented' (DR Kelley 1984, 274).

[8] M de Montaigne 1991, III 13, 1215.

[9] M de Montaigne 1991, II 12, 653–654.

In this passage later taken up by Pascal and which brings us back to the heart of Montaigne's thought, laws are explicitly and strictly recognised as historical: their foundation is geographically and historically limited, marked out by epochs, rivers and mountains. In this context, Montaigne strongly opposes the medieval tradition that consists in bringing back any feudal institution to Roman law, and this leads him to join the critique of Roman law put forward by some of his contemporary French humanist lawyers (such as Pasquier), praising that 'Gascon gentleman from my part of the country whom Fortune led to be the first to object when Charlemagne wished to impose Imperial Roman law on us'.[10]

As mentioned above, the main emphasis of legal humanism was on the historical study of legal texts, the most famous example being Lorenzo Valla's demonstration of the falsity of Constantine's donation: there was no donation, the document attesting it being a forgery dating from the eighth century, as he demonstrated with the help of various historical arguments.[11] Although this falsity had previously been evoked without depreciating the text (its *a posteriori* approbation by the Pope sufficed to render it authentic), Valla opposed the idea that this historical falsification could be erased by inevitably posterior arguments of authority. In other words, Valla insisted on exposing the true historical origin of the text independently of its posterior political 'harnessing'.

This emphasis on the historically contingent character of legal texts undoubtedly found its most important application in the historical study of the *Corpus Iuris Civile*, whose aim was to establish clearly the original text and to clarify it solely with the help of historical and philological analyses (in contrast to the glossators' endless commentaries). At a time when Roman law and custom (which began to be codified) coexisted as two parallel

---

[10] M de Montaigne 1991, I 23, 132.
[11] Regarding this issue, I rely on Thomas Berns' analysis (T Berns 2000, 223 and 269), which quotes the full references to the works of Valla.

and competing sources of law in France, underlining the historically contingent value of the *Corpus* had obvious political implications, supporting the Gallican aspiration to a national law.[12] Along this line, François Hotman laid great stress on the necessity of going beyond the simple aesthetic concern of restoring the original Latin text (that characterised most legal humanists), emphasising that the law being the product of history, France had to codify itself with the help of its own laws and customs and not through infinite commentary upon Justinian's law.[13] Montaigne certainly shared this concern for going beyond a purely textual historicity whose implications would be exclusively theoretical (the historicity of a legal text indeed does not yet demonstrate the historicity of law as such), and to that extent distanced himself from the humanist movement.

From a broader perspective, Montaigne's originality in relation to his contemporaries essentially consists in having integrated his century's growing interest in the historicity of law into a specifically philosophical reflection about the sources of legal authority. If he does take part in the humanist movement through his critique of the medieval gloss,[14] and if he does support the Gallican demand that Roman law as an absolute reference be rejected, for Montaigne these contemporary issues are only the aspects of a much deeper question: how can one think of the authority of law within, and despite, its essentially historical

---

[12] Arising mainly out of a deep dissatisfaction with the obscurity bred by a dual system of justice (Roman law versus custom), legal Gallicanism mainly aimed at establishing the freedom of regional parliaments in relation to Roman law as well as asserting the preponderance of regional customs (see A Tournon 2000, 189–190 and ff).

[13] On this point see T Berns 2000, 225.

[14] 'Can anyone deny that glosses increase doubts and ignorance, when there can be found no book which men toil over in either divinity or the humanities whose difficulties have been exhausted by exegesis? The hundredth commentator dispatches it to his successor prickling with more difficulties than the first commentator of all had ever found in it. Do we ever agree among ourselves that "this book already has enough glosses: from now on there is no more to be said on it"? That can be best seen from legal quibbling' (M de Montaigne 1991, III 13, 1210).

value? In other words, for Montaigne the historicity of law, instead of requiring a demonstration, presents him with a fundamental problem. The challenge by which he is confronted amounts to understanding how law, with the authority that accompanies it, can emerge from the contingency of power and the arbitrariness of human activities. The 'revolution' that the emphasis on the historicity of law represents thus consists in thinking of the normative dimension of law *on the basis* and *from* the contingency of human activities, without this contingency being erased by a pre-established normative reference such as a pre-existing concept of the Good. Now, the perspicacious reader may notice that this challenge actually presents quite a few of the ingredients associated with a genealogical type of story. Can Montaigne's work be deemed an early precursor of a method traditionally associated with Nietzsche's 19th-century *coup*? Let me reserve this question for chapter four, once I have had the chance to put Montaigne's works and his 'story of the normative' in perspective with Kelsen's and Hart's accounts of normativity. For now the question that lies at the core of the next section can be formulated thus: is Montaigne going to succeed in reconciling law's claim to bindingness with a consciousness of its contingent origins? Can one inquire into the *sources* of legal normativity without denigrating it?

1.2 Montaigne's Inquiry into the Sources of Legal Normativity

For the sake of clarity, I propose to distinguish three steps within Montaigne's inquiry into the sources of legal normativity (the steps obviously do not appear as such within Montaigne's works). First, I shall analyse the philosophical bases that led Montaigne to reject any reference to pre-existing natural laws that would precede and thus guarantee the authority of the lawgivers. I shall then consider Montaigne's unveiling of law's empirical sources[15] and the difficulties with which they confront

---

[15] On the origins/sources distinction, see note 18 in the Introduction.

him. As a third and final step, Montaigne's endeavour to reconstruct a theory of the authority of law on the basis and *despite* the weakness of these sources will be examined.

1.2.1 What do I Know?

'We do not doubt much, because commonly received notions are essayed by nobody'.[16] In a sceptical refusal to take anything for granted (a refusal that characterises his whole body of work, and for which he is renowned, having inspired authors such as Descartes and Bacon), Montaigne devotes a significant part of his *Essays* to demonstrating the unreliability of our senses and judgement, which condemns us to a state of permanent uncertainty: 'to be convinced of certainty is certain evidence of madness and of extreme unsureness'.[17] With the help of many examples, Montaigne shows that our senses are necessarily subject to illusion,[18] and that we ourselves are constantly changing as our physical and emotional conditions alter: 'Now, since our state makes things correspond to itself and transforms them in conformity with itself, we can no longer claim to know what anything truly is: nothing reaches us except as altered and falsified by our senses'.[19]

If we truly had access to the essence of things, if they came to us 'by the force of their own authority', then, argues Montaigne, 'we would all react to them in the same way: wine would taste the same in the mouth of a sick man and a healthy one; a man whose hands were calloused or benumbed would find the same hardness in the timber or iron he was handling as anyone else'.[20]

[16] M de Montaigne 1991, II 12, 605.

[17] M de Montaigne 1991, II 12, 607.

[18] 'Take those rings wrought in the shape of plumes which are called in heraldry *Feathers without ends*. Can any eye ever be sure how wide they are and avoid being taken in by the optical illusion? For they seem to get wider on one side, narrower and more pointed on the other, especially if you turn them round your finger; yet to your touch they all appear to have the same width all the way round' (M de Montaigne 1991, II 12, 677).

[19] M de Montaigne 1991, II 12, 678.

[20] M de Montaigne 1991, II 12, 633–634.

But, as a matter of fact, the perception of our surrounding world varies to such an extent from one person to the other that it is impossible to decide which, of all these impressions, is the right one. In order for us to be able to settle the issue and thus determine the true nature of every thing (within the incredible diversity of a world constantly changing), we would need an 'instrument of judgement'. If our senses give way, can we then count on our reason?

> We want to find out *by reason* whether fire is hot, whether snow is white, whether anything within our knowledge is hard or soft [. . .] They [the philosophers] must not tell me: 'This is true; you can see it is; you can feel it is.' What they must tell me is whether I really and truly feel what I think I feel; and if I do feel it, they must go on and tell me why and how and what [. . .] Otherwise, let them abandon their professional intention, which is to accept nothing and approve nothing except by following the ways of reason. When they have to assay anything, reason is their touchstone. But it is, most surely, a touchstone full of falsehood, error, defects and feebleness. How better to test that than by reason itself. If we cannot trust reason when talking about itself, it can hardly be a judge of anything outside itself.[21]

Reason turns out to be as deceptive as the information gathered by our senses, and on that ground is of no recourse to us in our desire to understand the world, which only offers itself to us through misleading appearances. Are we then condemned to live in a world of illusions? As Starobinski puts it: 'Once pessimistic philosophy has repudiated illusory appearances, what then? What remains to be discovered by an author who has denounced artifice and dissimulation on all sides? Will he be allowed to achieve the truth, being and identity, in whose name he has deemed the veiled world unsatisfactory and bidden it farewell?'.[22] Montaigne's scepticism (at first[23]) results in a

---

[21] M de Montaigne 1991, II 12, 608 (emphasis added).

[22] J Starobinski 1985, ix.

[23] At the end of this section (and in the last section of this chapter), we will see how Montaigne turns this negative into a positive conclusion by recommending that one accept appearances as legitimate (which makes his scepticism very special).

negative conclusion: 'We have no communication with Being; as human nature is wholly situated, for ever, between birth and death, it shows itself only as a dark shadowy appearance, an unstable weak opinion'.[24] The truth of things is thus out of reach, and the world of essences is totally foreign to human experience, which can only progress within phenomena.

Since Being amounts to 'that which is eternal — meaning that which has never been born; which will never have an end; to which Time can never bring any change',[25] we cannot reach it, we who are always 'between birth and death'. We can only grasp things 'that are subject to pass from change to change' (like positive laws), and 'Reason is baffled if it looks for a substantial existence in them, since it cannot apprehend a single thing which subsists permanently, because everything is either coming into existence (and so not fully existing yet) or beginning to die before it is born'.[26]

Besides God, 'who has no beginning and no end',[27] natural laws are typically another instance of what lies beyond our experience. Montaigne's argument, for what regards natural laws, goes as follows: 'it is quite believable that natural laws exist: we can see that in other creatures. But we have lost them; that fine human reason of ours is always interfering, seeking dominance and mastery, distorting, confounding the face of everything according to its own vanity and inconsistency'.[28] Even if natural laws existed, we would not have any communication with them, as with everything that belongs to the world of 'Being'. Only the inconstancy, the diversity, and the deceptive appearance of positive laws offer themselves to our knowledge. As highlighted in the previous section, such a statement represents, at the time of Montaigne, a major intellectual revolution that leads to a reconsideration of positive laws in their historical dimension. If natural

---

[24] M de Montaigne 1991, II 12, 680.
[25] M de Montaigne 1991, II 12, 682.
[26] M de Montaigne 1991, II 12, 680.
[27] M de Montaigne 1991, II 12, 683.
[28] M de Montaigne 1991, II 12, 655.

laws cannot be deduced from positive laws (and vice versa), the only essence of these positive laws is to have a beginning, an end, and to be subject to mutations.

By stating that it is impossible to go beyond positive laws, which have no connection with Being or truth, Montaigne's aim is not to denigrate positive law, thus encouraging a certain trend to anomie. On the contrary, Montaigne seems willing to encourage a critical and reflective return to these laws considered in their positive and historical dimension, wisdom consisting precisely in not seeking to find a hidden truth behind positive law. From this perspective, at the end of his long essay *An Apology for Raymond Sebond*, Montaigne quotes a passage from Seneque, which he considers 'a pity saying; a most useful aspiration, but absurd withal': 'Oh, what a vile and abject thing is Man, if he does not rise above humanity'.[29] Such a statement is a 'pity saying' because, according to Montaigne, it is useless and vain to claim to 'mount above oneself or above humanity'; man indeed 'can see only with his own eyes, grip only with his own grasp'. Similarly, no matter how vile or abject humanity can be, it is still in the name of this humanity and 'from' this humanity that we create positive laws. For Montaigne, one of the worst human faults consists in thinking of oneself as possessing the true image of things. When one claims to deduce positive laws from natural laws, all one actually does is fabricate them at one's convenience.[30]

Montaigne's sceptical inquiry, aiming at emphasising the limits that, in a world of artifice and illusion, our senses and reason impose on us, ultimately encourages a reflective acceptance of the real world's appearances. Thus freed of the concern to seek a hidden truth in the name of which we would despise them, we can then try to win over these — potentially disgusting — semblances.

[29] M de Montaigne 1991, II 12, 683.
[30] M de Montaigne 1991, II 12, 653–654.

1.2.2 Unveiling Law's Empirical Sources

'Laws are often made by fools, and even more often by men who fail in equity because they hate equality: but always by men, *vain authorities* who can resolve nothing'.[31] If the importance of such a statement within Montaigne's works is relatively easy to grasp (this assertion marks the transition to a conceptualisation of the sources of normativity grounded in human activity), the understanding of its full implications is, however, more delicate. A hasty reading could easily lead one to conclude that Montaigne's sceptical critique ultimately leads to a strictly historical understanding of the origins of law, given his dismissal of any pretense at seeking its rational or 'natural' foundation. To avoid such misunderstanding it seems worth underlining here the importance of distinguishing between, on the one hand, Montaigne's inquiry into the sources of legal normativity, and, on the other, his emphasis on the precariousness of the historical birth of the law, which is a means rather than an end in itself. Montaigne indeed does not at any point suggest that he is looking for the *starting point* or chronological beginning of law's normativity. If Montaigne does devote an important part of his works to underscoring the arbitrariness pervading the sphere of human activities (and thus the emergence of law), his aim is above all to distance himself from classical natural law theories, according to which the legislators' claim to authority need not be arbitrary, as it is backed up by pre-existing natural laws. By contrast, the point of Montaigne's sceptical critique is to emphasise that law's authority cannot call on any other necessity than the one of history and empirics: 'necessity associates men and brings them together: afterwards that fortuitous bond is codified into laws'.[32]

Because Montaigne refuses to grant law's empirical sources any other value than their strict fortuitousness, the authority of law cannot rely on any justification linked to its birth, being too

---

[31] M de Montaigne 1991, III 13, 1216 (emphasis added).
[32] M de Montaigne 1991, III 9, 1083.

lightweight and tenuous in comparison with the 'grandeur' of what flows from it — the law in all its authoritativeness. Given the disproportion existing between the object of his study and its sources, Montaigne then seems to be willing to concentrate on the *established* authority of law, based on 'possession' and 'custom': 'laws gain their authority from actual possession and custom: *it is perilous to go back to their origins*; laws, like our rivers, get greater and nobler as they roll along: follow them back upstream to their sources and all you find is a tiny spring, hardly recognisable; as time goes by it swells with pride and grows in strength'.[33]

The 'peril' from which Montaigne wants to protect us consists in loathing the authority of law out of disgust for its tenuous and arbitrary beginnings: 'I once had the duty of justifying one of our practices which, far and wide around us, is accepted as having established authority; I did not wish to maintain it (as is usually done) exclusively by force of law and exempla so I traced it back to its origins: *I found its basis to be so weak that I all but loathed it* — I who was supposed to encourage it in others'.[34] In his endeavour to seek a foundation of law beyond the mere acceptance of its authority, Montaigne was led to discover such a weak and tenuous source that he could not but warn us against such an undertaking. Indeed, one way of reacting to the discovery of this 'tiny spring' — the precariousness of law's empirical sources — amounts to rejecting all this pretence that is supposed to magnify the law and make it grow in stature (custom and usage), thus refusing to take part in the masquerade that consists in inflating what is — and what should remain — only a tiny spring. According to Montaigne, this attitude can only lead to trouble, as

> those who refuse to be drawn away from the beginnings and sources fail even worse [than those dons who do not even dare to handle them] and find themselves bound to savage opinions [. . .] A man

---

[33] M de Montaigne 1991, II 12, 658 (emphasis added).
[34] M de Montaigne 1991, I 23, 131 (emphasis added).

who wished to loose himself from the violent foregone conclusions of custom will find many things accepted as being indubitably settled which have nothing to support them but the hoary whiskers and wrinkles of attendant usage; let him tear off that mask, bring matters back to truth and reason, and he will feel his judgement turned upside-down, yet restored by this to a much surer state.[35]

According to Montaigne, anyone who, undertaking to go beyond the sole accepted authority of law, concludes that this authority is not only fortuitous but also illegitimate (given the weakness of its sources) 'fails even worse' than someone who accepts the authority of law uncritically. In both cases (blind obedience and refusal of authority), 'one is at fault towards the law, for in one case as well as in the other, one believes in its truth (or one questions it in the name of its truth)'.[36] Only the refusal of authority is dangerous, though, for it means leaving the way open to all sorts of abuses and 'savage opinions'. In line with his general philosophy as presented in the previous section, Montaigne thus recommends the attitude of the 'wise sceptic' who, at once respectful and critical towards the law, chooses to reconstruct the authority of law on the basis and despite the weakness of its sources.[37]

1.2.3 Reconstructing the Precarious Authority of Law

The Problem: 'These Foolish Men who can Resolve Nothing'

Montaigne's undertaking — aiming at systematically questioning commonly received opinions, overcoming commonly admitted appearances — leads him to consider what lies at the source of law's authority. The 'tiny spring' he unveils is of such weakness, such precariousness, that it confronts Montaigne with a question that forces him to go about it in the reverse way, to

---

[35] M de Montaigne 1991, I 23, 131.

[36] T Berns 2000, 276 (my translation).

[37] Because of (and thanks to) this reconstruction, a logical and fundamental dimension will be added to the empirical character of these origins, as the principle in whose function a reconstructed theory of authority will be possible.

attempt to explain how the law, with the authority that accompanies it, can arise out of mere arbitrariness. The reality in whose function (and despite which) Montaigne seeks to reconstruct a theory of the authority of law essentially consists in this crude but inevitable truth: 'laws are often made by fools [. . .] but always by men, *vain authorities* who can resolve nothing'.[38]

Montaigne does not explicitly state what would need to be solved in order for these 'authorities' not to be in vain, but one can guess at least two elements that make men's (and women's) task problematic. The first one, the most obvious, is referred to by Montaigne as the 'foolishness' of legislators. The lawgiver would indeed need to be quite an 'extraordinary man' (in the words of Rousseau) in order to have no particular views vitiating 'the sanctity of his work',[39] in order to be protected against the passions depraving the soul. Laws are made by ordinarily weak and perverted men, and nothing but feigned appearance can raise them above their corrupted humanity. The second element contributing to making the task of the legislators difficult amounts to their being 'always between birth and death', thus subject to finiteness, which does not fit easily with the purported permanence of their task. The will of men and women, as finite beings, is doomed to change and to that extent raises the issue of the alterability of the law. If men (and women) are the exclusive authors, without any other guarantor, of their own laws, they can undo what they have done. What kind of authority would these laws have, which would be at the mercy of a change of will from their subjects (and authors)?[40]

Rousseau's famous statement, 'it would require Gods to give men laws'[41] could be taken as indicating that only God can 'resolve' the problem of lawgiving, thus denying the ability of men and women — as 'vain authorities' — to give themselves

---

[38] M de Montaigne 1991, III 13, 1216 (emphasis added).
[39] JJ Rousseau 1997, II 7, 70.
[40] See GA Cohen 1996, 167.
[41] JJ Rousseau 1997, II 7, 69.

laws. Such a construction would nevertheless forget to take into account the conditional mode adopted by Rousseau, suggesting more the weakness of men in relation to the greatness of the lawgiving task than the necessity for the laws to be given by Gods. Such a perspective rejoins and, in my sense, echoes that of Montaigne, whose emphasis on the disproportion existing between the grandeur of the law — its binding character — and the weakness of human condition tends to present the lawgiving enterprise as an undertaking beyond human power. Along the same line, it is interesting to note here a passage from Kant's *Metaphysics of Morals*:

> A law that is so holy (inviolable) that it is already a crime even to call it in doubt in a practical way, and so to suspend its effect for a moment, is thought *as if it must have arisen not from men but from some highest, flawless lawgiver*; and that is what the saying 'all authority is from God' means. This saying is not an assertion about the historical basis of the civil constitution; it instead sets forth an Idea as a practical principle of reason.[42]

Kant's *as if* construction is particularly important here, as it puts forward what may be considered a common theoretical device linking together these three authors in their endeavour to acknowledge the weakness of law's empirical sources. Rousseau's reference to an 'extraordinary man', or Kant's evocation of a 'flawless lawgiver' both suggest, by contrast, the sad reality with which any thinking of the authority of law is confronted: laws are made by ordinary men, 'full of flaws'. If they cannot raise themselves above humanity, one can at least call for that possibility, using the conditional mode or an 'as if' construction: although we know that the law arises out of the arbitrariness of human actions, it is still conceived *as if* it must have arisen from some highest, flawless lawgiver. The conditional or hypothetical formulation used by Rousseau or Kant essentially aims at *correcting* the imbalance caused by the weakness of the origins in comparison

[42] I Kant 1991, §49 A, 130 (emphasis added).

with the grand authority of the law. With a similar aim in mind, Montaigne, for his part, refers to a 'law of pure obedience'.

The Remedy: A 'Law of Pure Obedience'

Knowing that the original weakness of law is not susceptible of being overcome, and wanting above all to avoid the peril that the 'wild opinions' aiming at denigrating the authority of law represent, Montaigne is faced with the necessity of 'reconstructing' law's authority. According to Montaigne, the matter is first and foremost to see to it that the law does not only amount to the product of its historical birth, or at least that its authority does not flow from there. From this perspective, Montaigne puts forward 'The first commandment which God ever gave to Man [. . .] *the law of pure obedience*. It was a bare and simple order, leaving man no room for knowing or arguing'.[43]

Such a reference is at the least surprising coming from Montaigne, as it indeed suggests a grounding of the authority of law in precisely the kind of ontological principle whose inaccessible and thus illusory character he emphatically denounced. Are we to understand this 'law of pure obedience' as the starting point for a natural justice of divine inspiration? Obviously, such an interpretation would be directly at odds with Montaigne's general perspective, and besides, it would directly contradict his explicit rejection of any kind of natural law justice ('Nothing is just per se, justice being a creation of custom and law'[44]).

By contrast, if one keeps in mind the Kantian formulation ('law [. . .] is thought *as if it must have arisen not from men but from some highest, flawless lawgiver*; and that is what the saying "all authority is from God" means'), this reference to a 'law of pure obedience' may be understood in a way similar to Kant's 'all authority is from God'. The point of such a reference would be to provide this supplement of authority without which thinking of

---

[43] M de Montaigne 1991, II 12, 543 (emphasis added).
[44] M de Montaigne 1991, III 13, 1215.

the authoritative dimension of law does not seem viable, as it is desperately too grand in comparison to the weakness of its sources. From Kant's *as if* construction to Montaigne's legitimate fictions — 'even our system of Law, they say, bases the truth of its justice upon legal fictions'[45] — the step is easily taken. The essential aim of both Montaigne's 'law of pure obedience' and Kant's 'all authority is from God' is to provide the logical principle thanks to which one can theoretically establish the authority of law.

From this perspective, one can understand the putative divine origin of Montaigne's first law as essentially aiming at cancelling its iterative and performative character. The point of this law of pure obedience would above all consist in being ultimate, thus avoiding an infinite — and dangerous — regress in its motives. To that extent, the quasi-tautological character of its formulation (obedience to the law would be justified by a law of pure obedience) would merely confirm the necessity of avoiding developing any interest in this last and ultimate law. Montaigne's concern is indeed — let's repeat it — to spare us the peril that the disgusting appearance of the origins of law could constitute. On this basis, Montaigne's law of pure obedience probably amounts to the best way of stopping inquiry into the sources of law at a 'safe' point, a point referring to law alone, thus excluding the precariousness of power and the origins it represents.

At this stage, it is difficult not to mention a tempting parallel with one of the outstanding figures of 20th-century legal positivism — Hans Kelsen. This ambition of founding the authority of law on law alone, thus excluding any consideration of political or moral legitimacy, constitutes one of the striking features of the Kelsenian theory, which also gives a first norm — the Basic Norm — the task of founding the binding character of the laws flowing from it.[46] Both Montaigne and Kelsen choose to

[45] M de Montaigne 1991, II 12, 603.

[46] It is worth noting here that in Kelsen's work this first norm ultimately takes the form of a *fiction*, asking us to proceed *as though* the law were irreducibly normative.

proceed on the basis of the acknowledgement that there is no remedy to our search for the sources of the authority of law but the necessity of a rigorous attachment to the law in its positivity. On this basis, the famous statement from Montaigne — 'Now laws remain respected not because they are just but because they are laws [. . .] If anyone obeys them only when they are just, then he fails to obey them for just the reason he must!'[47] ('*les lois se maintiennent en crédit non parce qu'elles sont justes, mais parce qu'elles sont lois. [. . .] Quiconque leur obéit parce qu'elles sont justes, ne leur obéit pas justement par où il doit*'[48]) — may be considered one of the cornerstones of legal positivism, underlining the necessity of distinguishing between law's bindingness and law's justice.[49]

One could stop at this point. One could conclude by showing how Montaigne's sceptical critique, leading him successively to unveil the weakness of law's empirical sources and then reconstruct a theory of authority *despite* the precariousness of these sources, finally results in what may be considered one of the first positivist formulations of a theory of the authority of law. But Montaigne adds something, an element that, in this positivist framework, might appear at the least incongruous. In the middle of his above-mentioned famous statement, Montaigne adds: 'That is the mystical basis for their authority. They have no other' *C'est le fondement mystique de leur autorité.*[50]

[47] M de Montaigne 1991, III 13, 1216. This English translation (perhaps too aesthetically concerned) can be quite misleading. In the French version, it appears clearly that Montaigne criticises any obedience to laws that would be founded on the *justice* of the laws. If anyone obeys the laws because they are just, then he does not obey them *for the right reason* ('*par où il doit*'). Montaigne leaves open the reasons why we should obey the laws, but sets one *wrong reason* out: the justice of the laws, because in any case we don't have access to the concept of justice as such, which takes a different appearance in every kingdom.

[48] M de Montaigne 1965, 362.

[49] This 'positivist' tradition later bifurcates into a Hobbesian stand, distinguishing law's moral bindingness from the justice of its content, and a Kelsenian or Hartian stand, distinguishing legal from moral bindingness.

[50] M de Montaigne 1991, III 13, 1216.

If only from a terminological perspective, such a statement is exceptional. It is not only the sole occurrence of the term 'mystical' in the works of Montaigne, but the term 'mystical' as such seems to be rare at his time. Its meaning is relatively uncertain.[51] Originally, the Greek term '*mustikos*' meant 'relating to mysteries', referring more particularly to the religious domain accessible only to the initiated. From the time of Montaigne (his own works having certainly contributed to that development), this meaning extended to the vaguer idea of a mystical 'discourse', expressing the limit between a hidden and ineffable essence and the endless description of the visible.[52]

One of the clues to understanding this reference to a 'mystical basis', as regards the authority of law, consists in recalling the 'peril' against which Montaigne wants to protect us, having discovered how off-putting the precarious appearance of the origins of law could be for the uninformed (who are then led to 'savage opinions' denigrating the authority of law). In order to stop the inquiries into the sources of law's authority at a 'safe' point, Montaigne refers to a 'law of pure obedience', by virtue of which one has to obey the law 'because it is the law' without asking any further question. Thus drawing a line between what can be inquired into and what has to be kept at a distance, surrounded by mysteries, this first and ultimate law stands precisely where the theoretical discourse is brought to an end[53] in order to give way to the domain of the mystical (accessible only to the 'wise' such as Montaigne).

This link between the problem of the weakness of law's sources and its alleged 'mystical' basis is confirmed by several passages in the *Essays* where Montaigne refers to the necessity

---

[51] For a synthesis of the history of the term 'mystical', see T Berns 2000, 386–389.

[52] See the brilliant analysis of Michel de Certeau in M de Certeau 1982, 132 (for the English translation, see M de Certeau 1992).

[53] In *Force de loi*, Derrida endeavours to explain Montaigne's reference to the term 'mystical' by reference to that founding point where 'the discourse comes up against its limit', enclosed in the 'performativity' of its enunciation: 'Here a silence is walled up in the violent structure of the founding act' (J Derrida 1992, 14).

of voluntarily surrounding the origins of power with mysteries, given the inadequacy of its justifications: 'If we are to safeguard the authority of the Privy Council we do not need laymen participating in it nor seeing further than the first obstacle. If we want to maintain its reputation it must be taken on trust, as a whole'.[54] Montaigne further develops this distinction between 'laymen' who are to stay 'behind the first obstacle' (behind the law of pure obedience) and initiates who alone have access to the mysteries, by referring to the 'temple of Pallas' (alluding to Athena, taken here in her capacity of protector of the city, goddess of authority justice, etc.[55]): 'I reckon that in the temple of Pallas (as can be seen to be the case in all other religions), there were open secrets, to be revealed to the people, and other hidden higher ones, to be revealed only to initiates'.[56]

In the context of Montaigne's reconstructed theory of law's authority, these 'higher secrets' amount to the precarious sources that were unveiled by his sceptical critique. Given that their raw reality is not a spectacle within everyone's capability, Montaigne is led to isolate the arbitrariness of law's empirical sources in a 'non-discursive' field that stands beyond what can be expressed or inquired about.[57] From this perspective, the

[54] M de Montaigne 1991, III 8, 1058.

[55] T Berns 2000, 371, note 2.

[56] M de Montaigne 1991, III 10, 1138.

[57] It seems worth mentioning here as an interesting echo the propositions of Wittgenstein regarding 'what is mystical':

6.44 – Not *how* the world is, is the mystical, but *that* it is.

6.45 – The contemplation of the world *sub specie aeterni* is its contemplation as a limited whole.

The feeling of the world as a limited whole is the mystical feeling.

6.5 – For an answer which cannot be expressed the question too cannot be expressed.

The *riddle* does not exist.

If a question can be put at all, then it *can* also be answered.

6.51 – Scepticism is *not* irrefutable, but palpably senseless, if it would doubt where a question cannot be asked.

For doubt can only exist where there is a question; a question only where there is an answer, and this only where something *can* be *said* [. . .]

6.52 – There is indeed the inexpressible. This *shows* itself; it is the mystical. [. . .]

7 – 'Whereof one cannot speak, thereof one must be silent.'

(L Wittgenstein 1981, 187 and 189).

introduction of a 'law of pure obedience' as a first and ultimate law allows one to locate the foundation of authority in a field that does not require any discernment on the part of the layman, who cannot but 'religiously' obey the law 'because it is the law', without asking any further question.[58]

The source of law's normative dimension nevertheless remains located *within* human activities, which the wise, through their sceptical critique, unveil (while nevertheless remaining unable to explain how this initial precariousness can give rise to the 'grand' authority of laws). Such an explanation indeed requires one to ask on what basis the authority of the lawgiver — however foolish she might be — can escape its 'doomed' futility, ie how some people have managed to 'confer' authority upon themselves without this enterprise being predestined to fatuity. Montaigne could have taken that route; he had all the ingredients for it. The anxiety raised by the sense of having unveiled an all-too-shameful reality in comparison with what is meant to be, and what is to remain, the grand authority of law, nevertheless stopped Montaigne in his 'genealogical path'.

Montaigne's commitment to locating the source of legal normativity within human activity (thus rejecting any reference to pre-existing natural laws) was bound to give rise to a new kind of theoretical challenge: explaining the authority of law (and thus its normative character) despite the arbitrariness of the practices from which it stems. Among the many factors that led Montaigne to reverse the classical natural law trend, I have tried to underscore both the 16th-century humanist movement, reasserting the value of law's historicity, and Montaigne's sceptical attitude, emphasising the world's deceitful appearances (in

---

[58] This insistence that obedience to the law can only be conceived independently of any discretion, out of pure 'subjection' and not out of choice (obeying the law on the basis of one's will would, according to Montaigne, question the obligatoriness of the law itself) establishes another connection with the works of Kelsen, who rejects any kind of 'theory of recognition', which 'consciously or unconsciously, presupposes the ideal of individual liberty as self-determination, that is, the norm that the individual ought to do only what he wants to do' (H Kelsen 1967, §34 I, 218, note 83).

contrast to the *Being* of natural laws for instance). The result of this reversal appears most obviously through this central statement in Montaigne's works: 'Laws are often made by fools, and even more often by men who fail in equity because they hate equality: but always by men, vain authorities who can resolve nothing'.[59]

The problem that is to be 'resolved' essentially consists in asserting the normative character of law despite the futility of human activities, despite the fact that the authority of the law-giver always seems to be in vain when it is not guaranteed by a superior instance. To 'save' the authority of law from the disgust that the discovery of its arbitrary origins could bring about, Montaigne resorts to a law of pure obedience, enjoining one to obey the law 'because it is the law' without asking any further question (thus stopping the inquiries as to the origins of law at a 'safe point', a point beyond which one must fall silent).

This first law conveniently curbing the range of appropriate questions must nevertheless come from somewhere. Its coming from God might seem disconcerting given Montaigne's explicit dismissal of classical natural law theories. Is Montaigne suddenly moving backwards, unexpectedly joining the 'opposite side', endorsing the classical natural law stand and locating the source of legal normativity *beyond* human activity? Such an interpretation would overlook Montaigne's numerous assertions aimed at underlining that the source of normativity does indeed lie within human activity. This source is, however, too shameful to mention, as a 'tiny spring' whose disproportion in relation to the grandeur of the law can only cause disgust.

So it must be surrounded by mysteries; it must be relegated to the domain of the mystical. The purpose of the 'law of pure obedience' chiefly consists in stopping the theoretical discourse in time. From this perspective, its absence of any content (see 'Now laws remain respected not because they are just but because they are laws [. . .] If anyone obeys them only when they

---

[59] M de Montaigne 1991, III 13, 1216.

are just, then he fails to obey them for just the reason he must!'[60]) confirms the pertinence of constructing this first law's divine origin in parallel with Rousseau's 'it would require Gods' or Kant's 'all authority is from God': it is *as if* laws couldn't arise from the actions of men. And yet they do. We just haven't found (or are not willing to provide) any way of conceptualising the passage from the arbitrary sphere of human activities to the normative sphere of legal rules. We thus have to — provisionally[61] — stop all inquiries as to the source of legal normativity at a fundamental and original norm, just as Kelsen does, a few centuries later.

[60] M de Montaigne 1991, III 13, 1216. See note 47 above regarding the merits of this English translation.

[61] See chapter 5 for such an endeavour.

2
Kelsen

Like Montaigne, Kelsen is opposed to the classical natural law model. Referring to some order 'independent from and given to us' in order to explain the normative dimension of law will not do. While the theoretical challenge he takes up is thus similar to Montaigne's, Kelsen does not need to go through the same 'sceptical' enterprise, aiming at disputing commonly received opinions and unveiling law's empirical sources. In Kelsen's time, during the Weimar Republic, one knows well enough that 'laws are made by fools'. This basic truth is nevertheless put aside within Kelsen's theory, not in the name of the peril that the discovery of the arbitrary origins of the law would constitute, but in the name of a 'Neo-Kantian' methodological dualism, strictly separating *is* from *ought*. As elements belonging to the factual sphere, the human activities from which the law stems are, according to Kelsen, the concern of sociology and cannot have any part to play within a 'pure' theory of law.

Kelsen is thus led to explain the normative dimension of law without referring either to law-creating facts or to anything transcendent embodied within natural laws; his explanation can only proceed *from within* legal normativity. Kelsen therefore postulates a highest, 'basic' norm, which grounds the normative dimension of all the other norms of the system. Formulated as a transcendental presupposition, the Basic Norm allows one to interpret normatively, that is, in terms of *ought*, the empirical material that presents itself as law.

This endeavour to construct the law as an autonomous object, explainable by reference to normative considerations alone (without recourse to either moral or factual considerations) is fraught with difficulties. Throughout Kelsen's works, there were two theoretical questions for the treatment of which Kelsen had no choice but to refer to extra-normative considerations. These questions concern the problem of lawmaking and, related to it, the attribution of some 'content' to the Basic Norm. The analysis of Kelsen's treatment of these two questions will aim at emphasising the tensions resulting from his desire to isolate the normative sphere from any extraneous consideration. These tensions are crystallised in the Basic Norm, as the ultimate point closing the field of 'purely' normative considerations on itself.

Before considering the nature and the origins of these internal tensions, I shall first examine the demand of purity that conditions the whole works of Kelsen and prevents any consideration of the moral or factual contexts surrounding the concept of normativity (in section 2.1). In the second section I shall analyse Kelsen's numerous attempts to define the concept of legal normativity, as well as his awareness of the difficulties flowing from his ambition to construct the normative sphere in an autonomous way. Finally, in the third section, an analysis of Kelsen's 'problem of positivity' and his attribution of a 'content' to the Basic Norm should allow us to grasp the impasse Kelsen faces given his rejection of both the classical natural law model (thus committing him to locating the source of legal normativity *within* human activity) *and* any reference to initial law-creating facts.

2.1 The Prerequisites of Kelsen's Inquiry into Legal Normativity

2.1.1 The Programme: The Purity of the Pure Theory

Kelsen set himself the task of 'purifying' legal science from his very first work in legal theory — *Hautprobleme der Staatsrechtslehre* (1911). This purification endeavour may be seen as a continuation of the work of his predecessors (such as Laband and Jellinek), which essentially aimed at freeing legal science from the 'vice of methodological syncretism': the illegitimate combination of different methods of cognition.[1] Kelsen nevertheless radicalised this trend by supporting an expansive version of methodological dualism, separating the worlds of normativity and facticity by an 'insuperable abyss', corresponding to two independent spheres that are epistemologically unbridgeable. In opposition to Jellinek, Kelsen rejects the idea that a theory of law can comprise both a legal and a sociological perspective on its object. His aim is to secure the autonomy of law as an object of specifically legal cognition.

In his Foreword to the second printing of *Hautprobleme*, Kelsen sets out the outline of his programme with remarkable clarity:

> the purity of the theory or — amounting to the same thing — the independence of the law as an object of scientific cognition is what I am striving to secure, specifically in two directions. The purity of the theory is to be secured against the claims of a so-called '*sociological*' point of view, which employs causal, scientific methods to appropriate the law as a part of natural reality. And it is to be secured against the *natural law theory*, which, by ignoring the fundamental referent found exclusively in the positive law, takes legal theory out of the realm of positive legal norms and into that of ethico-political postulates.[2]

The second part of this 'programme', aiming at distinguishing the *Pure Theory* from natural law theories, is the most predictable side of Kelsen's argument, which in this matter contributes nothing new to the tradition of his predecessors. Kelsen mentions besides that 'in general, it is taken for granted that legal theory can only be a theory of positive law, and the many dangers threatening legal science through the often unconscious insinuation of ethico-political points of view are simply mentioned in passing'.[3] Throughout his works, Kelsen nevertheless has to reiterate more than once his opposition to any form of

[1] See below for more details on the epistemological background underlying Kelsen's concept of 'purity'.

[2] H Kelsen 1998a, 3–4.

[3] H Kelsen 1998a, 4.

moralisation of law,[4] the loss of the traditional landmarks embodied by the pre-war empire as well as the general feeling of disruption and unsettlement having brought about a strong desire to secure the stability of law by linking it to moral considerations. For Kelsen, this association of law with the sphere of morality (taking the form of a necessary bond) could only be seen as a dangerous compromise, threatening to conceal the specificity of legal normativity.

Undoubtedly, it is the first part of Kelsen's project, aiming at securing the purity of legal theory 'against the claims of a so-called "*sociological*" point of view' which stands at the forefront of Kelsen's inquiry and distinguishes it from other theories. This particular trend may be understood as the answer to a growing realist movement, endeavouring to explain the law by reference to predictive statements about the likely behaviour of individuals dealing with it. This reduction of law to mere concatenations of fact (based on a predictive analysis of adjudication) denies altogether the possibility of law's existing independently of its concrete realisations, and deems its supposed 'normative' status to be some kind of illusion. Against this factual analysis of law,[5] Kelsen opposes the force of a conviction, emphasising 'the specific lawfulness, the autonomy of the law, as the legal counterpart to the law of nature — the "law of the law", so to speak, the law of normativity (*Rechtsgesetz*)'.[6]

---

[4] Note that generally Kelsen does not develop much of an argument towards sustaining the separability of law and morality, to the point that Paulson actually holds that 'nothing remotely like an argument for rejecting natural law theory — for rejecting, that is to say, the morality thesis — has been offered by Kelsen. On the contrary, on this front he offers only a crass and vulgar relativism' (SL Paulson 2000a, 293).

[5] Kelsen's case against empirico-positivist theories is illustrated in the following passage: 'If one deprives the norm or the "ought" of meaning, then there will be no meaning in the assertions that something is legally allowed, something is legally proscribed, this belongs to me, that belongs to you, X has a right to do this, Y is obliged to do that, and so on. In short, all the thousands of statements in which the life of the law is manifest daily will have lost their significance' (H Kelsen 1992, §16, 33).

[6] H Kelsen 1998a, 5.

Kelsen's project, however, would be misunderstood if it were brought back to the mere ambition of defending the specific normativity of law against any attempt at reduction, be it to a 'moral' type of normativity or to no normativity at all. Kelsen's 'purity programme' indeed involves more than just distinguishing the object of legal cognition from the objects of other sciences, such as sociology or ethics. It also requires this object to be 'autonomous' or somehow 'self-standing'. In contrast to Hart's theory, for instance, which ultimately explains legal normativity by reference to social facts, Kelsen seeks to construct the law as an autonomous object, explainable by reference to normative considerations alone, without having to resort to either moral or factual considerations. Kelsen's project, aiming at securing the independence of law *qua* object of cognition, must thus be restated as not only striving to defend the irreducible normativity of law against any construction denying its specificity and restating it in moral or factual terms. His project also rejects any attempt to explain this normativity by reference to moral or factual considerations.

Kelsen is opposed to natural law theories not only in asserting the separability of law and morality, but also, more importantly, in dismissing any attempt to explain law's normativity by reference to some pre-existing natural laws. Kelsen refuses to locate the source of legal normativity in a concept of the good that would precede human action, be it given by God or incarnated in Nature or Reason.[7] 'For the norms of natural law, like those of morality, are deduced from a Basic Norm that by virtue of its content — as emanation of divine will, of nature, or of a pure reason — is held to be directly evident'.[8] By resisting the

---

[7] An example of a theory defending the separability thesis while locating the source of legal normativity in a transcendent concept of the good might be that of John Finnis, although one could discuss whether or not Finnis actually locates the source of normativity in a concept of the good that *precedes* human action or rather *flows* from it.

[8] H Kelsen 1992, §28, 56.

temptation to give an absolute basis for the validity[9] of law, Kelsen consciously goes against the current of his time, seeking to restore social confidence[10] by providing a substantial justification of the legal order.

On the other hand, Kelsen's opposition to the claims of a so-called 'sociological point of view' not only implies that the law is not reducible to factual propositions: it also entails that its normative dimension cannot be *explained* by reference to facts. Kelsen thus rejects any kind of fact-based positivism, the most prominent example being Hart's theory, which seeks to explain legal normativity by reference to social facts (the reductive trend among these fact-based positivist theories, which does not even seek to explain this normative dimension at all, being ruled out anyway[11]). In support of this normativist position (claiming to explain the law independently of facts[12]), Kelsen invokes his strict version of methodological dualism, separating *is* from *ought* by an 'insuperable abyss'.[13] In this view, the worlds of facticity and normativity are not only *differentiable* but also and above all totally unconnected, corresponding to two different spheres of knowledge.[14] Any

---

[9] In Kelsen's works, the concepts of validity and binding force are often used interchangeably. See H Kelsen 1967, 193: '[that] a norm referring to the behaviour of a human being is "valid" means that it is "binding" — that an individual ought to behave in the manner determined by the norm'.

[10] Kelsen explicitly addresses this state of social disturbance and lack of self-confidence in H Kelsen 1949a, 445.

[11] On this matter, see Paulson's useful distinction between 'empirico-reductive positivism' and 'non-reductive positivism'. In opposition to the reductive version of positivism (see for instance Austin's theory), the non-reductive version develops an explanation of legal normativity based on *social facts*, which, by contrast to Austin's habits of obedience, 'lend themselves to explication apart from a rule-governed scheme' (SL Paulson 1993, 240).

[12] SL Paulson 1993, 231.

[13] On the root of this methodological dualism, and its Neo-Kantian influence, see 'The epistemological background', in section 2.1.2.

[14] Note that 'on one reading [. . .], Sein and Sollen mark two points of view, the explicative and the normative; they are modalities de re, addressing what can be said about the thing (which is, then, either natural or normative in character). On another reading, Sein and Sollen are modes of thought — modalities de dicto, which, like grammatical modes, address what can be said not about the thing itself but about propositions of judgements (that are in turn addressed to things)' (SL Paulson 1998a, 157).

attempt at deriving legal norms from social practices proceeds from a gross misunderstanding of the different epistemological status characterising legal norms and social facts.

Kelsen's endeavour to secure the autonomy of law *qua* object of cognition thus not only leads him to ascertain the specificity of this object as compared to other sciences, it also leads him to reject any appeal to both moral considerations and social facts in order to explain legal normativity. Now, if the source of legal normativity can neither be located in some pre-existing concept of the good, nor in some human practices, one may legitimately wonder if the normative dimension of law can actually have any source at all. Kelsen's attempt at locating this 'source'[15] *within* legal normativity itself relies on an argument of transcendental import: in order to interpret normatively the empirical phenomenon that presents itself as law, one needs to presuppose a highest, 'basic' norm, which stands as the ultimate 'reason of validity'[16] of all the other norms of the system. Formulated as a transcendental presupposition, the Basic Norm represents 'the common source for the validity of all norms that belong to the same order'.[17] If, in this latter quotation, one replaces the word 'validity' with 'binding force' (see above note 9), one can then appropriately characterise the Basic Norm as 'the source of the normativity of the law, transmitting, by means of delegation, the quality of "ought" (*Sollen*) to the other norms of the system'.[18]

[15] In this context, one might better speak of the 'conditions of possibility' of legal normativity, given Kelsen's ambition to explain the normative dimension of law *from within*.

[16] Kelsen's argument goes as follows: given that the reason for the validity of a norm cannot be a fact but only the validity of another, higher norm, ultimately the normative dimension (ie the 'reason of validity') for every norm of the system can only be explained by reference to a last and highest norm which 'must be presupposed, because it cannot be "posited", that is to say: created, by an authority whose competence would have to rest on a still higher norm' (H Kelsen 1967, 195).

[17] H Kelsen 1967, 195.

[18] UU Bindreiter 2001, 147. See H Kelsen 1992, §29, 58: 'Rooted in the Basic Norm, ultimately, is the normative import of all the material facts constituting the legal system'.

Kelsen's location of the 'source' of legal normativity (which is of a very particular kind, given the *presupposed* nature of the Basic Norm) within this normativity itself allows him to isolate the object of legal science in its very specificity but also, and above all, in its *negative* autonomy. It is not only distinct from its factual and moral counterparts but also totally independent from them. Whether the closed and self-sufficient concept of legal normativity that is supposed to flow from such an autonomous conception of legal science is actually viable will be addressed in the third section of this chapter. Before that, let me consider the epistemological, political and anthropological backgrounds underlying Kelsen's ambition to secure the 'purity' of the normative sphere.

2.1.2 Why does Kelsen's Theory need to be Pure?

At the root of Kelsen's work stands his sharp distinction between the order of value and the order of reality, between *Sollen* and *Sein*, allowing no passage from one order to the other. If Kelsen's arguments in support of this fundamental split are of an essentially epistemological nature, one may nevertheless understand this separation in the light of other considerations that are not necessarily formulated explicitly by Kelsen. His upholding of a problematic distance between *is* and *ought* may be read as preserving the possibility of a critical assessment of the legal system's legitimacy. It may also be interpreted as flowing from Kelsen's mistrust of the human ability to make (sound) normative choices.

The epistemological background

The concept of purity that Kelsen puts forward as fundamentally directing the 'programme' of his theory ultimately flows from the Kantian endeavour to define a concept of cognition that is 'uninfluenced by any empirical element'. Taken up by the Heidelberg Neo-Kantians, this project is reformulated so as to apply to specifically *legal* cognition. Denouncing as illegitimate any amalgam of different methods of cognition, Georg Jellinek observes: 'If one has comprehended the general difference between the jurist's conceptual sphere and the objective sphere of natural processes and events, one will appreciate the inadmissibility of transferring the cognitive method of the latter over to the former. Among the vices of the scientific enterprise of our day is the vice of methodological syncretism'.[19]

Kelsen fully endorses Jellinek's position, while he nevertheless adds a supplementary requirement: to be pure, legal theory should not only avoid methodological confusion, it should also isolate its object as the object of a specifically *legal* cognition, which does not lend itself to any other kind of approach.[20] In other words, against Jellinek's 'two-sides' theory of law, one side being examined from a legal point of view while the other is apprehended sociologically, Kelsen rejects the idea that the same object can be the focus of two different methods.

This position is supported by his expansive version of methodological dualism, separating the worlds of *Sein* and *Sollen* by an 'insuperable abyss': 'The opposition between *Sein* and *Sollen*, between "is" and "ought", is a logico-formal opposition, and in so far as the boundaries of logico-formal enquiry are observed, no path leads from one to the other; the two worlds are separated by an insuperable abyss'.[21] In this matter, Kelsen was notably influenced by Wilhelm Windelband and Georg Simmel, whom he acknowledges in his *Foreword* to the second printing of *Main Problems in the Theory of Public Law*: 'Following Wilhelm Windelband's and Georg Simmel's interpretation of Kant, *I take the "ought" as the expression for the autonomy of the law* — with the law to be determined by legal science — in contradiction to a social "is" that can be comprehended "sociologically"'.[22]

Kelsen however cannot just assert the autonomy of law *qua* object of a specifically normative science. He first needs to demonstrate that such a 'purely normative' object is epistemologically

---

[19] G Jellinek 1979, 17 (translation by SL Paulson, in SL Paulson 1998b, 28).

[20] SL Paulson expresses the issue very clearly in SL Paulson 1998b, 28.

[21] H Kelsen 1911, 7 (translated and quoted by SL Paulson 1998b, 30).

[22] H Kelsen 1998a, 4 (emphasis added).

possible.[23] To this end, Kelsen adopts a resolutely Kantian strategy, drawing an explicit analogy between Kant's transcendental question and his own inquiry: 'Kant asks: "how is it possible to interpret without a metaphysical hypothesis, the facts perceived by our senses, in the laws of nature formulated by natural science?" In the same way, the Pure Theory of Law asks: "How is it possible to interpret without recourse to meta-legal authorities, like God or nature, the subjective meaning of certain facts as a system of objectively valid legal norms describable in rules of law?"'.[24] As an answer to this last question, Kelsen puts forward the concept of the Basic Norm, as the presupposition allowing one to interpret normatively the empirical material that presents itself as law. Implicit in the Basic Norm,[25] however, is a further argument drawing on the concept of 'imputation' as the *a priori* category conditioning our knowledge of the normative phenomenon.

In order to account for the possibility of isolating the law as a specifically normative (and thus non-causal) sphere, Kelsen introduces the notion of peripheral imputation[26] as his fundamental category, constructed as a counterpart to the category of causation: 'Just as laws of nature link a certain material fact as cause with another as effect, so positive laws [in their basic form] link legal condition with legal consequence (the consequence of a so-called unlawful act). If the mode of linking material facts is causality in the one case, it is imputation in the other, and imputation is recognised in the Pure Theory of Law as the particular lawfulness, the autonomy of the law'.[27]

---

[23] Note that Kelsen does not seek to demonstrate the *necessity* of law as a 'purely normative' object. Indeed, Kelsen does not aim at refuting reductivist theories, based on a categorical denial of the normative dimension of law. Rather, he acknowledges these theories as one possible theoretical attitude.

[24] H Kelsen 1967, §34(d), 202.

[25] SL Paulson 2000b, 1790 and SL Paulson 1992b, 325. See as well S Hammer 1998, 184.

[26] For a detailed analysis of the concept, see SL Paulson 2001.

[27] H Kelsen 1992, §11(b), 23.

Kelsen's point, then, consists in demonstrating that in the same way as the category of causation conditions our knowledge of the natural phenomenon, so, likewise, the category of imputation conditions our knowledge of legal propositions. From this perspective, Kelsen's reasoning starts from the fact that one has indeed cognition of legal norms (premise I), to assert that this cognition is possible only if the category of normative imputation is presupposed (premise II), and concludes that cognition of legal norms necessarily presupposes the category of imputation.

As Stanley Paulson has argued, the sceptic is actually unlikely to assent to the first premise — the fact of normative cognition — as these knowledge claims are precisely the target of his scepticism. 'Kelsen, however, pays no heed to the sceptic, pointing out that he does not mean to answer him'.[28] Kelsen acknowledges the position of the 'theoretical anarchist' as an alternative to his own view which he does not mean (and does not have the means) to counter: 'the Pure Theory is well aware that one cannot prove the existence of the law as one proves the existence of natural material facts and the natural laws governing them, that one cannot adduce compelling arguments to refute a posture like theoretical anarchism, which refuses to see anything but naked power where jurists speak of the law'.[29] In order to adduce such 'compelling arguments' (and thus show that the category of imputation is a necessary condition of legal cognition), Kelsen would have had to resort to the *progressive* version of Kant's transcendental argument, starting from a weak premise — the 'uninterpreted' data of consciousness — to then conclude the possibility of cognition conditioned by an *a priori* category (by opposition to the regressive version, which considers the possibility of cognition as given). Such a progressive version of the transcendental argument obviously does not fit Kelsen's purposes. He wants to defend a specifically *normative interpretation* of the raw

---

[28] SL Paulson 2000a, 288.
[29] H Kelsen 1992, §16, 34.

material that presents itself as law, and cannot start his demonstration with raw or 'uninterpreted' data.[30]

Kelsen thus ends up using the regressive version of the transcendental argument independently of its progressive counterpart (in Kant's doctrine, the two versions go together, Kant considering the regressive version as a summary statement awaiting full demonstration through the progressive version found in the *Critique of Pure Reason*[31]). As a result, Kelsen finds himself unable to demonstrate the necessity of his second premise — the claim that the possibility of legal or normative cognition presupposes the application of a category of normative imputation — which must then be merely *assumed*: '*whoever aspires* to treat the law as something normative can do so only if he presupposes a Basic Norm, understood simply in terms of a normative *category* of the hypothetical "ought"-judgement'.[32]

According to Paulson, such a use of the regressive argument form *sans* any appeal for support to the progressive version of the transcendental argument 'robs it of its transcendental force'[33] and is appropriately characterised as 'Neo-Kantian' (rather than properly Kantian). From a more general perspective, it is worth underlining here that 'Kelsen's Kant is the Kant of the Neo-Kantians, that is to say, the Kant of the *Critique of Pure Reason* and of the *Prolegomena*'.[34] Following the lead of the *fin de siècle* Neo-Kantians, seeking to extend Kant's transcendental inquiry to fields outside the realm of natural science (ie to specialised disciplines such as ethics, history or law), Kelsen's main concern is to establish the possibility of a specifically *legal* cognition, free of any empirical or moral admixture, by applying Kant's transcendental method.

That Kant rejected the application of this method to the fields of law and ethics, which are the object of the second Critique based on the concept of practical Reason, does not much bother

---

[30] On this issue see SL Paulson 2000a, 287, as well as S Hammer 1998, 186.

[31] See I Kant 1997, sec. 5, 31.

[32] S Hammer 1998, 186.

[33] SL Paulson 1992b, 331.

[34] S Hammer 1998, 183.

Kelsen, who sees in Kant's abandonment of the transcendental method a sign of weakness:

> A complete emancipation from metaphysics was probably impossible for a personality still as deeply rooted in Christianity as Kant's. This is most evident in his practical philosophy [. . .] At this point, Kant abandoned his method of transcendental logic [. . .] So it happens that Kant, whose philosophy of transcendental logic was pre-eminently destined to provide the groundwork for a positivistic legal and political doctrine, stayed, as a legal philosopher, in the rut of the natural-law doctrine.[35]

Kelsen's quick dismissal of Kant's moral philosophy has of course been severely criticised by many authors,[36] and Kelsen's rejoinder to that kind of criticism, which he had anticipated, is breathtaking: 'The appeal to Kant made by the Pure Theory of Law, then, can of course be contradicted by those who look upon his ethics as the true Kantian philosophy. *It is easily shown that the ethics is utterly worthless*, a claim that can be made even by those who look upon the Kantian transcendental philosophy as the greatest philosophical achievement of all'.[37]

The epistemological arguments 'which Kelsen deploys in order to establish the possibility of a pure and autonomous legal science, *borrow* from the authors which they invoke, without it being possible to establish a direct filiation between a certain epistemological current and Kelsen's theory. In relation to *fin de siècle* Neo-Kantians, Kelsen systematically radicalises the position of the authors that preceded him, such as Laband[38] or Jellinek,[39] judging that they did not go far enough in their

[35] H Kelsen 1949b, 444–5.

[36] See notably A Wilson 1982, 47–50.

[37] H Kelsen 1998b, 173 (emphasis added).

[38] 'The claim of some that the Pure Theory of Law amounts to nothing other than "Labandism" is especially absurd because of Laband's utter failure in his effort to separate the depiction of the positive law from politics' (H Kelsen 1998b, 170).

[39] 'Kelsen, like his predecessors, is committed to the purity of method but, unlike them, he has no truck with the idea that one and the same object might be the focus or subject-matter of different methods. And his critique of Jellinek's "two-sides" theory of law is scathing. A substratum holding the two sides together, Kelsen argues, is required by Jellinek's theory, but no explication of the notion is possible within the confines of the theory' (SL Paulson 1998b, 28).

enterprise of 'purification' of legal science. If it is this concept of purity that sets apart the Kelsenian theory as a unique epistemological position, one may wonder what motivates his striving towards a legal science that is detached from any moral or empirical element.

The Political Background

Kelsen presented his first sketch of a pure theory of law in his critique of legal reasoning in 1911.[40] Two major contexts underlined the elaboration of this work. On the one hand, as explained above, Kelsen was deeply influenced by the turn of the century Neo-Kantian movement. On the other hand, Kelsen was writing during the decline of the Austro-Hungarian empire, in the politically unstable period before World War I. As Peter Caldwell[41] notes, liberalism had lost much of its strength as a political current at the end of the 19th century, while authoritarian state socialism and social democracy gained public support with their calls for an interventionist state. Nationalist movements demanding that state borders correspond to lines of ethnicity threatened the existence of the multi-ethnic Austro-Hungarian Empire. The young Kelsen fiercely criticised these new currents leading to an identification of the abstract state with the nation or race. His liberal scepticism and criticism of radical nationalist or socialist politics, which compressed state and society into a unity, translated into his radical and total distinction between 'causal' and 'normative' reality.[42] Hence his rejection of any kind of sociological approach to jurisprudence, which was becoming fashionable by the turn of the century.

The disarray following the World War I brought about a strong desire for an absolute justification of the given social order, its traditional foundations — and, with them, the self-confidence of the individual — having been deeply shaken.[43] The natural law

---

[40] H Kelsen 1911.
[41] PC Caldwell 1997, 40 ff.
[42] See PC Caldwell 1997.
[43] This is Kelsen's explanation (see H Kelsen 1949b, 445).

theories providing an absolute (*contra* 'hypothetical') basis for the validity of law were one possible answer to this need for absolute justification. 'For the norms of natural law, like those of morality, are deduced from a Basic Norm that by virtue of its content — as emanation of divine will, of nature, or of a pure reason — is held to be directly evident'.[44] The Schmittian theory of the sovereign people provided another kind of absolute and indisputable basis for the legitimacy of the legal order, with its potential totalitarian drifts.[45]

Both these theories were severely attacked by Kelsen, first on epistemological grounds, as these doctrines were clearly at odds with his principle of the autonomy of the normative. In the case of natural law theories, the *ought* is derived from the *is* of God's commands or laws of nature. In the case of Schmitt's doctrine, the *is* takes the form of the ever-present people or the absolute will, 'closing off investigations of the relation between fractured society and unified state by bluntly asserting the unity of life and law'.[46]

Kelsen also opposed these theories in recognition of the danger they represented as models of a-critical legitimisation of the state.[47] In the annihilation of any problematic distance between *is* and *ought,* the very possibility of a critical assessment of the legal system's legitimisation basis is ruled out, making it prone to manipulations on behalf of any kind of absolute. Schmitt's doctrine is exemplary in showing the ravaging effects that such a simplifying strategy can have. Kelsen clearly chose his camp, even if it made his theory less attractive: 'The pure theory aims to depict the law *as it is*, without legitimising it as just or disqualifying it as unjust'.[48]

In a typically anti-positivist stance, Kelsen's theory has often been denounced for lacking an ethical moment. Kelsen's refusal to take part in the efforts of the lawmaker to have the law

[44] H Kelsen 1992, §28, 56.
[45] See chapter 4, section 4.2.
[46] PC Caldwell 1997, 102.
[47] H Kelsen 1967, §13, 69. This is an old ground of critique regarding natural law theories.
[48] H Kelsen 1992, §9, 18.

accepted as just,[49] however, elaborates a healthy critical distance. As Agostino Carrino puts it: 'The pure theory of law demystifies the will of the sovereign revealing his nakedness'.[50] It is interesting to note here that Kelsen had indirectly been in this position of 'nakedness' when Karl Renner gave him the assignment of writing a draft of the new republican constitution of Austria. On that occasion, he had to face the perplexities linked with the absence of any legal ground ultimately capable of legitimising his action (although of course Kelsen was only 'theoretically' sovereign).[51] One possible solution lay in the theory of the social contract made by the citizens to decide how they wanted to be ruled. Legality would then be derived from a pre-legal will, thus resolving the tension between *Sein* and *Sollen* in an autonomous, foundational act. Kelsen rejected that solution.

'One could only view an attempt to bridge the "is-ought" gap by means of the all-encompassing general will as a fiction in the troubled years after World War I in Austria and Germany'.[52] The connection between real people and the normative legal system could not be proven true. Kelsen kept it (highly) problematic, his extreme methodological dualism transforming this 'gap' between *is* and *ought* into an abyss.

Kelsen's conscious refusal to enter into the problem of praxis thus served a practical purpose by emphasising that the legal system was not reducible to social and natural reality. 'The dualistic conception of norm and fact, ideal and nature, reflected Kelsen's insistence on the existence of human freedom to

[49] 'If the question as to the reason for the validity of positive law [. . .] aims at an ethical-political justification of this coercive order [. . .] then the Basic Norm of the Pure theory of law does neither yield such a justification nor such a standard' (H Kelsen 1967, 217).

[50] A Carrino 1998, 514. Note the parallel with Montaigne's own enterprise of demystification, revealing the arbitrariness or the 'nakedness' of power.

[51] In that instance, the revolutionary break in legal continuity consisted in the fact that the Austro-Hungarian emperor's agreement in 1918 to recognise any decision by the National Council on the state's form was illegal according to existing law, since it was not approved by the Austro-Hungarian Imperial Council (*Reichsrat*).

[52] PC Caldwell 1997, 92.

issue ethical judgements regarding the contingent realm of necessity'.[53] By making all positive law subject to moral, ethical, and political criticism, Kelsen placed the responsibility for judging positive law in human hands. Do they have the means to take up this responsibility? Kelsen's sceptical appraisal of the judging capacities of humans makes the answer a delicate one.

The Anthropological Background[54]

Kelsen's systematic avoidance of any reference to some practical attitude or commitment on the part of citizens, and more generally society, constitutes one of the most striking features of his legal theory.

This isolation from the sphere of the citizen's normative choices and attitudes manifests itself not only with regard to the chain of validity structuring the legal system, which is constituted by norms and norms only: 'Ultimately all positive laws owe their validity to a non-positive law, a law *not created by human action*'.[55] It also makes Kelsen's understanding of legal authority most problematic. From this perspective, Bruno Celano emphasises the impossibility for Kelsen to explain what conditions the possibility of law's authority by reference to its recognition on the part of the legal subjects.[56] Indeed, for Kelsen, this kind of explanation would amount to regarding the law as having its *geltungsgrund* (its reason for validity) in something different from positive law itself. He thus explicitly rejects this interpretation in a footnote in the second edition of *The Pure Theory of Law*: 'the doctrine of the Basic Norm is not a doctrine

---

[53] PC Caldwell 1997, 89. By 'contingent realm of necessity', I take Caldwell to refer to the man-made character of the legal system, presented as a 'realm of necessity' in the sense that its propositions are not facultative.

[54] I should perhaps make clear that I understand here the term 'anthropological' as 'referring to a certain theory of human nature'.

[55] J Raz 1979, 125.

[56] Bruno Celano considers the statement according to which 'legal science merely represents the law as something which may be represented as a system of valid norms, ie as authoritative [. . .] by anybody who, for some reason or other (on the basis, namely, of any relevant ideologico-political assumptions), regards the Basic Norm of the legal system as valid' (See B Celano 2000, 187).

of recognition[57] as is sometimes erroneously understood. According to the doctrine of recognition positive law is valid only if it is recognised by the individuals subject to it [. . .] The theory of recognition, consciously or unconsciously, presupposes the ideal of individual liberty as self-determination, that is, the norm that the individual ought to do only what he wants to do'.[58]

This stark rejection of any claim to the effect that the existence of a legal order depends on the subject's recognition of it (*Anerkennungstheorien*) can be explained, in epistemological terms, as a direct consequence of Kelsen's commitment to the autonomy of the normative (which cannot depend on anything but *ought* statements). In that sense, *Anerkennungstheorien* simply fail to understand law itself as a specific *Sinnsphäre*, confusing the legality of a legal order with its efficacy.

This rejection can also be associated with a deeper disillusion, linked to a fundamental mistrust of the human ability to make normative choices (Kelsen would probably agree with Montaigne's statement: 'laws are made by fools, and even more often by men who fail in equity because they hate equality: but always by men, vain authorities who can resolve nothing'[59]). From that perspective, one could consider Kelsen as still influenced by the Judeo-Christian understanding of law as a *command*. The Basic Norm as a transcendental presupposition would therefore ensure that the normativity of law is understood independently of any subjective choice; that is: 'the Basic Norm is not presupposed arbitrarily, in the sense that there is a choice between different basic norms'.[60] Introducing any such *political choice* at the ground of the legal system would amount to rooting it in the domain of 'irrationality'. As David Dyzenhaus puts it: 'the thought that ethics and politics are deeply irrational [. . .]

---

[57] On the doctrine of recognition: 'it says that legal norms are valid only because, and only to the extent that, they are recognised as such by those at whom they are aimed.' (A Jacobson and B Schlink 2000, 60).

[58] H Kelsen 1967, §34 i, 218, note 83.

[59] M de Montaigne 1991, III 13, 1216.

[60] H Kelsen 1967, §34 d, 201.

is an article of faith which Kelsen and Schmitt share'.[61] If one does not trust the human ability to engage in judgement, then indeed ethics and politics, as the products of this very ability, are bound to be deemed 'irrational' (to use Dyzenhaus's words — I would rather say 'non-rational').

The systematic exclusion of any ideological or political consideration from the 'pure' theory may be understood as answering a situation of crisis that Kelsen couldn't help but sense (and of which he will personally bear the brunt). What reasons would lead Kelsen to trust a political arbitrariness that, in the Weimar Republic, could only be perceived as more and more threatening? By keeping the arbitrariness of power at a distance, Kelsen's work allows for a critical appraisal of the law's basis of legitimisation (by contrast with Schmitt's bringing back 'power to law and law to power'). The distance he imposes is, however, such that any passage from the sphere of power (*Sein*) to the sphere of law (*Sollen*) is ruled out, dooming the legal sphere to a 'negative autonomy', detached from any external (moral or empirical) element. The object of legal science thus isolated in its 'pure purity', Kelsen still has to define positively what he understands by normativity: cut from any empirical or moral context, this definition is doomed to circularity.

2.2 Explaining Legal Normativity 'From Within'

If one analyses Kelsen's attempts to define the concept of legal normativity throughout his works, one is necessarily struck by the number of circumlocutions and obscure formulations Kelsen uses in order to remain consistent with his ambition to secure the autonomous character of the normative sphere. Before considering Kelsen's awareness of the difficulties linked to this ambition, as well as the factors that led him to sustain such a project of autonomy, I propose to analyse, in chronological

[61] D Dyzenhaus 1997, 105.

order, the different formulations[62] Kelsen gave to the concept of legal normativity.

2.2.1 Defining the 'Specific Lawfulness' of the Law

In *Hautprobleme der Staatsrechtslehre*, his first work in legal theory, Kelsen explicitly formulates what will become the basis of an enduring impasse: 'logically speaking, enquiring into the "why" of a concrete *Sollen* can only lead to another *Sollen*, just as the answer to the "why" of a *Sein* can only be another *Sein*'.[63] In this very early work, Kelsen starts by providing a definition of the concept of normativity in exclusively negative terms, as opposed to facticity. The normative phenomenon is thus trapped in the dualistic opposition between *is* and *ought* which, as 'ultimate categories', cannot be explicated: 'Just as one cannot describe what . . . *Sein* is, so likewise, there is no definition of *Sollen*'.[64]

Later, in *Natural Law Doctrine and Legal Positivism*, Kelsen discusses the concept of normativity as the 'common form' of both positive and natural law, insisting that, by contrast with natural law, the *ought* of positive law can only have a relative meaning. '*We unavoidably find an "ought" expressed in positive law if we take it inherently to convey a norm or rule*. It is an "ought", however, which can only have a relative meaning. It follows that the category of "ought" (normativity) has a formal meaning only, unless it is related to a determinate content which alone is qualified as "good" or "just"'.[65] The circular structure of the first sentence of this quotation — *we find an 'ought' in positive law if we take it to convey a norm or rule* — constitutes a good illustration of the impasse Kelsen is trapped in, given the 'detached autonomy' to which he confines the normative sphere.

---

[62] Karl Leiminger (in K Leiminger 1967, 63–66) would have presented what he claims to be 18 distinct 'definitions' of Kelsen's *Sollen* (quoted by SL Paulson 2001, 59).

[63] H Kelsen 1911, 8.

[64] H Kelsen 1911, 7.

[65] H Kelsen 1949b, 394 (emphasis added).

If we go a step further, in the first edition of *Reine Rechtslehre*, Kelsen seeks to establish a parallel between the 'law of nature' (*Naturgesetz*), which links a certain material fact as cause with another as effect, and the 'law of normativity' (*Rechtsgesetz*), which links legal condition with legal consequence. 'If the mode of linking material facts is causality in the one case, it is imputation in the other, and imputation is recognised in the Pure theory as the particular lawfulness, the autonomy, of the law'.[66] As we have seen previously,[67] Kelsen does not understand the term 'imputation' in its common sense. As a counterpart to the category of causation, Kelsen puts forward the category of imputation as 'conditioning *a priori* our knowledge of the normative phenomenon'. Unfortunately, deprived of any reference to the progressive version of the transcendental argument, Kelsen has no means of establishing the necessity of this *a priori* category, and thus cannot account for the concept of normativity but through self-referential definitions.

From that perspective, the *General Theory of Law and State* does not bring any major innovation: 'the statement that an individual "ought to" behave in a certain way means that this behaviour is prescribed by a norm [. . .] The "ought" simply expresses the specific sense in which human behaviour is determined by a norm'.[68] In the second edition of *Reine Rechtslehre*, Kelsen goes on to distinguish between the subjective and the objective meaning of an 'ought', specifying that if the command of a legal organ also has the objective meaning of an ought — by contrast with the command of a robber gang which is only 'subjectively' normative — it is because we presuppose the Basic Norm. 'But why do we interpret the subjective meaning of the one act also as its objective meaning, but not so of the other act? Why do we suppose that of the two acts, which both have the

---

[66] See H Kelsen 1992, 23 (§11 b, 'Ought as designating a transcendental category').

[67] See 'The epistemological background', in section 2.1.2.

[68] H Kelsen 1949a, 37.

subjective meaning of an "ought", only one established a valid, that is, binding, norm?'[69] This is a typical example of a 'Kelsenite' sentence, linking together concepts as different as normativity, validity and binding force.[70] Lacking a definition, Kelsen thus mixes up these notions, to the detriment of the credibility of the concept of legal normativity, which some modern authors have qualified as simply incompatible with Kelsen's positivist ambitions.[71]

2.2.2 Kelsen's Awareness of the Theoretical Limits Striking his Project of Autonomy

Given Kelsen's dualistic premise, strictly separating 'is' from 'ought', and his rejection of natural law theories (locating the source of normativity in a pre-existing concept of the good), the conceptual vagueness that surrounds legal normativity may be deemed inescapable, as it is necessarily cut off from any extraneous explicative resource. In this, Kelsen has been described as 'a characteristic representative of normativism given his concern to consider law as an order closed on itself'.[72] Kelsen is not unaware, though, of the difficulties linked to such closure. In one of his very early works, *Das Problem der Souveränität* (1920), he reveals a surprising awareness of the theoretical limit inevitably striking his ambition of closing in an autonomous way the formal legal system: 'to want to determine the choice of

[69] H Kelsen 1967, 45.

[70] Joseph Raz underlines that confusion in *The Concept of a Legal System*, asserting that 'Kelsen is trapped by his identification of validity with the existence of a norm on the one hand and its justification on the other. The statement that legal norms are only conditionally justified is synonym for him with the statement that legal norms are only conditionally valid, ie that they enjoy only conditional existence' (J Raz 1980, 135).

[71] E Bulygin 1998, 315: 'Either we will want to preserve the idea of *normative validity* [note the confusion, which is indeed allowed by Kelsen] (but then true principles or norms must be substituted for the Basic Norm, which implies the rejection of positivism and the acceptance of some sort of natural law), or else we will choose to be thoroughgoing positivists (but then we must reject the idea of validity as binding force)'.

[72] JF Kervégan 1995a, 238.

juristic starting point juristically would be tantamount to standing on one's shoulders, [and] would be equivalent to Munchausen's attempt to pull himself out of the swamp by his own pigtail'.[73]

In his subsequent writings, Kelsen's way of coming to terms with this enigmatic sentence amounts to insisting on the extra-systemic character of the Basic Norm, as a way of ensuring that, indeed, the Basic Norm as a juristic starting point is not 'juristically determined'. In *Das Problem der Souveränität*, Kelsen above all underlines the 'borderline status' of the 'Origin-Norm' (*Ursprungsnorm*)[74] as the fundamental presupposition that the legal system as a whole is valid, which cannot itself derive from that system. Later, in *Allgemeine Staatslehre* (1925) Kelsen takes pains to emphasise that the 'hypothetical norm' 'actually *does not stand inside the system* of positive legal propositions but first of all founds these systems'.[75] He reiterates this view in the second edition of the *Pure Theory of Law*, where he explicitly rejects interpretations according to which the Basic Norm is inside the legal order, declaring that the Basic Norm is 'actually "outside the constitution"'.

Do these explicit assertions about the extra-systemic character of the Basic Norm spare it the solipsistic status that would unavoidably flow from its being 'juristically determined'? First, one has to remember, with Julius Stone, that despite Kelsen's explicit declarations, 'he has regularly attributed functions to the

---

[73] H Kelsen 1960, 96. Note that Kelsen uses the same 'Munchausen' image a few years later, in Kelsen 1949b, 419, but this time to characterise 'the elementary kernel of all metaphysics and religion', ie 'this strange hypothesis' referring to 'a sphere which is said to hide the grounds and causes he [the human being] seeks, the ideas or archetypes of all earthly things experienced, the things as they are. . .' [. . .] 'by which man produces the illusion of growing beyond himself, this curious attempt of the eternal Munchausen to climb on his own shoulders'. Can we say then that the 'auto-foundation attempt' is as paradoxical as the attempt to ground the legal system in some metaphysical beyond?

[74] Kelsen does not yet use the term 'Basic Norm'. See H Kelsen 1960, 97.

[75] H Kelsen 1925, 104 (emphasis added).

basic norm which implied that this norm *was* a part of the respective legal order. He has kept on saying that this norm brings about the unity of the legal system [. . .] he has said that the hierarchy of legal norms "runs into the Basic Norm" and that this Basic Norm "sets up". . . a law creating organ'.[76] Moreover, the very fact that Kelsen found it necessary in the second edition of the *Pure Theory of Law* to repudiate the idea that the Basic Norm is part of the legal system suggests that he too felt discomfort at the implications of his own language. Secondly, even if one takes seriously Kelsen's explicit assertions about the extra-systemic status of the Basic Norm, one can still ask how the Basic Norm — which has repeatedly been characterised by Kelsen as the 'starting point' of legal cognition — is supposed to be 'determined', if not 'juristically'. Kelsen must have been aware that his aiming at a detached autonomy for the concept of normativity actually does not leave any alternative to 'juristic' determinations. Given the importance of Kelsen's methodological dualism, which rules out any determination by social facts or ethical principles, the Basic Norm is bound to be either simply *undetermined*[77] or, indeed, 'juristically' determined.[78] Kelsen would thus have been trapped in the very logical impasse he was warning against in one of his earliest works.

The extreme epistemological position of Kelsen is at the root of his difficulties in defining what he calls 'the specific lawfulness of the law' or 'the law of normativity'. The degree to which Kelsen was actually aware of the theoretical impasses introduced by his striving for a detached autonomy of the normative sphere remains unclear. What is certain is that his works are pervaded by tensions that he was never able to reconcile: the

---

[76] J Stone 1963, 45 (referring to Kelsen 1925, 84 and 249).

[77] Hence perhaps the final characterisation of the Basic Norm as a fiction.

[78] Kelsen's presentation of the Basic Norm as 'merely raising to the level of consciousness what all jurists are, even unconsciously, doing when [. . .] they reject natural law and yet consider the data of their cognition not as mere facts of power, but as laws, as norms' (H Kelsen 1949b, 395) corroborates this point.

unavoidable reference to the sphere of human activity in order to account for the possibility of law's normativity ultimately foils his ambition to secure the purity of the normative sphere.

2.3 Where Kelsen's 'Purity Project' gets Defeated: Acknowledging Specific Forms of Conditionality

In section 2.1, I considered Kelsen's two-sided 'purity programme', aiming at securing the autonomy of the normative sphere as the object of a specifically *legal* cognition, detached from both empirical and moral considerations. The strict methodological dualism underlying such a striving towards a *pure* theory of law made any attempt at defining the normative phenomenon thus 'purified' particularly challenging.

Throughout Kelsen's works, there were two theoretical questions for the treatment of which Kelsen had no choice but to refer to extra-normative considerations. These questions concern the problem of lawmaking as well as the attribution of a 'content' to the Basic Norm, to which Kelsen will give the most diverse formulations, until finally suppressing it.

2.3.1 'The Problem of Positivity'

When, in 1917, Kelsen adopted Merkl's doctrine of hierarchical structure,[79] leading him to a dynamic characterisation of law, he was faced with the delicate question of lawmaking (as distinct from the question about the validity of law already made). 'The law is made by human will'[80]: Kelsen could not escape the acknowledgement of this fundamental truth at the basis of what he called 'the problem of positivity'. For Kelsen, the problem consists in the fact that 'the law appears as ought and is at the same time, while *logically* these two categories are mutually exclusive'.[81] Indeed, on the one hand, positive laws

---

[79] It is worth noting that this adoption corresponds to the time when Kelsen was actually involved in the drafting of the Austrian constitution.
[80] H Kelsen 1949b, 392.
[81] H Kelsen 1949b, 394 (emphasis added).

are made by an act of will that occurs in the realm of being (*is* dimension of law); on the other hand, 'positive law, as a norm, is from its own immanent point of view an *ought*'.[82] When these empirical acts of will take the form of legislative acts, this tension can be resolved by considering these acts as somehow endowed with law-creating status by a higher authorising norm. These law-creating facts are then part of the chain of validity, embodying the condition of effectiveness, necessary to the existence of a legal system. When, however, there is no higher authorising norm to endow the (initial) empirical act of will with law-creating status, Kelsen is faced with a problem. For fear of falling into an idealism that he deems untenable,[83] Kelsen cannot simply ignore the *initial* law-creating facts, 'the social practice which ties the ultimate legal rule to social reality'.[84] Likewise, these initial law-creating facts cannot be *logically* linked to the norm they have created (the historically first constitution) as indeed, given Kelsen's methodological dualism, an *ought* cannot possibly derive from an *is*. As we shall see in the next section, Kelsen initially finds a way out by making these initial law-creating facts the *content* of the basic norm. Kelsen will nevertheless have to abandon that solution, and the problem of lawmaking will remain a source of tension throughout his work.

Interestingly enough, Kelsen emphasises that the positivity of a legal system is 'a ground of validity thoroughly alien to natural law because, as a "natural" order, it is not created by man and by its own assumption cannot be created by a human act'.[85]

---

[82] H Kelsen 1949b, 393.

[83] 'The first [idealistic theory of law] is wrong for it is undeniable that a legal order in its entirety, and an individual legal norm as well, lose their validity when they cease to be effective; and that a relation exists between the *ought* of the legal norm and the *is* of physical reality also insofar as the positive legal norm, to be valid, must be created by an act which exists in the reality of being' (H Kelsen 1967, 211).

[84] See J Raz 1998, 251.

[85] H Kelsen 1949b, 392.

One may wonder, though, in what sense the 'positivity' of law can provide a ground of validity for the *positive* legal system as understood by Kelsen (ie as detached from any factual element). The true ground of validity, in Kelsen's system, is the Basic Norm. As he himself acknowledges, the Basic Norm somehow constitutes a 'limitation to the idea of legal positivity' as 'the Basic Norm is *not valid because it has been created in a certain way*'.[86] By considering the ultimate consequences of this 'limitation', one could hold that, as a transcendental hypothesis beyond which one cannot go,[87] the Basic Norm actually makes positivity 'thoroughly alien' to Kelsen's concept of validity. And yet, every valid law can only be made by a human act, an empirical act of will . . . As Joseph Raz phrases it: 'Though every law is created by human action, it derives its validity not from the act, but from another law authorising its creation'.[88] The ultimate element in this chain of 'authorisation' is the Basic Norm, which is charged with the important task of avoiding any consideration of the factual origins of law (thus ensuring the normative closure of the system). In order for this fundamental norm to be exempted from this ineluctable 'law of foundation'[89] without breaking the unity of the system, it has to be of a nature different from all the other rules composing it.

This 'special status' of the Basic Norm notably shows through the 'content' Kelsen first attributed and then denied to it.

2.3.2 The 'Content' of the Basic Norm

The need for an 'ultimate' or 'basic' norm was expressed by Kelsen as early as 1914.[90] The first reference to a *content* of the Basic Norm is nevertheless to be found in *Allgemeine Staatslehre* (1925): 'It [the Basic Norm] has for its typical content that an

[86] H Kelsen 1949b, 401.
[87] H Kelsen 1949b, 396.
[88] J Raz 1979, 125.
[89] According to which each norm has to find the ground of its validity in another norm.
[90] See H Kelsen 1914, 215–220.

authority, a source of law, is set up whose expressions have to obtain as valid: *behave as the legal authority commands*'.[91] This imperative characterisation of the content of the Basic Norm is, however, relatively rare and will never reappear in later works.

The reference to the content of the Basic Norm in *Natural Law Doctrine and Legal Positivism* is most interesting as it brings to light a major tension Kelsen had to deal with. Indeed, as Kelsen himself acknowledges — under the heading 'The limitation of positivism' — 'the Basic Norm is not valid because it has been created in a certain way, but its validity is assumed by virtue of its *content*. It is valid, then, like a norm of natural law, apart from its merely hypothetical validity'.[92] Kelsen is thus aware that the attribution of content to the Basic Norm makes it dangerously close to the natural law model, first target of his double-sided purity programme. The relatively confused characterisation he suggests testifies, I think, to his efforts to get rid of this ambiguity: 'the content of the Basic Norm — that is, the particular historical fact qualified by the Basic Norm as the original law-making fact — depends entirely upon the material to be taken as positive law, on the wealth of empirically given acts subjectively claiming to be legal acts'.[93]

In the first edition of the *Pure Theory of Law*, Kelsen is more cautious, taking care to establish a clear-cut distinction between 'the norms of natural law [which] are deduced from a Basic Norm that by virtue of its *content* [. . .] is held to be directly evident' and 'the Basic Norm of a [positive] legal system, which has a *thoroughly formal*, dynamic character [. . . being] simply the basic rule according to which the norms of the legal system are created'.[94] Kelsen then characterises the content of the Basic

---

[91] H Kelsen 1925, 36.

[92] H Kelsen 1949b, 401.

[93] H Kelsen 1949b, 436. Note that one can interpret the 'facts' that determine the content of the Basic Norm as, simply, those facts about the spatial and temporal dimensions of a legal system (dimensions which are 'affixed' to the Basic Norm), so that one can still maintain that the Basic Norm has, as it were, a 'constant content' (its formulation remains the same in any case).

[94] H Kelsen 1992, §28, 56.

Norm as depending 'on a certain material fact, namely, the material fact creating that system to which actual behaviour corresponds to a certain degree'.[95] Now, this 'facts-oriented' characterisation of the Basic Norm is at the root of another major tension, which will become even more tangible in *General Theory of Law and State*.

In that work, Kelsen characterises the content of the Basic Norm as 'determined by the facts through which an order is created and applied, to which the behaviour of the individual regulated by this order, by and large, conforms'.[96] According to Julius Stone, this grounding of the content of the Basic Norm in these 'foundational facts' may be interpreted as a reaction to the criticism of Hersch Lauterpacht — a former pupil of Kelsen — who pointed out in 1933 that 'there must be a certain parallelism' between what is and what ought to be: 'The tension between the factual and the normative must not be too great [. . .], just as it ought not be too small'.[97] This time what is at stake is the implication of Kelsen's second movement of rejection, which creates an 'unbridgeable abyss' between *is* and *ought*. Kelsen's last and most adventurous characterisation of the content of the Basic Norm indeed clearly conflicts with his ideal of 'purity'.

In the second edition of the *Pure Theory of Law*, any reference to the content of the Basic Norm has completely disappeared.[98] It is as if Kelsen had realised that ultimately this notion of 'content' would necessarily lead him either to provide a satisfactory conceptualisation of these 'social practices' which he had left to the province of legal sociology (and thus force him to renounce — or at least to temper — his methodological

---

[95] H Kelsen 1992, §30, 59.

[96] H Kelsen 1949a, 120.

[97] H Lauterpacht 1933, 111.

[98] See eg H Kelsen 1967, 219, which has an equivalent in H Kelsen 1949b, 401, except that any reference to the *content* of the Basic Norm has disappeared.

dualism), or would introduce an internal point of contradiction threatening the coherence of his whole system.

In order to determine the phenomena by reference to which the content of the Basic Norm is to be defined, one can consider that the content of the Basic Norm either is implied in or is in some way to be deduced from the existing norms of the particular legal order.[99] But then the affirmation that the legal order can only be identified by reference to its Basic Norm becomes dangerously circular (and, besides, Kelsen has expressly rejected that solution in the *Pure Theory of Law*[100]). Or one can consider the existential facts of social life in a given community, possibly accompanied by (non-legal) normative judgements.[101] But then it is the very purity of the Kelsenian method that is threatened. From this perspective, Ernesto Garzon Valdes suggests yet another formulation of the dilemma linked with the determination of the *content* of the Basic Norm: 'The question of the content of this Basic Norm is, of course, a complicated matter. If the Basic Norm merely says, "one ought to behave as the constitution prescribes",[102] it does not seem to be very different from the command of divine law [. . .] If, on the other hand, the content of the Basic Norm is "determined by the facts" that accompany each act of creation in a positive system of norms, then it becomes hard to understand the sense in which the Basic Norm can be seen as a Kantian category'.[103]

Kelsen was certainly most aware of the complexities linked to the determination of the content of the Basic Norm. His ultimate turn to a characterisation of the Basic Norm as a *fiction*

[99] See J Raz 1980, 95–96, underlining that 'Kelsen tends to succumb to the temptation to make every Basic Norm include in its content all the conclusions of his theory of norms'.

[100] 'The content of a positive legal order is entirely independent from its Basic Norm' (H Kelsen 1967, 217).

[101] This would amount to taking the genealogical route, advocated in chapter 5.

[102] See Kelsen's first characterisation, as well as H Kelsen 1967, §34 c, 201.

[103] EG Valdes 1998, 270.

testifies, somewhat dramatically,[104] to Kelsen's awareness of the impossibility for the Basic Norm to be at the same time this transcendental presupposition free of any ideological or factual consideration and the element that, via its content, intrinsically refers to the factual sphere.

In 'The Function of a Constitution', published in 1964, Kelsen already prepares what will be his ultimate position in *General Theory of Norms*: 'to the assumption of a norm not posited by a real act of will but only presupposed in juristic thinking, one may validly object that a norm can be the meaning only of an act of will and not of an act of thinking. One can meet this objection only by conceding that, along with the Basic Norm, presupposed in thought, one must also think of an *imaginary authority* whose (figmentary) act of will has the Basic Norm as its meaning'.[105] This last quotation, marking Kelsen's distance from the Kantian traditional doctrine, sanctions his adoption of a 'will theory of law',[106] which leaves the Basic Norm in desperate need of an author. If the Basic Norm cannot have a 'real' author (with a real and thus arbitrary will), one is left with *imagining* one[107] (who, in his quality of 'imaginary' being, can only produce a fiction).

From the status of 'transcendental hypothesis', the Basic Norm goes to a status of (legitimate) fiction: '*Notre droit-même, dit-on, a des fictions légitimes sur lesquelles il fonde la vérité de sa justice*'.[108] The concept of *legitimate fiction* is, I think, particularly relevant here as it points towards a kind of heuristic device

---

[104] This last shift has been described by John Finnis as a 'débâcle', see J Finnis 1996, 204.

[105] H Kelsen 1986, 115.

[106] Note that Kelsen vehemently criticised these 'voluntaristic' theories of law in his earlier phases (see SL Paulson 1998c, xxvii).

[107] It is worth noting here that this need for an author marks a shift from Kelsen's Kantian phase since a 'transcendental hypothesis' certainly does not need any author.

[108] 'Even our system of Law, they say, bases the truth of its justice upon legal fictions' (Note that this translation unfortunately does not quite render the idea of *legitimate* fictions) (M de Montaigne 1991, II 12, 603).

acknowledging the need to close the theoretical discourse on an object which, however, is not sufficient unto itself (ie whose full understanding necessitates the reference to extraneous elements). 'According to Vaihinger, a fiction is a cognitive device used when one is unable to attain one's cognitive goal with the material at hand. The cognitive goal of the Basic Norm is to ground the validity of the norms forming a positive moral or legal system [. . .] this goal can be attained only by means of a fiction'.[109] In other words, Kelsen could not sustain (or explain) the irreducibly normative character of law in strictly legal terms, ie exclusively by means of the elements contained in his system of norms as he had defined it. By means of the (fictitious) Basic Norm, Kelsen suggests proceeding *as though* the material of the law were irreducibly normative. From this perspective, Kelsen could be taken as recognising that a positive affirmation of the irreducibly normative character of law would necessarily bear on factual (and possibly moral) arguments, which he nevertheless wishes to keep apart from his *Pure* theory.

Kelsen's resort to his theory of the Basic Norm as a fiction is, I think, mistakenly characterised as 'irrational'. It could rather be interpreted as an acknowledgement of the impossibility of conceiving the 'specific lawfulness' of the law in exclusively legal terms, while preserving the separability of the legal from the moral and factual spheres. The concept of 'fiction' may be the confused recognition of these specific forms of conditionality that the Basic Norm (problematically) crystallises through its unavoidable confrontation with the sphere of factuality.[110] It is worth recalling here Kelsen's early statement: 'For to want to determine the choice of juristic starting point juristically

---

[109] H Kelsen 1991, ch 59, §I, D, 256 (note that I have preferred to give Paulson's translation).

[110] The ultimate characterisation of the Basic Norm as a fiction may be considered as a way of conceptualising the 'incompleteness' of the legal sphere, 'living through the awareness that there is virtually no end to the reasons that could underpin and undermine the allegedly supreme norm' (B VanRoermund 2000, 211).

would be tantamount to standing on one's own shoulders'.[111] Would Kelsen have ultimately realised that the application of methodological dualism to his concept of Basic Norm had led him to execute the acrobatic feat he had been warning against in one of his earliest works? The sudden disappearance of the notion of 'content' of the Basic Norm testifies to Kelsen's uneasiness regarding its unavoidable dependence upon the factual sphere, which is yet made unintelligible by his epistemological position strictly separating *is* from *ought*.

For Kelsen, to posit a *fictitious* Basic Norm as a 'juristic starting point' is a way of closing and ensuring the 'purity of the pure theory', while leaving critical thinking a clear field. For theories less concerned with 'purity' and equally committed to locating the source of legal normativity *within* human activity, Kelsen's Basic Norm could indicate the field beyond which it is necessary to consider what enables the normative character of legal norms. This task is at the centre of the 'story' I develop in chapter 5.

Conclusion

If there is one element unfailingly pervading Kelsen's work, despite its numerous turns, it is Kelsen's determination to secure the purity of his pure theory, isolating its object in the etheral sphere of strictly normative propositions. Beyond arguments of an epistemological nature, relying on an expanded version of methodological dualism, one can understand Kelsen's concern to ensure the independence of his theory from moral, political or ideological considerations in the light of the tormented political realities surrounding the elaboration of his work. While, in the case of Montaigne's theory, the initial law-creating practices were set apart in consideration of the danger they represented for the layman, who couldn't but be

---

[111] H Kelsen 1949b, 96.

disgusted by their precarious and arbitrary appearance, in the case of Kelsen's theory, a similar kind of danger is at stake, involving the more-than-ever threatening *compromission* of law with politics.

Having thus excluded any appeal to either moral or factual considerations to explain the normative dimension of law, Kelsen is left with the task of accounting for the normativity of law 'from within', without appealing to any external element. This ambition to define an autonomous legal *ought* ultimately fails. Kelsen's rejection of the classical natural law model indeed commits him to locating the source of legal normativity *within* human activity, while his methodological dualism rules out any reference to the very 'fabric' of human activity: factual and moral elements. Hence Kelsen's reference to the Basic Norm as a 'presupposed' starting point, an 'origin' that makes any inquiry into the sources[112] of legal normativity conveniently superfluous. The numerous difficulties contravening this project and Kelsen's ultimate turn to a characterisation of the Basic Norm as a *fiction* testifies to the impossibility of grounding legal normativity in a singular point allegedly free of any moral or factual elements. In chapter 4, I will contrast this hope of singular or original foundation (the 'pedigree approach') with an approach seeking to establish the 'genealogy' of legal normativity": the multiple, interconnecting social processes enabling the emergence of legal norms.

---

[112] For the distinction between 'sources' and 'origins', see 18 in the Introduction.

3
Hart

Hart and Kelsen share a common concern to defend the specificity of legal normativity against any attempt to reduce it to either mere factuality or to moral normativity. Like Kelsen, Hart is committed to accounting for the normative dimension of law while rejecting the classical natural law model. His explanation of this normative dimension nevertheless differs drastically from Kelsen's. The aim of this chapter is to highlight the reasons underlying such a difference of understanding and the implications of this contrast in the general context of legal theory.

In the first section of this chapter, I consider the different factors that have contributed to the elaboration of Hart's and Kelsen's contrasted understandings of legal normativity, starting with their respective positions as to the relationship between law on one hand, and factuality and morality on the other. As one would expect, these methodological assumptions determine the shape of their account of legal normativity. I shall hence try to underline the very different aims Hart and Kelsen have in mind when they seek to account for the normative dimension of law. While Kelsen is trying to grasp what conditions the possibility of the normative status of legal rules, Hart, in contrast, is concerned with emphasising the *context* within which legal normative utterances can have meaning. Finally, I shall consider the respective roles that the Rule of Recognition and the Basic Norm, as 'ultimate rules', play in explaining the normative dimension of law.

As the general picture ensuing from my account of the contrast existing between Hart's and Kelsen's understandings of legal normativity differs importantly from Raz's account of the same contrast, I shall devote the second section of this chapter to developing Raz's understanding of the difference of outlook between the two authors. The main source of my disagreement with Raz's analysis consists in his examining Hart's and Kelsen's conceptions of legal normativity on the basis of his own cognitive understanding of the normativity problem, and applying this specific perspective to Kelsen's account, which results in a misinterpretation of Kelsen's project.

Finally, in a third section, I shall sketch an account of what unites the three theories we have considered so far. Montaigne, Kelsen and Hart indeed all face the same kind of theoretical difficulty. It flows from their common commitment to explaining the normative dimension of law while rejecting the classical natural law model, thus having to locate the source of legal normativity *within*, rather than *beyond* human activities. All three theories are reluctant to confront the apparent arbitrariness of these 'human activities', most of the time embedded in an ideological or political context that might seem best kept apart from the field of legal theory. While Montaigne invokes the precariousness and ridiculous futility of the practices conditioning and enabling the existence of law, Kelsen refers to methodological considerations, and Hart to the mere irrelevance of the initial law-creating facts, in order to relegate them to the scope of inappropriate questions.

The point of the second part of this book is to show that this effort to *separate* the normative and social aspects of law into two distinct 'explanatory targets' is both unnecessary and counterproductive.

3.1 Hart's and Kelsen's Understandings of Legal Normativity Contrasted

In this section I consider the different factors that contribute to the important difference of outlook characterising Hart's and Kelsen's conceptions of legal normativity. I shall first expose the methodological premises underlying Hart's and Kelsen's approaches, which mainly show through their respective conceptions of the link between, on the one hand, law and facts, and on the other, law and morality. I shall then emphasise the very different aims Hart and Kelsen have in mind when they try to explain the normative dimension of law. In contrast to Kelsen, who seeks to understand the conditions of possibility of legal norms (considered as normative entities), Hart seeks to capture the normative status of law by describing how certain people *treat* it as normative (thus concentrating on what I shall call the 'downstream side' of normativity). Finally, I shall consider the role that the Rule of Recognition and the Basic Norm respectively play, as 'ultimate norms', in Hart's and Kelsen's accounts of legal normativity.

3.1.1 Underlying Methodological Assumptions

Kelsen departs from the traditional positivist view of his time by rejecting the 'reductive semantic thesis', which reduces law's normative dimension to mere concatenations of fact. Hart clearly shares this anti-reductivism, devoting a significant amount of his work to criticising John Austin's analysis of law in terms of commands and habits. This shared conviction about the normative dimension of law commits both authors to providing an explanation — if not a definition — of what they understand by 'normativity'. Is there a specifically legal concept of normativity? Is the normative dimension of law somehow 'constituted' or is it inherent in the law itself?

I have emphasised in the last chapter how Kelsen's difficulties in providing a definition of the concept of normativity flow from his methodological dualistic premise, strictly separating *is* from *ought*. This epistemological position leads Kelsen to sustain what Paulson calls the 'normativity thesis', 'the idea that the import of such concepts as legal norm, "ought", and obligation has to be explicated, at every juncture, independently of any appeal to fact — in contrast, say, to HLA Hart's appeal to social facts'.[1] Hart does not associate his conviction about the

---

[1] SL Paulson 1998c, xxxiv.

normative character of law with such a methodological dualism; which allows him to explain legal normativity by reference to social facts.[2]

Another factor crucially determining Hart's and Kelsen's approach is their common adoption of the 'separation thesis', namely the idea that there is no conceptually necessary connection between law and morality. Hart's and Kelsen's interpretations of this thesis, however, differ significantly in that Kelsen understands this absence of necessary connection as a relationship of radical *independence* of law from morality (this construction is linked to Kelsen's understanding of autonomy in terms of independence, see previous chapter). The importance attributed by Kelsen to his ideal of purity, conjoined with his moral scepticism,[3] leads him to defend a vision of legal theory as — apparently — *value-free*.

Hart does not hold such an extreme position, and in an attempt to accommodate Dworkin's views about the role played by moral arguments in legal discourse, he explicitly endorses in his *Postscript* what he calls a 'soft positivism',[4] acknowledging that 'the rule of recognition may incorporate as criteria of validity conformity with moral principles or substantive values'.[5] In contrast to Kelsen's theory, which fiercely rejects any reference

---

[2] 'I share with him [Kelsen] the conviction that a central task of legal philosophy is to explain the normative force of propositions of law [. . .] None the less [. . .] my main effort in these two essays is to show that references to both psychological and social facts, which Kelsen's theory in its excessive purity would exclude, are in fact quite indispensable' (HLA Hart 1983, 18).

[3] See H Kelsen 1967, 59–69.

[4] This form of positivism is most commonly referred to as 'inclusive legal positivism' (by contrast with Raz's exclusive legal positivism). Jules Coleman also calls it 'incorporationism' (see J Coleman 2001a). Matthew Kramer takes these two different terms to refer to two different positions, depending on whether consistency with a moral principle is considered a *necessary* or a *sufficient* condition for the status of a norm as a legal norm (M Kramer 2000). I will come back to this inclusive/exclusive positivism debate in further details in section 5.2.2.

[5] HLA Hart 1994, 250.

to moral considerations in order to determine the validity[6] of legal rules, Hart thus ultimately recognises the *possibility* of such a reference. Interpreted in various ways,[7] such a move does not carry any direct consequence for Hart's conception of normativity, as indeed the criteria of validity incorporated in the Rule of Recognition first and foremost aim at determining the membership quality of legal rules, not their normative dimension.

Hart's and Kelsen's respective premises, conditioning their accounts of legal normativity, may thus be summarised as follows: whereas, for Kelsen, any explanation of the normative dimension of law must necessarily proceed from a non-factual starting point and needs to be independent of the moral value of the law, for Hart, this explanation is bound to be grounded in social facts, and 'need not be moral' (ie may, but need not, be independent of moral considerations). Now, the contrast between Hart and Kelsen does not stop at their distinctive methodological premises. It also shows through the very different objectives they respectively have in mind when they account for the normative dimension of law.

3.1.2 Telling Different Sides of the Story

According to Hart, one of the central issues underlying any speculation about the nature of law shows through questions such as 'what are rules?', 'what does it mean to say that a rule

---

[6] As I have tried to underline in the previous chapter, Kelsen's concept of validity encompasses both the membership *and* the normative quality of a rule, by contrast with Hart's understanding of validity as referring exclusively to the membership quality of a rule.

[7] While Jules Coleman claims that Hart's embracing incorporationism is inconsistent with the core theses of his positivist commitment (ie the conventionality thesis and the practical difference thesis) (see J Coleman 2001a, 101), Scott Shapiro argues that Hart's 'soft positivism' offends his view that the primary function of the law is to guide conduct: 'for Hart, legal norms must not only result *from* norm-guided behaviour but must also possibly result *in* norm-guided behaviour and, as I argued, this cannot be the case for moral principles, which are valid solely in virtue of their content' (SJ Shapiro 2001, 186). For an answer to the latter argument, see notably M Kramer 2000 and M Kramer 2002.

exists?'.[8] Behind the fairly straightforward appearance of such questions lies, according to Hart, a fundamental problem underscored (*a contrario*) by the development of 'rule sceptic' theories. Such theories indeed question the extent to which law is at all an affair of rules, either by condemning the very notion of a binding rule as confused or fictitious, or by reducing the law to a set of predictive statements as to the behaviour of courts or officials.[9] Against such 'reductionist' accounts, Hart puts forward his 'conviction that a central task of legal philosophy is to explain the normative force of propositions of law which figure both in academic legal writing and in the discourse of judges and lawyers'.[10]

Hart starts off his investigation of the normative character of law by underlining 'the crucial difference between merely convergent habitual behaviour in a social group and the existence of a rule of which the words "must", "should", and "ought to" are often a sign'.[11] Beyond the mere predictability of punishment (which constitutes one factor of differentiation), Hart emphasises the 'internal aspect of rules', which implies that some people at least 'must look upon the behaviour in question [to which the rule refers] as a general standard to be followed by the group as a whole'.[12] The normative statement 'it is a rule' can thus only have sense in the context of regular behaviour combined with a reflective critical attitude shared by at least part of the population. These normative statements are, typically, what 'imperative theories' cannot account for, ignoring the specific 'internal' dimension conditioning the meaning of normative utterances.[13]

[8] HLA Hart 1994, 8.
[9] HLA Hart 1994, 11–12.
[10] HLA Hart 1983, 18.
[11] HLA Hart 1994, 10.
[12] HLA Hart 1994, 56.
[13] 'The imperative theory, however, also fails to account for a feature of statements of legal obligation [. . .] this feature is what is now called the "normativity" of such statements and statements *of the law* or the legal position of individuals under the law' (HLA Hart 1982, 144).

Hart's explanation of 'the normative force of propositions of law' thus focuses above all on the *context* within which normative propositions can have a sense, underlining the various elements conditioning the meaning of these statements. In the case of legal rules, Hart adds to the components already identified in the case of social rules an extra dimension, consisting in the acceptance of a 'Rule of Recognition'. The point of legal utterances such as 'it is the law that' is to invoke the Rule of Recognition and the precepts stemming from it as standards that *ought* to be observed.[14]

Now, at this stage, very little is said about what this *ought* exactly consists of, what conditions a claim such as 'this standard ought to be observed'. And that is precisely what Hart is not seeking to explain. In his inquiry into the nature of law, Hart mainly tries to clarify certain uses of language,[15] and notably its normative use, which is 'the standard normal form of description of the content of law'.[16] From a naturalist perspective (which Joseph Raz deems to characterise Hart's approach[17]), the explanation of a proposition such as 'it is the law that' indeed raises particular difficulties, since law is not 'a thing located in space'. Hart's analysis of legal statements as statements from an internal point of view refers to the *attitude* of part of the population in order to account for the normative dimension of the statements in question. This approach tackles the problem *from*

[14] Of course Hart underlines that one can also speak of the law 'from an external point of view', either referring to the way in which the people accepting the rules view their own behaviour, or referring to mere observable regularities of behaviour, in which case one's 'description of their life cannot be in terms of rules at all' (HLA Hart 1994, 89).

[15] Hart's allegiance to JL Austin's method, aimed at elucidating even the most complex concepts by reference to the 'things people do with words', will be examined in section 4.3.

[16] HLA Hart 1982, 145.

[17] In 'The Nature of the Theory of Law', Joseph Raz indeed maintains that Hart's approach would be characterised by a naturalist outlook, 'according to which the only things there are (or the only things whose existence has duration) are things located in space, knowledge about which is gained by the natural sciences, or at any rate is subject to correction by them' (J Raz 2001, 4).

downstream, seeking to put forward the meaning that a normative proposition might have for the people confronted with it.[18] Such an approach, focusing on the *conditions of enunciation* of legal propositions, is not as such concerned with the *conditions of possibility* of law's normativity, ie what allows and conditions the passage from social facts[19] to legal norms.

To put it another way: Hart's aiming to capture the normative status of law by describing how certain people *treat* it as normative and adopt a 'critical reflective attitude' towards legal rules does not commit him to explaining what it is about law, or about the context of interaction in which it is embedded, that would give rise to the adoption of such an attitude. Hart's specification in the *Postscript* that the Rule of Recognition should be understood as a *conventional rule* may be regarded as the beginning of such an explanation, which Stephen Perry nevertheless deems to be 'incomplete', 'because he does not say why general conformity could be part of a reason for accepting a rule'.[20] Regarding Hart's account of legal normativity generally, Perry observes: 'As far as these latter concepts [obligation and authority] are concerned, Hart is content simply to make the observation that officials and perhaps others accept the Rule of Recognition, meaning they *regard* it as obligation-imposing. This is to describe the problem of the normativity of law rather than to offer a solution'.[21] In my opinion, Hart probably never

---

[18] Along this line, see Hart's emphasis on the need for a 'hermeneutic' method, 'which involves *portraying rule-governed behaviour as it appears to its participants*, who see it as conforming or failing to conform to certain shared standards' (HLA Hart 1983, 13, emphasis added).

[19] If indeed law is deemed to be made possible by social facts, a thesis which Coleman deems one of the main commitments of legal positivism (see J Coleman 2001a, 116).

[20] SR Perry 2001, 341.

[21] SR Perry 2001, 353 (see also 334 and 351). Along a similar line, Coleman emphasises that 'the internal point of view is an existence condition of a social rule, and it marks the fact that people treat the rule as reason-giving. It does not explain why or how the rule does so. This means that Hart never really gives an account of how the Rule of Recognition in particular, or how a social rule in general, create reasons for action or guide behaviour' (J Coleman 2001a, 119).

intended to offer the kind of 'solution' to the problem of normativity that Perry suggests. Such a solution would indeed require Hart to develop and explain how the 'context of social interaction' in which the law is embedded can *give rise* to the establishment of social and then legal rules, a problem which, given Hart's specific perspective on the problem of normativity, was not part of his theoretical concerns.

By contrast, Kelsen's theory does seek to understand what conditions the possibility of legal normativity. His methodological dualism, strictly separating *is* from *ought*, however, does not allow him to ground the *ought* dimension of law in factual propositions. Kelsen thus has to resort to the transcendental argument I have presented in the previous chapter, relying on the Basic Norm as the last (and presupposed) *reason of validity* for all the norms of the system. Allowing one to interpret the *subjective* meaning of the initial acts of will as their objective meaning, that is, as normative, the Basic Norm is what allows the passage from *is* to *ought*, or rather what takes the place of such a passage. Indeed, one can understand the Basic Norm as what allows Kelsen to avoid having to provide the type of philosophical argument suggested by Korsgaard in *The Sources of Normativity*[22] (such an argument would necessarily lead him either to locate the source of legal normativity beyond human activity to or renounce his methodological dualism and refer to factual propositions).

Kelsen's concerns are nevertheless not so far removed from Korsgaard's insofar as, like her, he seeks to understand what allows the existence of (legal) norms. One can thus characterise Kelsen's perspective upon the 'normativity problem' as an *upstream perspective*, in contrast to Hart's *downstream* approach, which basically tells another side of the story. One way of understanding this stark difference of outlook consists in thinking of Kelsen's and Hart's respective accounts of normativity as

[22] CM Korsgaard 1996 — see my general introduction.

telling respectively the beginning and the end of the 'story of the normative', Kelsen accounting for the conditions of possibility of legal norms, and Hart accounting for their 'conditions of enunciation' (ie the context within which propositions about norms can have a meaning).

3.1.3 The Role of the 'Ultimate Norm'

Given the distinctive aims Hart and Kelsen have in mind when trying to explain the normative dimension of law, the roles which the Basic Norm and the Rule of Recognition respectively play in this explanation are bound to be different. Aware of the potential confusions linked to the fact that, in both theories, the Basic Norm and the Rule of Recognition are presented as 'ultimate', Hart underlines the importance of carefully defining the ultimate character of the Rule of Recognition. His aim is to 'disentangle' it from the misleading understandings developed by Austin's theory of sovereignty as well as by Kelsen's theory of the Basic Norm as a transcendental hypothesis.

In this context, Hart shows how, at some point, inquiries concerning the validity of a rule are brought to a stop, 'for we have reached a rule which, like the intermediate statutory order and statute, provides criteria for the assessment of the validity of other rules; but *it is also unlike them in that there is no rule providing criteria for the assessment of its own legal validity*'.[23] In contrast to Kelsen, who expresses the ultimacy of the Basic Norm by saying that, contrary to other rules, its own validity cannot be demonstrated but is 'assumed' or 'postulated', for Hart the Rule of Recognition is ultimate in the sense that there is no rule providing criteria for the assessment of its validity. Hart rightly underlines this important point of differentiation in relation to Kelsen's theory, as it carries significant consequences for the understanding of such concepts as validity, existence and binding force.

---

[23] HLA Hart 1994, 107 (emphasis added).

According to Hart, 'no question concerning the validity or invalidity of the generally accepted Rule of Recognition as distinct from the factual question of its *existence* can arise'.[24] The word 'validity', in Hart's theory, is used to ascertain whether or not a certain rule satisfies certain criteria of membership within the legal system. To apply this test of validity to the rule which posits these criteria amounts either to nonsense or misunderstanding, for 'it [the Rule of Recognition] can neither be valid nor invalid but is simply *accepted* as appropriate for use in this way'.[25]

While for Hart the question of existence alone can sensibly be applied to the Rule of Recognition, for Kelsen, the question of the existence of the Basic Norm is of very little significance. Conceived as a 'transcendental presupposition' allowing the normative interpretation of 'the empirical material which presents itself as law',[26] the Basic Norm merely exists 'in juristic consciousness' (if it exists at all — see Kelsen's shift to the characterisation of the Basic Norm as a fiction). One could actually maintain that the question about the existence of the Basic Norm is just as relevant (that is, not at all) for Kelsen as the problem of the validity of the Rule of Recognition is for Hart. These wrongheaded questions merely testify to a serious misunderstanding of either Hart or Kelsen's theory.

What about Kelsen's statement that the 'validity' of the Basic Norm cannot be demonstrated but is 'presupposed'? To understand this assertion, one has to relocate the concept of validity within the context of Kelsen's understanding. When Kelsen asks: 'Why does a norm belong to a certain order?',[27] he does not expect a statement of the kind 'because this norm is to be held valid in view of certain criteria', as Hart would probably suggest, but rather a statement underlining that this norm has the same *reason for its validity* as the other norms belonging to

---

[24] HLA Hart 1994, 293 note 2.
[25] HLA Hart 1994, 109 (emphasis added).
[26] H Kelsen 1949a, 116.
[27] H Kelsen 1967, 193.

this order.[28] Odd as it may sound, for Kelsen the central issue is not so much the concept of validity itself but rather the 'reason for validity' of a norm, which actually amounts to the questioning of the origin of the normative status of a norm. The use of the same term 'validity' thus refers to totally different concerns in the minds of Hart and Kelsen. While for Hart it merely states a 'membership quality', for Kelsen it refers to the normative or binding status of a norm. Hence the common characterisation of Hart's and Kelsen's 'ultimate norm' as the ground of validity of all the rules of the system actually refers to very different properties.

While in Kelsen's theory, the Basic Norm stands at the source of the normative dimension of every rule of the system and thus truly *conditions* the normative interpretation of the legal phenomenon, in Hart's theory the Rule of Recognition does not perform any 'foundational task' regarding the normative dimension of law, but merely provides the criteria needed to identify which rules may be held valid. In a way, one may hold that the Rule of Recognition merely plays a 'secondary role' in relation to Hart's explanation of normativity, being the object of the phenomenon of acceptance which alone grounds the normative dimension of law.

To conclude this review of the respective roles of the Basic Norm and the Rule of Recognition in Hart's and Kelsen's theories, it is worth noting at least one point of similarity between these two fundamental norms: they both mark a 'limit point' within the scope of theoretical investigations. Indeed, by pointing to the end of a 'chain of validity' or of a chain of *reasons for*

[28] The difference between these two kinds of answer might be difficult to understand. Indeed, to say that a rule is to be held valid in view of certain criteria amounts to saying that the reason for the validity of this norm is its corresponding to the validity-ascertaining criteria. The difference lies in the fact that in this type of answer, the reason put forward does not refer to any extraneous element in relation to the concept of validity, but merely states its constitutive elements (ie the validity-ascertaining criteria). In Kelsen's type of answer, the validity of a norm truly finds its 'reason' in something else, ie the Basic Norm.

validity (that is, binding force), the Basic Norm and the Rule of Recognition indicate a will to confine the theoretical discourse to a certain type of question, formulated in terms of validity/ existence or binding/normative force. Any question involving a semantic field whose scope goes beyond that which the Basic Norm and the Rule of Recognition are supposed to close will systematically be considered meaningless or irrelevant within the system thus defined. From that perspective, Kelsen under-lines: 'that a norm of the kind just mentioned is the Basic Norm of the national legal order *does not imply that it is impossible to go beyond that norm.* Certainly one may ask why one has to respect the first constitution as a binding norm. The answer might be that the fathers of the first constitution were empow-ered by God. The characteristic of so-called legal positivism is, however, that it dispenses with any such religious justification of the legal order'.[29] Similarly, Hart stresses, 'there are many questions which we can raise about the ultimate rule [. . .] we can ask whether it is a satisfactory form of legal system which has such a rule at its root. Does it produce more good than evil? Are there prudential reasons for supporting it? Is there a moral obligation to do so? These are plainly very important questions; but, equally plainly, when we ask them about the rule of recog-nition, we are no longer attempting to answer *the same kind of question about it as those which we answered about other rules with its aid*'.[30]

In other words, the 'basic rule' allows and defines one set of questions beyond which any further investigation will be devoid of any relevance to the theoretical inquiry. So the questioning of the binding force of the first constitution or the value of the Rule of Recognition might raise very interesting issues, but they cannot receive any attention within Kelsen's or Hart's theory, as they amount either to an attempt at justification of the legal

[29] H Kelsen 1949a, 116 (emphasis added).
[30] HLA Hart 1994, 107 (emphasis added).

order (according to Kelsen[31]) or to a statement of value, which legal theory supposedly can avoid.

As ultimate rules, the Rule of Recognition and the Basic Norm not only put an end to a derivative chain of validity or reasons for validity. They also set the *boundaries* of the legal system as conceptualised by legal theory. Before considering what 'lies behind' these boundaries, as well as the reasons underlying such an attempt at closing the scope of legal discourse (in section 3.3.), I propose to turn to Raz's characterisation of the contrast between Hart's and Kelsen's conceptions of legal normativity. Raz's account of this contrast is indeed very different from mine, and in the next section I shall try to expose the assumption underlying his account.

3.2 Raz's Account of the Contrast Between Hart's and Kelsen's Concepts of Normativity

The gap that separates Hart's and Kelsen's conceptions of legal normativity flows from a different outlook on the normativity problem. While Hart seeks to understand the context within which normative utterances have a sense, Kelsen focuses on what allows and conditions a normative interpretation of the legal phenomenon, referring to the Basic Norm and the category of imputation. In another context, Joseph Raz suggests quite a different way of accounting for Hart's and Kelsen's contrasted understandings of the concept of normativity, based on a distinction between what he calls a 'justified' and a 'social'

[31] It is interesting to note that when Kelsen considers the possibility of going *beyond* the Basic Norm, he immediately refers to a justificatory approach, with God's seemingly unavoidable 'authorisation'. I think that this tendency to see immediately a matter of — allegedly divine — justification behind the Basic Norm partly explains Kelsen's obstinate determination to secure the *autonomy* of the normative sphere, without realising that 'beyond' the Basic Norm one can also find social practices which do not need any divine guarantee to be meaningful. François Ost and Michel van de Kerchove develop an interesting analysis of this reference to God in Kelsen's theory in F Ost and M van de Kerchove 1985.

conception of normativity. According to the justified conception of normativity, 'legal standards of behaviour are norms only if and in so far as they are justified'. On the other — social — view, 'standards of behaviour can be considered as norms regardless of their merit. They are social norms in so far as they are socially upheld as binding standards and in so far as the society involved exerts pressure on people to whom the standards apply to conform to them'.[32]

Given their respective premises, it is easy to guess which conception, in Raz's scheme, Hart and Kelsen each endorse. Kelsen's principle of the autonomy of the normative (*ought* cannot be derived from *is*) categorically rules out any 'social' conception of normativity. According to Raz, Kelsen must hence be regarded as adopting a *justified* conception of normativity (a conception typically endorsed by natural law theorists). Let me follow his arguments step by step.

First, Raz endeavours to show that Kelsen rejects the concept of social normativity as 'not being really a concept of normativity or at any rate as not being appropriate for legal theory'.[33] Indeed, for Kelsen, the concept of social normativity would necessarily be based on 'subjective' value judgements. These judgements, expressing 'the relation of an object to the wish or will of an individual directed at this object',[34] are in stark opposition to 'objective' value judgements, which alone can describe the relation between a fact and an 'objectively valid norm'.

According to Kelsen, an act of will directed at the behaviour of another can only be called a norm if it has the *objective meaning of an ought*.[35] A subjective ought can become an objective

---

[32] J Raz 1979, 134.

[33] J Raz 1979, 135.

[34] H Kelsen 1967, §4 e, 19.

[35] '"Ought" is the subjective meaning of every act of will directed at the behaviour of another. But not every such act has also objectively this meaning; and only if the act of will has also the objective meaning of an "ought", is this "ought" called a "norm"' (H Kelsen 1967, §4 b, 7).

ought only by presupposing the Basic Norm, which invests the subjective meaning of the historically first constitution with an objective ought, that is, with legal normativity. Kelsen's introduction of this (otherwise rather obscure) distinction between objective and subjective oughts is meant to justify epistemically his conviction about the *irreducible*[36] normativity of law: 'without the presupposition of the Basic Norm — this is the argument — that which we know to be the case (namely, that the law *is* normative) could not be the case'.[37] In other words, without the presupposition of the Basic Norm, the normative dimension of legal rules — their objective claim to influence my conduct — could fail to be established. This said, one '*may* but *need not*' presuppose the Basic Norm. If one does not presuppose the Basic Norm, then one does not interpret as 'normative', that is as imposing obligations, granting powers or rights, the relevant interhuman relationships. In other words, without the Basic Norm, all one can consider is power relations ('subjective oughts'), not legal norms. The concept of normativity and the concept of Basic Norm are thus closely interrelated, to the point where one can maintain that the existence of legal norms (and thus normativity) is made conditional upon the Basic Norm.

Now, this distinction between subjective and objective *oughts* still does not explain why Kelsen could be said to refer to a justified concept of normativity. As a next step, Raz quotes a passage where Kelsen refers to the law as an ideology: 'This is the *reason* why it is possible to maintain that the idea of a norm, an "ought", is merely ideological . . . In this sense the law may be considered as the specific ideology of a certain historically given power'.[38] Knowing that the 'reason' Kelsen refers to merely

---

[36] By contrast with subjective oughts whose normative claims can easily be dismissed, Kelsen wants to defend the irreducibly normative character of legal norms (hence his introduction of a split between the subjective and the objective meaning of an ought, which the Basic Norm as a transcendental presupposition is meant to bridge).

[37] U Bindreiter 2001, 148.

[38] H Kelsen 1971b, 227.

acknowledges that 'there is no necessity to presuppose the Basic Norm',[39] it is difficult to see in what sense Raz's statement according to which 'the law is normative, that is, justified and good for everyone who regards it as normative' is supported by the above quotation. Indeed, it is one thing to suggest that the presupposition of the Basic Norm is ideological in the sense that one is free to abide by it and that it is obviously in the interest of the power in place that such a presupposition is made, and it is another to maintain that 'the Basic Norm is presupposed, that is, accepted, and the law is regarded as normative only by people who consider it to be just'.[40] Its being in the interest of the power in place does not entail that anybody presupposing the Basic Norm and considering the law as normative necessarily does so out of a political or moral conviction in the justice of the system.

From this perspective, Kelsen's treatment of the case of the anarchist — who considers the claim to authority of the law unjust — is particularly interesting, as Kelsen's views as to whether or not the anarchist can nevertheless be seen as possibly presupposing the Basic Norm change drastically over the years. Whereas in *Value Judgments in the Science of Law*, Kelsen maintains that the anarchist 'will decline to speak of "lawful" and "unlawful" behaviour, of "legal duties", or "delicts". He will understand social behaviour merely as a process whereby one forces the other to behave in conformity with his wishes or interests ... He will, in short, *refuse to presuppose the Basic Norm*',[41] in the second edition of *The Pure Theory of Law*, Kelsen explicitly withdraws his previous statement that the anarchist 'refuses to presuppose the Basic Norm', maintaining that actually an anarchist can object to the law and yet 'describe positive law as a system of valid norms, *without having to approve of this law*.[42] Kelsen thus seems to have realised that 'disapproval of law in general, by virtue of a moral attitude (anarchism), or of a certain type of legal system, in view of a political attitude (communism), constituted, for this theory, a practical stance such as could co-exist with the juristic view, without affecting it or being affected by it'.[43]

Surprisingly, although he is aware of Kelsen's explicit change of mind on the question,[44] Raz refers to Kelsen's early statement — maintaining that the anarchist will 'refuse to presuppose the Basic Norm' — in order to support his claim according to which 'for an individual to presuppose the basic norm is to interpret the legal system as normative, *ie as just*'.[45] Beyond the questionability of the method which consists in referring to a statement on which Kelsen had explicitly gone back, the accuracy of the logical process which consists in deducing[46] from the statement that the anarchist will not presuppose the Basic Norm the conclusion that anyone who presupposes the Basic Norm considers the law just is at least contestable.

Raz's endeavour to explain why Kelsen's conception of normativity should be regarded as justified (rather than 'social') thus relies on a rather disputable interpretation of Kelsen's

[42] H Kelsen 1967, 218 note 82.

[43] A Wilson 1982, 53.

[44] In the chapter immediately following that on Kelsen, Raz refers to Kelsen's later statement, which he reads as pointing towards the possibility of 'statements from a point of view' (J Raz 1979, 156). In *The Concept of a Legal System*, Raz also quotes a passage where Kelsen explicitly states that normative statements do not imply 'any approval of the described legal norm' (H Kelsen 1967, 79). Regarding Kelsen's change of mind in relation to his earlier statement, Raz claims that 'there was no reason for [Kelsen] to contradict [himself] as anyone who does not presuppose the Basic Norm can still describe the law using normative statements' (J Raz 1980, 137).

[45] J Raz 1979, 138.

[46] J Raz does not explicitly present his reasoning as a 'deduction', but it seems clear that Raz refers to the above-cited quotation in order to support his claim according to which 'for an individual to presuppose the Basic Norm is to interpret the legal system as normative, ie as just', which immediately follows the quotation (J Raz 1979, 138).

works. Raz's central claim — 'The Basic Norm is presupposed, that is, accepted, and the law is regarded as normative only by people who consider it to be just'[47] — is indeed at odds with Kelsen's late but explicit recognition that the Basic Norm can indeed be presupposed by the anarchist: 'In earlier publications I used as an example for the fact that the presupposition of the Basic Norm is possible but not necessary: an anarchist does not presuppose the Basic Norm. This example is misleading [. . .] Anarchism is a political attitude, based on a certain wish. The sociological interpretation, which does not presuppose a Basic Norm, is a theoretical attitude. Even an anarchist, if he were a professor of law, could describe positive law as a system of valid norms, without having to approve of this law'.[48]

As one would expect, Joseph Raz nevertheless does not see this statement as contradicting his theory. On the contrary, Raz suggests a highly inventive reading of the above-cited passage, indicating the possibility of presupposing the Basic Norm in an 'uncommitted way'. Joseph Raz indeed draws a distinction between, on the one hand, judging norms valid from a *personal* point of view, which entails adopting them as just, and, on the other, judging the same norms valid from a *scientific* or *detached* point of view, which implies no consideration of their justice. According to Raz, legal science can 'be value-free, and at the same time regard the law as normative in the only sense admitted by Kelsen, ie that of justified normativity'[49] by adopting the point of view of the hypothetical legal man in a professional and uncommitted way (the legal man is defined as 'a person accepting from a personal point of view all and only the legal norms'). In the above-mentioned passage, Kelsen would thus have pointed towards the possibility for the anarchist to discuss the law 'from the point of view of legal science', leaving aside his personal point of view, according to which he would 'reject the validity of the law'.

[47] J Raz 1979, 137.
[48] H Kelsen 1967, 218 note 82.
[49] J Raz 1979, 140.

Beyond the problems that are raised, as such, by the doctrine of the legal man,[50] it is difficult not to be struck by the degree of contortion and manipulation necessary to Raz's maintaining that Kelsen does indeed adopt a 'justified' conception of normativity.[51] The only way Raz could sustain his interpretation of Kelsen's works despite his significant reversal consisted in suggesting this concept of a 'detached point of view'. Now, if one tries to understand the works of Kelsen for their own sake, without having any pre-defined understanding of the concept of normativity, the Razian construction appears rather like an ambitious (and ingenious) scaffolding. Indeed, for Kelsen, the normativity of law is not something that can or cannot be 'endorsed', depending on the individual's point of view. In this respect, Raz's statement, according to which 'for them [those who admit the concept of justified normativity] to judge the law as normative is to judge it to be just and to admit that it ought to be obeyed',[52] is a good instance of precisely the kind of conclusion Kelsen would have fought at all costs. According to Kelsen, the normative character of law is not susceptible to being 'judged' or acknowledged in the same way as one could 'judge' that the law is just. If, from a theoretical perspective, one can fail to recognise that the law is normative (which is the case of some reductivist theories for instance), it is not up to the individual to determine whether or not the law is normative. For Kelsen, if one does not consider the law as normative,

---

[50] SL Paulson notably underlines that, the moral beliefs of the legal man corresponding to whatever 'the law-making processes generate in the name of the law', the possibility of norm conflicts (entailed by the source thesis) 'may well be fatal to the doctrine of the legal man and the normativity that the doctrine represents'. The existence of conflicting norms would indeed lead us to attribute inconsistent beliefs to the legal man (see SL Paulson 1992a, 161).

[51] Along this line, Uta Bindreiter also remains unconvinced as to the conclusions Raz draws from the Kelsenian doctrine, and stresses that the 'detached' adoption of the Basic Norm 'only seems to produce statements the modality of which is essentially unclear — for what, exactly, does "detached" normativity mean?' (U Bindreiter 2001, 160).

[52] J Raz 1979, 137.

one simply does not speak of law at all, but instead one refers to power relations.[53] In other words, the law exists as normative, or does not exist at all. 'The most important concept is that of a point of view'[54] can be held true in the context of Raz's theory, but not in Kelsen's.[55]

Ultimately, it seems that Raz has been trying to understand Kelsen's works while proceeding from his own reason-based[56] and cognitive explanation of normativity, which essentially aims at understanding what it is for an individual to consider the law as normative (in opposition to what it is for a rule to be normative).[57] Indeed, if one looks at Kelsen's works with an understanding of the term 'normative' as 'capable of making a practical difference' in mind, it is difficult to grasp how the anarchist can presuppose the Basic Norm and thus consider the law as normative, given that, by definition, the law cannot make any practical difference for him. If, by contrast, one

---

[53] See Kelsen's important passage: 'The fact that the Basic Norm of a positive legal order may but need not be presupposed means: the relevant interhuman relationships may be, but need not be, interpreted as "normative", that is, as obligations, authorisations, rights, etc. constituted by objectively valid norms. It means further: they can be interpreted without such a presupposition as power relations — in other words, they can be interpreted sociologically, not juristically' (H Kelsen 1967, §34 I, 218 — parentheses omitted).

[54] J Raz 1979, 139.

[55] One could mention here Kelsen's rejection of any claim to the effect that the existence of a legal order depends on the subject's recognition of it (*Anerkennungstheorien*) (note that in this passage Kelsen is not specifically talking about the normative character of legal rules, but about their validity which, according to his terminology, is pretty similar) (see H Kelsen 1967, §34 i, 218 note 83). In that sense, A Wilson underlines that 'the notion of "justified normativity" or any demand for acceptance of law involves what Kelsen explicitly abjures in *The Pure Theory of Law*, namely the "theory of recognition", seen there as illegitimate syncretism foisting on law elements alien to it.' (A Wilson 1982, 51).

[56] 'Aspects of the world are normative in as much as they or their existence constitute reasons for persons' (J Raz 1999, 67).

[57] One could express this idea by saying that in Raz's works, the focus is very much on something's *normative significance* for someone, rather than on the normative status of the concepts or ideas that lead us to lend normative significance to something (see notably J Raz 1999, 67–89).

approaches Kelsen's works with a broad understanding of normativity, one may understand Kelsen's distinction between objective and subjective oughts as pointing towards the same problem as that emphasised by Korsgaard: 'the problems of philosophy always or at least very often take the form of trying to understand why some purported normative claim really is normative'.[58] Contemporary accounts of normativity tend to converge in basing their answer on some concept of practical deliberation, whether it be informed by some 'pre-existing standards' to be discovered in the fabric of the Universe or by values and principles that are themselves the product of socio-cultural practices. In contrast to this dominant model, what sets apart Kelsen's account is its characteristic refusal to give any role to practical deliberation. Kelsen's explaining why 'some purported normative claim [subjective oughts] really is normative [objective oughts]' is a theoretical move through and through, based on the Basic Norm as a transcendental presupposition. This means that the individual's practical stance towards the law, the result of his own deliberation as to whether law's claim to bind him should succeed, is entirely irrelevant to Kelsen's account of law's normativity.

The hazards linked to a misinterpretation of Kelsen's work show how important it is to grasp the difference in outlook characterising the respective approaches of Hart and Kelsen. If Kelsen does indeed reject any reference to social facts in order to explain the normative dimension of law, and in that sense can be opposed to Hart, his aim when trying to provide such an explanation is nevertheless so drastically different from Hart's that, with a bit of speculation, one could maintain that even if he were to refer to social facts, Kelsen's account of legal normativity would still diverge from Hart's. To refer back to the image I suggested previously, the contrast between Hart and Kelsen may be expressed in terms of upstream/downstream perspectives: while Hart focuses on the context within which normative utterances

[58] CM Korsgaard 2003a, 51.

such as 'it is the law that' have a meaning, Kelsen seeks to explain what conditions and allows a normative interpretation of the legal phenomenon. In this context, a reading of Kelsen's works based on a downstream approach of normativity (cf 'the most important concept is that of a point of view') can, in my opinion, only lead to a misrepresentation of Kelsen's project.

Now, beyond the stark difference of outlook characterising Kelsen's and Hart's respective accounts of legal normativity, there is also one important similarity between these two theories: the limits which both Hart and Kelsen impose on the scope of their theoretical discourse.

3.3 Where Hart and Kelsen Meet: The Scope of Appropriate Questions

Both Hart's and Kelsen's works are structured around the ambition to account for law's normative nature. Their common rejection of natural law theories forbids them to locate the source of legal normativity *beyond* the sphere of human activities. Yet neither of them can be said to be locating that source *within* human activities: Kelsen grounds legal normativity in the Basic Norm, and Hart does not 'ground' it at all. Should one conclude that the apparent arbitrariness of law-creating activities makes them inherently inappropriate in relation to law's power to bind us, to impose an obligation upon us?

Montaigne was quite explicit about it: the precariousness of the initial law-creating practices requires them to be 'set apart',[59] as their futile character makes them utterly disproportionate in comparison to the 'grandeur' of the law, that is, its normative dimension. As a result, Montaigne inaugurates an important distinction between the social practices that enable law's existence and what conditions law's normativity. While we

[59] The 'mystical status' attributed by Montaigne to the factual origins of law places them 'beyond what can be said', in a field accessible only to the 'initiates' (as opposed to laymen).

may discover that lawmaking practices are actually driven by 'fools', the normative status of law is to be explained by a 'law of pure obedience' that has nothing to do with these potentially off-putting social practices.

In another context, and a few centuries later, Kelsen also ends up isolating the arbitrariness of human activity from the sphere of the normative, this time not so much in the name of the danger of discovering the 'tiny spring' at the source of law's normativity, but in the name of a methodological dualism of Neo-Kantian inspiration, strictly separating *is* from *ought*. Any question going beyond the Basic Norm, inquiring about the initial law-creating facts, will systematically be dismissed as irrelevant, reaching *beyond* the scope of the pure theory: 'The problem of the origin of the law [. . .] is beyond the scope of this theory'.[60]

What about Hart? Is he confronted with a challenge similar to Montaigne's, attempting to explain the authority of law (and thus its normative dimension) *despite* the arbitrariness from which it stems? Does he share with Kelsen the ambition of closing in an autonomous way the sphere of legal normativity, thus isolating the social practices from which it flows? Hart does not endorse Kelsen's methodological dualism, and one of the main factors distinguishing Hart's theory from Kelsen's lies in his embrace of the *social facts thesis*, ie 'the claim that while law is a normative social practice it is made possible by some set of social facts'.[61] Hart nevertheless does not elaborate much on the link between the initial social practices and the normative dimension of law, leaving to the reader the task of constructing such a link, for instance through a conventional scheme of interpretation, as he explicitly suggests in his *Postscript*.[62]

---

[60] H Kelsen 1971a, 294. Similarly, see 'the question as to where the content of the positive legal order has originated [. . .] is beyond this cognition' (H Kelsen 1949b, 438).

[61] J Coleman 2001a, 116.

[62] 'But the theory remains as a faithful account of conventional social rules which include, besides ordinary social customs (which may or may not be recognised as having legal force), certain important legal rules including the rule of recognition' (HLA Hart 1994, 256).

Generally, Hart does not seem to be interested in developing an account of the factors contributing to the emergence (or renewal) of a legal system and in this respect shares at least some affinities with Kelsen's approach. From this perspective, Raz underlines what he considers to be a methodological parallelism between Hart and Kelsen, 'who sought to provide autonomous legal criteria for the definition of the continuity of law. Autonomous criteria are those derived from the content of laws, their interrelations, and their efficacy. Reliance on them presupposes that not only the internal working but also the precise *boundaries* of the law can be fixed on the basis of specifically legal considerations alone. But the law is an aspect of a political system [. . .] Both its existence and its identity are bound up with the existence and identity of the political system of which it is a part'.[63]

When the matter is precisely to determine what should count as a change in the identity of a legal system, such purportedly 'autonomous' theories are faced with important difficulties, linked to the temporal dimension of legal rules. In 'Revolutions and the Continuity of Law',[64] John Finnis has shown that neither the Basic Norm nor the Rule of Recognition could answer the question 'what is it about a sequence of sets of rules that entitles us to interpret it as an existing or subsisting system of rules with a lasting identity or duration?'.[65] As Finnis emphasises: 'the legal system, considered simply as a set of "valid rules", does not exist, since, considered simply as a set of rules, of interdependent normative meanings, there is nothing to give it continuity, duration, identity through time'. To be able to understand how a set of (valid) rules happens to come into existence, and eventually to wither away, one has to consider the legal system 'as something

---

[63] J Raz 1980, 210–211 (emphasis added).
[64] J Finnis 1973, 44 ff.
[65] J Finnis 1973, 66. For Finnis's detailed arguments (which I won't reproduce here) see 67 and 68.

importantly more than a set of rules'; one has to consider its inscription within the sphere of society.

These very general considerations find an important illustration in the way Hart and Kelsen describe the initial[66] law-creating facts, or, in other words, the 'social practices that tie the ultimate legal rule to social reality' (to borrow Raz's expression). As regards Kelsen, I have already underlined the difficulties he had to face when considering the *is* side of any norm, and particularly the Basic Norm. Unlike the other norms, the Basic Norm is not a positive norm, in the sense that it has not been created or posited by a human act. The 'facts through which an order is created and applied' cannot be said to bring the Basic Norm into *existence*, since it merely exists in 'juristic consciousness' (if it exists at all — see Kelsen's later shift to the Basic Norm as a fiction). These 'initial' social practices cannot be deemed to ground either the binding force or 'validity' of the Basic Norm, since ought cannot be derived from is. Yet these initial law-creating facts cannot be totally ignored, if Kelsen's theory claims to differ from idealistic theories.[67]

Given his determination to preserve the conceptual autonomy of the normative sphere, avoiding any reference to the factual background prevailing throughout the emergence of norms, Kelsen will never find a satisfactory way of conceptualising the social practices that lead to the construction of a legal system,[68] thus holding the phenomenon of law creation in a metajuridical sphere: '[the Basic Norm's] creation must therefore be seen as a material fact outside the legal system'.[69] How does this last quotation compare with Hart's view that the existence of the Rule of Recognition is a 'matter of fact'?

[66] Rather than 'original' (see the contrast I have suggested between the concept of 'origins' and the concept of 'sources' — in n 18 of the Introduction).

[67] Regarding such a claim, see Kelsen 1967, 211.

[68] Kelsen's initial 'way out' was to designate the 'facts through which an order is created and applied' as the *content* of the Basic Norm. In the last chapter I showed how Kelsen ultimately had to abandon such a solution, turning to a characterisation of the Basic Norm as a fiction.

[69] H Kelsen 1998a, 13.

A striking feature which Finnis has emphasised is Hart's scant concern for the *emergence* of the legal system and thus the creation of the Rule of Recognition: 'For Hart, the existence of a rule of recognition is simply a *present* matter of fact'.[70] Whenever Hart refers to the existence of the Rule of Recognition, he consistently reiterates his view according to which its existence is *established* by the judicial practices expressing the internal point of view, ie the acceptance of certain criteria of validity as *appropriate for use*.

If Hart does acknowledge the possibility for a legal system to be 'at one stage unborn, at a second not yet wholly independent of its mother, then enjoy a healthy independent existence, later decay and finally die',[71] these different organic stages of a legal system do not seem to imply any further qualification of the Rule of Recognition, which for its part always exists 'as a present matter of fact'. It is as if the Rule of Recognition could only accommodate *a posteriori* statements ascertaining its existence. To ask what social practices are at the source of the Rule of Recognition *as a rule* amounts to asking the wrong, or rather irrelevant, question: 'it's a matter of fact' will be the unavoidable answer, revealing little interest in the question.

As a conclusion, one could echo Kelsen's statement about the creation of the Basic Norm and maintain, this time about the Rule of Recognition, that 'its creation must therefore be seen as a material fact outside the legal system'[72]. In this context, the term 'creation' is meant to be understood widely, encompassing not only the historical genesis but also, most importantly, the process enabling and conditioning the Rule of Recognition's normative status. The 'matter of fact' to which Hart refers as what lies beyond the Rule of Recognition is not meant to account for that process. The 'internal point of view', for its part, can only explain the normative dimension of legal rules

---

[70] J Finnis 1973, 55 (emphasis added).
[71] HLA Hart 1994, 112.
[72] See above n 69.

from a 'downstream perspective', that is, one that *presupposes* the possibility of law's normativity, which only needs to be acknowledged. As Coleman notes, 'the internal point of view is an existence condition of a social rule, and it marks the fact that people treat the rule as reason-giving. It does not explain why or how the rule does so'.[73]

To explain why the Rule of Recognition is capable of giving reasons for action, one needs to look at what conditions and allows its existence as a normative rule. In other words, one needs to look at the Rule of Recognition *from upstream*: one needs to consider what allows the Rule of Recognition to emerge from a certain context of social interaction. One possible scheme of answer — and what Coleman considers to be the 'missing argument' in Hart's theory — is provided by constructing the Rule of Recognition as a convention,[74] creating a system of reciprocal, legitimate expectations, partly enabled by the internal point of view.

Now, one may wonder why Hart did not provide such an argument initially, knowing that in his *Postscript* he does refer to the conventional model.[75] The most plausible answer is in my opinion related to Hart's adoption of a 'downstream perspective' on the problem of normativity. His aim is indeed to emphasise the *context* within which normative utterances have a sense, explaining the fact that some people treat rules as reason-giving. From this perspective, accounting for what conditions law's normativity is only peripheral. This relegation of any inquiry into the sources of legal normativity to the range of irrelevant (or peripheral) questions establishes a link between the Hartian theory and the two theories that have been presented so far — Montaigne's and Kelsen's. Montaigne relegates the sources of legal normativity to the domain of the mystical, while for

---

[73] J Coleman 2001a, 119.

[74] On the conventional model in general, see section 5.2.1, para 2 (pp 170 *et seq*).

[75] HLA Hart 1994, 256.

Kelsen the problem lies 'beyond cognition' — ie beyond the scope of the pure theory, as it necessarily involves factual references. In Hart's theory, the sources of law's normativity are neither mystical, nor 'unknowable'. They simply point towards a 'matter of fact' which Hart does not deem necessary to develop further.

So why do these three theories systematically relegate any inquiry into the sources[76] of legal normativity to the scope of inappropriate questions? In the case of Montaigne's theory, the discovery that 'laws are made by fools' was deemed too dangerous, imperilling the authority (and thus the normative character) of law, which could not be conceived as flowing from such a 'little surgeon' — the futility of human practices. In Kelsen's theory, the practices conditioning and enabling law's normativity could not be accounted for either, the main argument for excluding them from the scope of the 'pure' theory being of an epistemological nature, the radical separation between the world of *is* and *ought* demanding that legal norms derive from norms and norms only. We have seen, however, that other considerations, based on the fear of the law being compromised by ideological or political discourses, are likely to have played a role in Kelsen's adoption of his extreme methodological dualism.

In Hart's case, one may argue, there need not be any reason explaining why his theory does not include an account of what conditions law's normativity. Such an issue just did not fall within Hart's concerns, which, as we have seen, had little in common with Kelsen's. One could stop the parallelisms here, and ascertain that, yes, Hart did not develop much of an argument towards accounting for what *conditions* law's normativity, this lack of interest being nevertheless quite independent of the kind of motives that led Kelsen to sustain the autonomy of the normative sphere. If, however, one questions Hart's apparent lack of interest in the 'matter of fact' conditioning the Rule of

---

[76] The concept of 'sources' is understood as what conditions or enables the existence of a given phenomenon, and need not be understood in a foundationalist way.

Recognition, one may venture a parallel between these two major representatives of legal positivism.

Beyond the acknowledged reasons respectively underlying Hart's and Kelsen's refusal to give theoretical relevance to the social practices enabling and conditioning law's normativity, there is a common wariness of the danger that compromise of the law with any kind of ideology or substantial morality represents. In *Natural Law Doctrine and Legal Positivism*, Kelsen evocatively expresses that concern, stressing that the content of a legal order always emerges from a 'struggle for power' which 'invariably presents itself as a struggle for "justice"; all the fighting groups use the ideology of "natural law". They never represent the interests which they seek to realise as mere group-interests, but as the "true", the "common", the "general" interest'.[77] If one takes into account this last quotation as well as the general spirit of defiance towards politics, which Kelsen evokes on many occasions (especially in *Natural Law Doctrine and Legal Positivism*,[78] which was published in 1928), the danger from which Kelsen seeks to preserve his theory by isolating it from any factual consideration does not seem so far removed from the 'peril' mentioned by Montaigne. Indeed, between the vexed acknowledgement that 'law is made by fools'[79] and Kelsen's underlining of the fact that law emerges from a 'struggle for power' led by 'group interests' which, in Kelsen's time, were likely to seem particularly threatening, there is not much of a difference. In the end, it all comes down to the wish to safeguard law's normative purity in the face of political

---

[77] H Kelsen 1949b, 438.

[78] See for instance: 'The social foundations and, with them, the self-confidence of the individual, have been deeply shaken in our time. Most values thus far taken for granted are questioned; the conflict between interest groups has been tremendously intensified, and with it the struggle for a new order is under way. In such times, a greatly deepened need for the absolute justification of the postulates put forth in the struggle will manifest itself' (H Kelsen 1949b, 445–6).

[79] And more generally the emphasis on the precariousness from which the 'grandeur of the law' flows.

struggles. Beyond their futile character, these struggles may prove particularly dangerous given the mimetic capacity of power, which has a gift for passing itself off as law.

The ideal of autonomy preventing Kelsen from conceptualising the law-creating facts is a way of ensuring the integrity of his *Pure Theory* against any ideological recuperation.[80] This attitude of distrust in relation to any political content, relegating any moral or ideological conviction to the sphere of private autonomy pervades Kelsen's work, and may be described as one of the key features of the liberal spirit which, a few years later, openly influenced Hart's work. Can one for all that state that Hart shares Montaigne's and Kelsen's determination to avoid any reference to the arbitrariness of initial law-creating facts? If Hart's work does not comprise any explicit allusion to the danger that such a reference would constitute, one may nevertheless venture to say that, when Hart deems the 'matter of fact' that is supposed to sum up the practices leading to the adoption of the Rule of Recognition not to be worth any further development, he might be driven by the same kind of concern as Kelsen's: a concern, that is, to avoid having to include within his theory any analysis of political or ideological reality.

The lack of interest Hart showed for the question of the emergence of the Rule of Recognition can be analysed along the same lines as Kelsen's determination to preserve the autonomy of the normative sphere. It results from the wish to exclude from the scope of legal theory any potentially compromising consideration (because it might refer to a determined ideological content). 'The purity of its knowledge in the sense of *political indifference* is its characteristic aim'[81] may be applied to both Hart's and Kelsen's theory, and this trend will constitute one of the main targets of Carl Schmitt's doctrine, which describes liberalism as 'the negation of politics'.[82]

---

[80] A recuperation which, according to Kelsen, would be allowed by a conceptualisation of the practices leading to the existence of a legal system.

[81] H Kelsen 1949b, 438.

[82] See section 4.2.

Part II
A Genealogical Endeavour

4
The Method

The choice of a given method to approach a philosophical problem has its potential pitfalls. On the one hand, just like a package one may have to stretch a bit to fit its intended contents, the object of one's study may at some point exceed the method's domain. On the other hand, until it has been 'practised', the chosen method can only be delineated by its name, whose meaning is to a large extent determined by its intellectual history. The more troubled or confused that history is, the more unstable its meaning, and the more risky it becomes to declare one's allegiance to that method. From this viewpoint, the concept of genealogy scores high on the scale of 'murky methodologies'. While it owes its status of philosophical method to Nietzsche, Nietzsche was neither the first nor the last philosopher to resort to a genealogical strategy: among the philosophers who recently re-appropriated that method, Foucault and Williams stand as the most notable — and contrasted — figures.

The point of this chapter is to consider the extent to which a genealogical methodology is conducive to my endeavour to account for what conditions and enables law's normative dimension. To this end, I could proceed from a detailed comparison of Nietzsche's, Foucault's[1] and Williams's understandings of

[1] Such a comparative analysis would prove particularly challenging when it comes to Foucault, given his rather loose use of the concept of genealogy, which varies considerably from one work to the other. 'At times, Foucault uses the term as a specific methodological term or title for a critical historical-philosophical project (namely his own), in other passages it is used rather broadly and synonymously with "history" or "genesis". And if the survey includes the books he himself called genealogical, ie mainly *Discipline and Punish* and *The History of Sexuality: Vol 1*, and some of the shorter texts of his "middle" period (ca 1970–1976 /77), this ambiguity is not resolved here either' (Saar 2002, 231).

genealogy, with the hope of isolating a few common denominators that would be applicable to my project. Although that approach would probably be the most rigorous one, I take a reverse way, putting forward my own objectives in adopting a genealogical approach, to see whether they find an echo in the works of authors who have previously had recourse to that strategy.

By contrast with legal theory's prevailing trend of adopting what I have called a 'downstream approach'[2] to the normative question, a genealogy of legal normativity looks in the right direction: its point is to question what conditions the possibility of law as a normative phenomenon. Its ambition is not, however, to find *the* starting point of legal normativity. A genealogy by definition proceeds from the awareness of the impossibility of finding the origin or 'degree zero' of the object it studies. Its ambition is to trace the social and cultural factors that have contributed to bringing about the phenomenon in question. In doing so, its hope is not to discover some 'founding principle' that would provide some definite grounding for that phenomenon, but to cast a new, challenging light upon it. This limit, essential to the genealogical project, makes it particularly suited to the study of legal normativity. As one will never be able to isolate a situation that is not in some way preceded by legal normativity, its 'origin' will always vanish to some further, inaccessible point. The genealogical method is thus particularly helpful in this respect, as it contributes to clearing up the ambiguities inherent to an inquiry into the 'sources' of legal normativity.

The other major asset of genealogy as a method is its commitment to debunking any form of realist metaphysics. The challenge underlying an account of law that brings together its

---

[2] I used this image in chapter 3 to describe the reluctance of theories such as Hart's to consider the context of social interaction that allows and conditions law's normative status. Understanding this context of social interaction would be the 'upstream side' of the normative problem, while accounting for the impact and meaning of (legal) normative utterances for individuals would constitute the 'downstream side' of the same problem.

social and normative dimensions in one continuous explanation is indeed to face up to the implications of social contingency for our understanding of normativity. The 'realist' temptation to instill some form of necessity in the background of that social contingency by way of intrinsically normative entities 'hanging out there' is strong, and the genealogical method leaves no room for it.

Now, the most difficult question which a genealogical endeavour must face is to explain the sense in which it differs from, or is not reducible to, mere history. The answer mainly lies in the specific purpose of a genealogy. Its reading of history is at the service of the re-evaluation of a given phenomenon. This critical[3] appraisal is not the accidental by-product of a project that is first aimed at reading history. A genealogical undertaking is a re-evaluation project whose tools include history, among others.

4.1 Hypotheses, History and Philosophy

4.1.1 What the Story is Made of: History and Hypotheses

In his preface to *On the Genealogy of Morality*, Nietzsche warns against 'English hypothesis-mongering *into the blue*. It is quite clear which colour is a hundred times more important for a genealogist than blue: namely grey, which is to say, that which can be documented, which can actually be confirmed and has actually existed, in short, the whole, long, hard-to-decipher hieroglyphic script of man's moral past!'.[4] According to Nietzsche, Rée's inquiry into *The Origin of Moral Sentiment* is a good example of 'English hypothesis-mongering': putting forward abstract hypotheses tracing back moral ideas to psychological impressions, they characteristically lack any historical dimension. This abstraction from historical circumstances typically allows these accounts to confirm or prolong the way these institutions think

---

[3] As I will argue in section 4.1.2, the use of the term 'critical' here does not necessarily imply a negative connotation.

[4] F Nietzsche 1994, 8–9.

of themselves by contributing abstract hypotheses that consciously or unconsciously share in their self-understanding.

A genealogy, by contrast, clears the ground for a renewed — and
potentially critical — understanding of these institutions by revealing the impact of the historical processes that brought them about.
The full power of a genealogy typically reveals itself when it is
directed at institutions whose self-understanding requires conceal-
ing the impact of these historical processes. The stronger their
claim to authority, the more reluctant these institutions are to
reveal their historical variability and contingency, 'both in the
sense that they are what they are rather than some others, and
also in the sense that the historical changes that brought them
about are not obviously related in a grounding or epistemically
favourable way to the ethical [or legal etc] ideas they encouraged'.[5]
By contrast with teleological understandings of history, the historical material of a genealogy indeed does not proceed from an identified *goal*, to then go on to show how it gradually emerged from
its embryonic beginnings. 'Rather, the genealogies chart the
processes that, by contingent confluence, produce a contemporary
result'.[6]

A genealogy cannot *just* proceed from history, though. In a
genealogical framework, history is at the service of an *interpretation*, which requires the formulation of hypotheses. The
genealogist's concern is to undermine ahistorical and inflation-
ary interpretations of human institutions. While these interpretations typically appeal to structures or norms which stand above
nature and history, a genealogical interpretation is characterised

---

[5] B Williams 2000, 155.

[6] RK Hill 1998, 1.

[7] Quotation marks are particularly important here, as 'naturalism' in ethics
has been used to characterise 'physicalistic reductionist' positions that are radically incompatible with a genealogical project. By contrast, Williams defines the
naturalist question about ethics as 'the question of how closely the motivations
and practices of the ethical are related to other aspects of human psychology —
to the way, as one can very loosely and inaccurately put it, human beings are
"anyway" [. . .] As one might put it, we are asking about human ethical life in
relation to the rest of human nature' (B Williams 2000, 154).

by a 'naturalist'[7] commitment to explaining its object 'in terms of an account of human beings which is to the greatest possible extent prior to ideas of the ethical [or the object to be explained]'.[8] A genealogy thus needs to proceed from some concerns or attitudes, which are taken as given, to then explain how these attitudes or intentions give rise to the phenomenon to be accounted for. Now, it is very unlikely that any actual society could ever be reduced to the characteristics and attitudes which the narrator isolates for the sake of her story; and it is very likely, in fact, that any actual society will always already 'present the features from which the abstraction has to be made'.[9]

The *raison d'être* of genealogy as a method is to translate the awareness that one cannot reach the starting point or 'degree zero' of the phenomenon to be accounted for. In order to make its point and explain how its object *came about*, a genealogy thus needs, in most cases, to proceed from an hypothesis that is *fictional* by definition, in that it has to imagine a state of affairs that is free of the phenomenon to be accounted for. Resorting to such a 'State of Nature' hypothesis (with all its possible variations[10]) does not always prove necessary, though. While a genealogy seeks to question the motives that underlie the existence of a given phenomenon, and to that extent needs to abstract from historical variations, it does not always have to rely on a fictional hypothesis for that purpose.

Legal normativity, for instance, is one of these phenomena whose existence is regularly suspended in the course of political upheavals or revolutions. The 'normative gaps' which these revolutions produce provide for the kind of calling into question which the 'State of Nature hypothesis' otherwise enacts for phenomena such as morality or truthfulness. The nature of these

---

[8] B Williams 2000, 154.

[9] B Williams 2002, 35.

[10] In his genealogical account of truthfulness, Williams for instance posits a State of Nature which, 'in contrast with some stories in that tradition, [. . .] does contain a society, a group of human beings who co-operate but are not kin' (B Williams 2002, 21).

concepts indeed does not allow for any kind of suspension or temporary bracketing. Yet one needs to consider a situation that is somehow free of the concept to be explained if one is to understand the demands and necessities that the concept answers. To bring out the functional elements that are key to interpreting the historical development of concepts such as morality or truthfulness, one thus needs to resort to the State of Nature fiction.[11] The concept of legal normativity, by contrast, lends itself to a functional interpretation on the basis of a non-fictitious but abstract hypothesis, underlying the various needs and concerns which it is deemed to address.[12]

Now, at this stage, most readers will — legitimately — ask: what is the need for a story? 'Why not just give a functional account without the story?' Does the diachronic aspect of a genealogy add anything 'except colour'?[13] The answer is: it does more than just 'add' something. A genealogy without history would be like a diving board without spring. The point of the genealogical method is to bring out the artificial character of a certain kind of institution. It typically aims at those institutions that seem to be able to construct their legitimacy only by 'forgetting' that they were brought into existence by a historical process. The moving forces underlying this historical process may have nothing to do with the official rhetoric legitimising those institutions. Going for a functional account *without* the story would comfort these institutions in their effort to detach themselves from any form of contingence. It would also be liable to unconsciously perpetuate the self-image of these institutions by failing to escape the logic of their legitimising discourse.

---

[11] 'We could not appeal to some actual, very early, hominid society instead, because any actual society would always already (as some thinkers are fond of saying) present the features from which the abstraction has to be made' (B Williams 2002, 35).

[12] For the development of such a hypothesis, see the next chapter.

[13] B Williams 2002, 34.

Going for a story *without* the functional account, on the other hand, would entail giving up on the genealogical project altogether. In asking 'why do we have this or that institution?' (and hoping to produce an elaborate answer), a genealogy indeed presupposes that the object it studies can meaningfully be treated as *functional*, that is, as serving an end other than itself.[14] The study of the 'driving forces' underlying the history of a given institution aims at unveiling the unexpected or hidden desires, ambitions and needs[15] which that institution serves. While this disclosure seeks to contribute a meaning that renews the understanding of that institution, it need not be detrimental to its perceived legitimacy. If anything is to measure the success of a genealogy, it would rather be its capacity to 'problematise' the allegedly self-evident assumptions of a given phenomenon.

4.1.2 Philosophy as the Art of Calling into Question

When can a story claim philosophical status? If the qualifications of the storyteller do not carry much weight, is it a matter of his or her ambition in telling that story? Does a story *become* philosophical if it induces in its readers an unexpected sense of wisdom? While a genealogy may not always achieve such a desirable goal, its philosophical pretensions are based on its capacity to call into question a phenomenon whose possibility is normally taken for granted. Whether it be applied to morality, Christianity,[16] truthfulness or legal normativity, a common feature of the genealogical project is its commitment to questioning the assumptions underlying the various forms of discourse

---

[14] The 'genealogical move' would for instance be opposed by those who deem art to exist for its own sake, for no other purpose than itself.

[15] The move from 'functional' to 'instrumental' is as frequent as it is detrimental to the understanding of the specificity of genealogy as a method.

[16] 'The traditional philosophical discussion of Christianity, whether critical or apologetic, primarily investigates the truth of the Christian doctrine, or the potential justification of the Christian faith. These traditional investigations tacitly presuppose that something like Christianity already exists as a unified, internally coherent, given phenomenon that presents itself as an object for possible discussion. Genealogy is designed to render precisely this presupposition problematic' (R Geuss 2002, 212).

dealing with these concepts. As for the concept of legal normativity, the point of the three first chapters of this book was to
emphasise legal theory's propensity to consider the normative
dimension of law as a *given*. From this traditional perspective,
explaining legal normativity involves considering its impact on
individuals, its potential conflicts with other forms of normativity, but never what conditions its possibility. By contrast, the
ambition of a genealogical account of legal normativity is to
challenge its axiomatic status by putting forward an account of
the context of social interaction that allows and conditions law's
normativity.

As a way of doing philosophy, the genealogical project can be
considered as working towards three distinct but complementary goals.

Genealogy as 'Critique'

In its everyday sense, the term 'critique' connotes a negative
stand towards a given phenomenon, backed up by some reasons
or arguments aimed at justifying the alleged falsity, invalidity or
inappropriateness of the phenomenon in question. The
genealogical project is *not* a critique in this everyday sense.[17] A
genealogy's concern is not to assess the validity or falsity of its
object, but to unveil the various factors that led to the emergence of a given phenomenon. This disclosure may, in some
cases, be damaging to the phenomenon's perceived legitimacy,
but this disobliging consequence is only the by-product of a
genealogy's 'true' critical ambition: to undermine the traditional resistance of some human institutions to revealing the historical processes that brought them about. As Williams points out:
'the concepts or values under explanation are likely to claim an
authority which rejects the appearance of contingency, and so
resist being explained in real terms at all. But this is true to a
greater extent of some values and institutions than others'.[18]

---

[17] Raymond Geuss develops the specific sense in which a genealogy is to
be understood as 'critique' in a much more elaborate way (R Geuss 2002).

[18] B Williams 2000, 159.

While some institutions will remain stable under genealogical explanation, others may face a necessary 'makeover', requiring a serious re-examination of their meaning or legitimation basis. In the 16th century, the genealogical movement initiated by Montaigne[19] shook the foundations of the natural law model. For want of being incorporated in a new account of legal normativity, the realities it came to unveil had the potential to seriously compromise law's authority. In the face of such a 'peril', and lacking the resources to construct an account of law that could encompass both its social, contingent aspect and its normative dimension, Montaigne recoiled from the consequences of the genealogical project he initiated.[20]

Denouncing Inadequacies

Constructing a genealogy is not a neutral philosophical project (if philosophy can ever be said to be 'neutral'). It is driven by an agenda, which typically involves stigmatising the way a certain concept, value or institution is commonly accounted for. Whether it be applied to the concept of justice, morality, the prison system or legal normativity, a genealogical endeavour seeks to trigger or renew reflections on the phenomenon to be explained.

As for the concept of legal normativity, Montaigne's 'genealogical twist' in the 16th century came at a dramatic moment, as it contributed to the progressive construction of an alternative to the classical natural law model. So one may wonder what is the point of developing a genealogy of legal normativity at this stage, in the 21st century, when the positivism/natural law debate has been extensively and exhaustingly repeated, rehearsed, reiterated, retold and duplicated? The point is clearly not to denounce the inadequacies of the classical natural law model any more, but rather to aim at legal theory's persistent lack of concern for the meta-ethical issues flowing from the rejection of that model.

---

[19] As to whether Montaigne can appropriately be said to have had recourse to a 'genealogical strategy', see section 4.2.

[20] See section 1.2.3.

The real challenge brought about by the adoption of a positivist understanding of legal normativity consists in coming to terms with the fact that the law-creating practices cannot be said to reflect or conform to some pre-existing natural laws.[21] Instead of natural laws 'reassuringly' imprinting some necessity upon these law-creating practices by virtue of their intrinsically normative character, all the positivist has at his disposal are — potentially — moral values[22] which cannot call on any other necessity but the social practices that engendered them. It is this shift in the ontological status of the moral values informing law-creating practices, and not what would be the 'sudden' realisation that laws are indeed made by fools, which led Montaigne and his followers to discount the study of the context of social interaction that allows and conditions law's normative status.

The fact that laws are made by men and women has always been an inescapable truth. The sense of contingency introduced by the turn to a positivist account of normativity is not related to the pseudo 'discovery' of law's positivity, but to the withdrawal of any meta-referent whose intrinsic normativity is taken to imprint some external necessity upon that positivity. As long as there were natural laws in the background, the law-creating practices could be seen as informed by a set of moral values that themselves instantiated natural law's 'higher order of necessity'. Once these natural laws are taken out of the picture, the difficulty consists in understanding the status of the moral values that are — still — taken to permeate law-creating practices. The turn to a positivist understanding of legal normativity indeed does not entail a strictly value-free understanding of law or of the process giving rise to law. If one seeks to understand the factors that make it desirable for a society to have law as a distinct

---

[21] Or to some moral values themselves deriving or conforming to natural laws.

[22] I do not seek to argue that law-creating practices are *always* informed by moral values, but rather that, in what one might consider the 'central case' of a legal system, law-creating practices typically are driven by moral concerns, among other types of ambitions.

form of governance, the contingent appearance of lawmaking practices may give way to various political and moral concerns that importantly shape what law is. In this context, the task faced by legal theory is not so much to keep asserting the separability of law and morality, but rather to *confront* the implications of social contingency for the moral values informing law-creating practices. A proper account of the relationship between law and morality cannot afford to remain agnostic on the status of morality itself.[23] The agenda driving my genealogical account of legal normativity consists in highlighting — and remedying — the 'understanding deficit' created by legal theory's reluctance to deal with the apparently 'abhorrent' arbitrariness of law-creating practices.

Branding Realist Metaphysics

As a philosophical tool, a genealogy is not only geared towards a critique of existing forms of discourse, it also carries an intrinsic commitment to a constructivist meta-ethics. Its ambition to give a 'naturalist'[24] account of its object makes it particularly hostile to any kind of realist metaphysics. The effort to explain a given phenomenon in terms of human attitudes, capacities or desires is meant to overcome the temptation to find the origin[25] of that phenomenon 'behind the world', in an order apart and distinct from how we conceive of ourselves.

In questioning the conditions under which we construct value judgements, and inquiring about their value, Nietzsche shows the 'moral good' to be reducible to human instincts of compassion, negation and self-abnegation. The disquieting impact his

---

[23] This agnostic position was most famously articulated by Hart himself: 'Legal theory should avoid commitment to controversial philosophical theories of the general status of moral judgments and should leave open, as I do in this book (p 168), the general question of whether they have "objective standing"' (HLA Hart 1994, 253).

[24] For the specific meaning of 'naturalist' in this context, see above n 7.

[25] Note that Nietzsche emphasises the contrast between his 'genealogy' and the term 'origin', which Rée employed in his own genealogical endeavour, which 'failed' due to its excessively 'blue' (or ahistorical) character.

genealogy had on traditional moral philosophy proceeds not only from the degrading aspect of his explanation, but also from his distancing from the traditional recourse to theology to 'wrap up' explanations of morality. From this perspective, David Couzens Hoy draws a parallel between Nietzsche and Hume's 'experimental reasoning', which allowed Hume 'to consign metaphysics to the flames, and to show reason to be the product of bodily instinct. The method allows him to inquire into the origins of morals without assuming as his contemporaries did that the virtuous dispositions were implanted in all of us by a divine creator'.[26]

While Couzens-Hoy argues that genealogy is 'a philosophical tool that is at once antimetaphysical and nonmetaphysical',[27] I would maintain that genealogy is rather a method committed to debunking *realist* metaphysics. To qualify it as 'nonmetaphysical' is misleading as indeed a genealogy does take a constructivist meta-ethical stand, working towards an understanding of values and institutions that grounds their possibility *within*, rather than *beyond* human activities. To confuse a constructivist meta-ethical position with the *absence* of metaphysics goes against the credibility of the constructivist model, however, as constructivism does assert the existence and possibility of normativity, which by definition is not part of the physical world, the world of matter. By contrast with a realist model however, a constructivist account of normativity does not seek to account for its possibility by reference to an order antecedent to and given to us.

Instead of appealing to a world of essences, 'natural laws' or 'intrinsically normative entities', a constructivist account endeavours to explain the possibility of our having values by reference to a certain understanding of human nature.[28] The

---

[26] D Couzens-Hoy 1994, 253.

[27] D Couzens-Hoy 1994, 252.

[28] For an idea of the role which Aristotle's account of human nature may be made to play in this context, and its chances of successfully establishing a foundation for our attempts to answer the question, 'how should one live?', see Nussbaum 1995.

concept of human nature upon which it relies is not going to provide the scientific kind of objectivity which 'an order antecedent to and given to us' promises. While the realist model can conceive of ethical thought as a process aiming at 'tracking the truth' of moral propositions by reference to the independent order it postulates, constructivism seems to leave ethical thought in need of some fixed 'object' or entity[29] by reference to which it could build the possibility of ethical objectivity. Such is the impression, at least, which has driven many of the realist reactions to constructivist proposals.[30] This impression is based on the wrong-headed belief that 'if a claim is objectively true, then there have to be objects to which the claim "corresponds"'.[31] Instead of 'yielding to the temptation to find mysterious entities which somehow guarantee or stand behind correct judgements of the reasonable or the unreasonable',[32] the challenge faced by moral constructivism is to build a theory of moral concepts that allows for our confidence in the objectivity of moral judgements in spite of the absence of any independent or external guarantee. As a philosophical tool, a genealogy can help clear the ground for such a challenge. Its commitment to deflating any form of mystification, exposing realist 'guarantees' for what they are — queer metaphysical objects — may initially sap one's confidence in the possibility of ethical objectivity. This initial disillusionment, however, need not be taken as the

---

[29] By contrast with the irremediable 'fleetingness' and variability of human nature.

[30] Christine Korsgaard has sketched an impressive survey of the constructivism/realism debate since the 18th century and throughout the 20th century in CM Korsgaard 2003b, where she notably argues that realism 'is a reactive position that arises in response to almost every attempt to give a substantive explanation of morality. It results from the realist's belief that such explanations inevitably reduce moral phenomena to natural phenomena. I trace this belief, and the essence of realism, to a view about the nature of concepts — that it is the function of all concepts to describe reality.' (CM Korsgaard 2003b, 99).

[31] H Putnam 2004, 52.

[32] H Putnam 2004, 70. (As for the possibility of defending a realist position without committing oneself to the existence of peculiar metaphysical entities, it is notably advocated by Thomas Nagel in T Nagel 1986, 144.)

last and final word of the story, and can, in the context of ethical (and legal) theory, be deemed the first and necessary step towards a constructivist understanding of moral values.

4.2 Pedigree or Genealogy?

A fairly instinctive way of making sense of things is to ask about their origins. If one is not familiar with this or that institution, one will inquire about the circumstances or phenomena that brought it about, and gave it its present shape. This reaction applies not only to social constructs, but also to the understanding of our 'natural' environment, whether it be the people who surround us (understanding their character traits) or the structure of biological phenomena. Beyond the archetypical 'Big Bang theories', much of our effort to understand the world that surrounds us is geared towards its origins. This effort can be characterised by two contrasted attitudes, translating very different expectations when inquiring into the origins of a phenomenon.

One possible attitude seeks to trace the 'pedigree' of a given phenomenon. In that case, one expects to be able to assign it a single, fixed point of origin, generally with a view to legitimising or justifying that phenomenon. From this perspective, Raymond Geuss refers to the endeavour to trace the pedigree of Agamemnon's sceptre[33] as one early example of such attitude: 'The pedigree of the sceptre traces Agamemnon's possession of it back through a series of unbroken steps of transmission to a singular origin. For the pedigree actually to discharge its function, the origin to which it recurs must be an actual source of

---

[33] 'Powerful Agamemnon stood up holding the sceptre Hephaistos had wrought him carefully. Hephaistos gave it to Zeus the king, son of Kronos, and Zeus in turn gave it to the courier Argeiphontes, and Lord Hermes gave it to Pelops, driver of horses, and Pelops gave it to Atreus, the shepherd of the people. Atreus dying left it to Thyestes of the rich flocks, and Thyestes left it in turn to Agamemnon to carry and to be lord over many islands and over all Argos'. (Homer 1951, book II, lines 100ff reference from R Geuss 1994, 289).

positive value, and each of the steps in the succession must be value-preserving'.[34] In the actual, 'non-mythical' world,[35] few phenomena can actually be traced to the *singular* origin required by a pedigree approach, except by limiting the scope of one's inquiry. One may, in that sense, trace the pedigree of a given legal system to its first 'enabling' constitution. This original constitution can be deemed the 'fixed' origin of a legal system only if a whole range of political, social and economical factors are dismissed as irrelevant. From this perspective, Kelsen's endeavour to trace the source of legal normativity to what he calls the 'Basic Norm' looks temptingly like a pedigree approach. Aware of the need to postulate some further source of normativity 'authorising' the first constitution, but wary of any reference to some transcendent order[36] Kelsen posits the Basic Norm as the point to which the normative status of all the rules of a legal system can be traced back. Except in the theorist's mind, this point does not exist. First formulated as a Kantian 'transcendental presupposition', and then as a fiction, the Basic Norm is what allows Kelsen to avoid any reference to the contingency of social practices, thus escaping, like Montaigne, the 'dangers' of a genealogical endeavour.[37]

[34] R Geuss 1994, 275.

[35] In some tribal societies, myth and reality are connected in such a way as to allow what is initially a genealogical movement tracing the filiation of families or clans to become a pedigree through the identification of a totemic ancestor or founding father in some mythological past.

[36] 'That a norm of the kind just mentioned is the Basic Norm of the national legal order does not imply that it is impossible to go beyond that norm. Certainly one may ask why one has to respect the first constitution as a binding norm. The answer might be that the fathers of the first constitution were empowered by God. The characteristic of so-called legal positivism is, however, that it dispenses with any such religious justification of the legal order' (H Kelsen 1949a, 116).

[37] Beyond the initial similarities that make it 'tempting' to characterise Kelsen's inquiry into the sources of legal normativity as a pedigree approach, there are some serious difficulties, related not only to the 'presupposed' character of the Basic Norm, but also to Kelsen's repeated emphasis on the 'neutral' — non-justificatory — character of his theory, which is at odds with the justificatory ambitions of a pedigree approach.

By contrast with the pedigree approach, there is no end to a genealogical enquiry into the origins of a phenomenon. As it progresses 'upstream', a genealogy reveals a conjunction of diverse processes which cannot be brought back to a singular origin. Whether they confirm or downplay the perceived legitimacy of the phenomenon in question, these processes are exposed for the sake of challenging common perceptions. Unlike a pedigree, a genealogy is not undertaken with a view to confirming the value of its object. A desire to scrutinise the understanding of a given phenomenon is what drives a genealogy. That desire can be motivated by curiosity, impertinence or audacity. In every case, a genealogy is not meant to be 'safe'. Its capacity to radically undermine the accepted understanding of a given phenomenon determines its degree of 'dangerousness'. The longer a phenomenon remains unquestioned, the more rigid its understanding, and the more 'dangerous' a genealogy can be.

From this perspective, Montaigne's initial endeavour to trace a genealogy of legal normativity came at a dramatic moment. Its potential to radically undermine law's accepted authority (based on the belief in the existence of natural laws) drove Montaigne to take a striking turn and ultimately rely on a pedigree approach rather than a genealogy. Montaigne's grounding the authority of law in a 'law of pure obedience' — the 'first commandment which God ever gave to Man'[38] — is indeed meant to 'save' legal normativity from the peril of its contingent beginnings. This safety comes at a price: the alleged divine origin of this law of pure obedience can be deemed a form of 'surrender' on Montaigne's part. After having shown that our finite nature — our always being 'between birth and death' — does not give us access to the true nature of things and condemns us to finding our way in a world of appearances, Montaigne reintroduces an absolute reference: God. This divine reference is not to be

[38] M de Montaigne 1991, II 12, 543. For further development of this idea see section 1.2.3.

accepted on the basis of rational judgement but on the basis of faith alone. Because of the deficiency of our natural faculties, we should not use them to judge of matters divine. Instead, we should yield to the authority of the Church.[39] The same leap of faith is asked of the layman when it comes to law's authority. The point of Montaigne's law of pure obedience is to introduce an ultimate and indisputable point of reference. The quasi-tautological character of its formulation (obedience to the law would be justified by a law of pure obedience) confirms the necessity of avoiding developing any interest for this last and ultimate law, and yielding to law's authority on the basis of 'obedient faith'.

This attempt to turn attention away from what is meant to 'stand as' the ultimate grounding of law's normativity is a trait characteristic of a certain kind of legal positivism. The link I traced from Montaigne to Kelsen[40] was meant to emphasise a pervasive concern to avoid a form of 'theoretical embarrassment'. In the particular context of this pedigree–genealogy contrast, this 'embarrassment' can be reformulated as flowing from the reluctant adoption of a pedigree approach in order to 'take over' an aborted or forbidden genealogical endeavour. Kelsen's Neo-Kantian methodology indeed committed him to preserving the absolute 'purity' of the normative sphere, thus forbidding any link to the socio-cultural practices a genealogy would need to build on. Introduced as a presupposition necessary to considering law as a normative phenomenon, the Basic Norm — unsuccesfully — seeks to keep out of the limelight (just like Montaigne's 'law of pure obedience'), while providing the 'stopping point' which Kelsen needs if he is to avoid the threatening arbitrariness of lawmaking politics.

Now, the problem lies precisely in this status of 'stopping point', a point where 'the *Sollen* suddenly stops and normativity breaks off; in their place one sees the emergence of the

---

[39] Montaigne was strongly opposed to Luther's reliance on the individual's conscience and 'rational capacities' to discern the truth in religious matters.

[40] See section 3.3.

tautology of a crude effectivity: something is valid if it is valid and because it is valid. This is positivism',[41] which Carl Schmitt targeted as the ultimate weakness of legal positivism. Instead of being the exalted starting point which a pedigree approach calls for, the Basic Norm, like the 'law of pure obedience', comes across as a stopgap measure. The reality it is meant to avoid — the context of social interaction that brings law into being — is highlighted by Schmitt as the necessary 'gesture that institutes normativity'. His nihilist decisionism, however, turns that 'gesture' into an inhuman one.[42] Schmitt's grounding law's normativity in the sovereign's absolute decision 'springing from the normative nothing and a concrete disorder'[43] indeed provides legal normativity with a 'mythical' pedigree leaving no room for an ethical dimension,[44] thus opening the door to a kind of political recuperation whose consequences were disasterously illustrated by the Nazi regime.

[41] C Schmitt 1928, ch 1, 9 (my translation): 'Hier hört plötzlich das Sollen auf und bricht die Normativität ab; statt ihrer erscheint die Tautologie einer rohen Tatsächlichkeit: etwas gilt, wenn es gilt und weil es gilt. Das ist Positivismus'.

[42] As a model of the social practices bringing law to existence, Schmitt's concept of decision 'springing from the normative nothing' indeed seems to fall above all within the domain of the political fable, which in this case is based on the idea of a sovereign people with quasi-divine powers. For more details on Schmitt's critique of Kelsenian positivism, see S Delacroix 2005. For a brilliant analysis of the pervasive theological pattern in Schmitt's works, see JF Kervégan 1995b.

[43] 'The sovereign decision is, therefore, juristically explained neither from a norm nor from a concrete order, nor incorporated into the sphere of a concrete order, because for the decisionist, it is, on the contrary, the decision which first establishes the norm as well as the order. The sovereign decision is the absolute beginning, and the beginning (also in the sense of arche) is nothing but sovereign decision. The sovereign decision springs from the normative nothing and a concrete disorder' (C Schmitt 2004, 62 — for the German text see C Schmitt 1934, 28).

[44] Schmitt's interpretation of the 'state of nature' as some kind of normative emptiness leaves no room for ethical references or moral principles. Along this line, Schmitt emphasises that '[the decision] can do without any justification derived from an ethical or legal norm, and takes its meaning from its political existence' (C Schmitt 1928, ch 9, 87 — my translation: 'Sie bedarf keiner Rechtfertigung an einer ethischen oder juristischen Norm, sondern hat ihren Sinn in der politischen Existenz').

The relevance of Schmitt's contribution to legal philosophy, however, does not lie in his 'decisionist' account of legal normativity, but rather in his stigmatisation of legal theory's pervasive trend to proceed from the assumption that the problem of how legal normativity is possible in the first place is only an apparent problem or a problem that does not need to be solved.[45] With his 'law of pure obedience', Montaigne inaugurated that trend. Kelsen's reliance on the concept of 'Basic Norm' to account for law's normativity while at the same time warding off any reference to what he perceived as the threatening reality of lawmaking politics can be deemed the epitome of that tendency. The ambivalent status of their respective 'grounds' for legal normativity (neither the exalted starting point of a pedigree, nor meant to exclude any genealogical endeavour) springs from their desire to escape a question they have themselves raised. Whether it be by 'stopping the discourse in time' or ensuring the 'purity' of the legal sphere, the law of pure obedience and the Basic Norm are meant to render any genealogical type of inquiry irrelevant. This trend inaugurated by Montaigne does not end with Kelsen.

4.3 The Irrelevance Objection

One major objection that may be raised against a genealogical account of legal normativity consists in dismissing the very relevance of such a project, arguing that if law's normative dimension is indeed an element essential to the understanding of law, this normative dimension does not in itself call for a specific, further explanation of its possibility. While this kind of argument may be considered a corollary of a realist understanding of normativity (as normativity is deemed part of the 'fabric' of

---

[45] According to Schmitt, this assumption, this temptation to act 'as if a norm could produce by itself the conditions of its effectuation' is the product of an old trend of bourgeois liberalism aiming at raising the law above any kind of political force in order to secure private property and bourgeois freedom.

the world, its possibility may be taken for granted), it is also invoked by theorists who reject the realist position. From their perspective, law's normativity is to be taken as an axiom whose possibility does not in itself require further explanation. If law were not normative, it would not be law. To try to explain what *makes* law normative, what allows or conditions its normative dimension, is to ask for the kind of trouble Montaigne and Kelsen ran into. At best, one may say that a complex web of social and cultural interactions somehow comes to confer special significance to a certain set of practices, which consequently acquire a normative status.

This is, roughly put, the kind of detached, unconcerned answer put forward by Hart. His inscription within a philosophical context dominated by JL Austin's theory of language, weary of abstract essences whose metaphysical status is supposedly independent of linguistic usage, predisposed Hart to appearing unconcerned about what conditions law's normativity. His late reference to a conventionalist framework to explain the emergence of the rule of recognition is made in passing, in a brief passage of his *Postscript*,[46] as if the study of the context of social interaction allowing and conditioning law's normative dimension were unlikely to yield any significant insight as to the meaning and properties of law itself. As if, more importantly, any such inquiry into its conditions of possibility would inevitably grant the concept of normativity a metaphysical status it should not and cannot have.

Hart's reliance on JL Austin's method, aimed at elucidating even the most complex concepts by reference to 'the things people do with words', was meant to provide him with the means to account for law's normativity without relying on any

---

[46] 'But the theory remains as a faithful account of conventional social rules which include, besides ordinary social customs (which may or may not be recognised as having legal force), certain important legal rules including the rule of recognition, which is in effect a form of judicial customary rule existing only if it is accepted and practiced in the law-identifying and law-applying operations of the courts' (HLA Hart 1994, 256).

of the metaphysical presuppositions often associated with natural law theories. His accounting for the difference between coercion and obligation by reference to the 'distinct normative attitude'[47] typically associated with the use of the word 'obligation' was taken to show that one may explain law's normativity without embarking on a meta-ethical reflection about the 'status' of norms.[48] Hart was indeed notably sceptical as to the possibility of preserving the objectivity of values without adhering to some form of moral realism, a metaphysical option he was committed to rejecting. His taking refuge in the belief that, to use Raz's words, 'the problems about the ontological standing of legal "things" such as law, rights and corporations [...] can be dissolved with the judicious application of speech-act theory'[49] allowed him to leave his meta-ethical concerns behind.[50]

One may, however, question the substance of these 'problems about the ontological standing of legal "things"'. The problem, or at least the need to 'dissolve' it, may lie precisely in its being

[47] This distinct normative attitude 'consists in the standing disposition of individuals to take such patterns of conduct both as guides to their own future conduct and as standards of criticism which may legitimate demands and various forms of pressure for conformity' (HLA Hart 1994, 255).

[48] It was also meant preserve a distinction in kind between legal obligation and moral obligation, as indeed Hart repeatedly emphasised that the critical attitude typically associated with the legal use of the term 'obligation' need not translate any moral conviction on the part of the utterer.

[49] J Raz 2001, 5. Note that Raz does add that 'by the time Hart published *The Concept of Law* many of these hopes had receded. But his faith in the benefits for legal analysis of learning the lessons of speech-act theory is manifested in his way of understanding legal statements as statements from what he called the internal point of view'.

[50] 'Even when there is agreement on this point and certain rules or principles are accepted as indisputably belonging to morality, there may still be great philosophical disagreement as to their *status* or relation to the rest of human knowledge and experience. Are they immutable principles which constitute part of the fabric of the Universe, not made by man, but awaiting discovery by the human intellect? Or are they expressions of changing human attitudes, choices, demands, or feelings? These are crude formulations of two extremes in moral philosophy. Between them lie many complicated and subtle variants, which philosophers have developed in the effort to elucidate the nature of morality. In what follows we shall seek to evade these philosophical difficulties'. (HLA Hart 1994, 168).

characterised in ontological terms. For Raz must mean something special by 'the problem of the ontological standing' of a thing like law. It has to be something different from the existence of law as a 'social' phenomenon, an issue with which Hart had no reason to feel particularly uncomfortable. Is this 'ontological standing' issue meant to refer to the existence of law as a normative phenomenon, with a claim to bind us? This interpretation would make sense, as indeed in another context, trying to grasp the implications of social contingency in relation to the objectivity of the moral values they give rise to, Raz also formulates the problem in ontological terms, as a problem about the *existence* of values. In his answer to Raz's lecture, Bernard Williams actually raises doubts about the appropriateness of such a vocabulary: 'Raz expresses his thesis, and the whole discussion, in terms of the conditions on *values existing* (at certain places, times, and so on). My problem is that I am not sure what this means.'[51] The problem, maybe, is that the meaning of this particular vocabulary crucially depends on the broader meta-ethical position Raz may be deemed to endorse.

Raz does seem, at times, to endorse a form of moral realism, whereby the truth of our moral concepts depends on their accurately 'tracking' some independent reality. His attempt to introduce a distinction between 'the concepts of true and false values' on the basis of whether or not a value V *exists* (if it does not, then 'the concept of V is a concept of a false or illusory value'[52]), does indeed seem to presuppose a realist framework. In such a framework, a judgement relying on some value or norm will be deemed 'objectively true' if it corresponds to some *object*, natural or non-natural (such as *good* as a non-natural property). This particular understanding of objectivity

[51] B Williams 2003, 108.

[52] 'Concepts of false values cannot have instances [. . .] if there is no value V, then the concept of V is a concept of a false or illusory value [. . .] Concepts that cannot have instances do not connect the concepts they are used to explain to the world or to anything in it, and thus they fail to explain them' (J Raz 2003b, 24).

has been criticised by Hilary Putnam, who associates it with a Platonic theory of Ideas, or what he calls 'Ontology': 'But there is something else wrong with Ontology, and that is the idea that each and every instance of objectivity must be supported by *objects*'.[53]

A realist interpretation of Raz's position throws a particular light on 'the problems about the ontological standing of legal things' which, according to Raz, Hart hoped to dissolve by recourse to speech-act theory. What Hart would have wanted to 'dissolve' with the help of Austin's philosophy of language are the metaphysical postulates implied by a commitment to moral realism. As an ontological thesis, moral realism conditions the truth of moral judgements to their accurately 'tracking' some entities or state of affairs that supposedly exist independently of our thoughts or feelings. His sharing the widely spread assumption that the possibility of ethical objectivity presupposes a moral realist position triggered Hart's scepticism as to the possibility of ethical objectivity. This scepticism had an indirect but important influence on his legal theory. Its impact can be traced back to two different strategies.

4.3.1 Moral Legitimacy made Irrelevant

One of Hart's major concerns was to account for law's normativity in a way that did not at any point have to presuppose a moral component. John Tasioulas analyses this concern[54] as flowing from an endeavour to assert the normativity of legal statements in a way that makes it independent of whether or not moral judgements can claim objectivity. To support this argument, Tasioulas contrasts Hart's theory with Raz's, or, more

---

[53] H Putnam 2004, 51.

[54] 'It was [. . .] the ambition [. . .] to preserve the normativity of legal statements in a way that did not compromise their truth or validity that explains why Hart, as someone sympathetic to ethical non-objectivism, sought to provide an explanation of legal normativity that did not include the moral endorsement of the rule of recognition as a necessary element' (J Tasioulas 2002, 231).

precisely, with Raz's 're-appropriation'[55] of Kelsen's account of normativity. Raz indeed attributes to Kelsen what he calls a 'justified' conception of normativity, according to which those who presuppose the Basic Norm, and thus consider the law as normative, do so out of a belief in the moral legitimacy of law.[56] This account of legal normativity makes it 'dangerously' dependent on the possibility of ethical objectivity: as James Harris pointed out, if one adopts the relativist position Kelsen endorsed at the end of his life,[57] then the belief in the moral legitimacy of law carries no weight (as it cannot be objective) and it consequently cannot ground law's normativity. Raz's linking up his account of legal normativity to a belief in law's moral legitimacy would thus require a meta-ethical position defending the possibility of ethical objectivity, a position which did not seem viable to Hart.

This need not have been so. Among the figures who had a profound philosophical impact on Hart was not only JL Austin but also Richard Hare, whose first book, *Language of Morals*, was published in 1952. In the spirit of Austin's 'speech-act theory', Hare's project is to explain the function of moral language. His fundamental premise is that the aim of moral language is *not* to describe or 'report' some facts about the world. Besides the 'factual or descriptive meaning' they may have, moral

[55] I think that the word 're-appropriation' in this case is more accurate than 'interpretation', given Raz's liberal reading, taking advantage of some of the pervasive ambiguities of Kelsen's works to 'impose' some conclusions which Kelsen would have resisted at all costs — see my detailed analysis in section 3.2.

[56] Except for those who presuppose the Basic Norm in a 'detached' way, to take Raz's expression. This qualification is meant to allow for the fact that Kelsen explicitly went back on his previous statement that the Basic Norm could not be presupposed by the anarchist (made in H Kelsen 1971b, 226–227), to maintain that the anarchist may indeed presuppose the Basic Norm, even though she obviously does not accept the law as a standard of conduct (H Kelsen 1967, 218 note 82).

[57] Kelsen's late 'will theory' according to which the normativity of legal statements is reducible to their being 'willed' by the appropriate authority indeed seems to collapse into a form of relativism.

judgements have an irreducible prescriptive dimension aimed at guiding our actions. Unlike statements about the colour or shape of objects, the moral injunction to care for one's elderly parents, for instance, does not state any fact about elderly parents. If it has a descriptive content on the basis of which it may be deemed true or false, it is, according to Hare, the moral principles by reference to which that moral injunction may be justified.[58] The moral principles enjoying a widespread recognition in a given society may indeed be deemed 'moral facts' about that society, conditioning the truth-value of moral statements in that society. These facts do not, however, have the same 'robustness' as, say, the redness of ripe strawberries. By contrast with the moral principles underlying the moral injunction to support one's elderly parents, which may be negated in a different society (or ultimately put into question in the same society), the redness of ripe strawberries is not supposed to leave much room for disagreement as to their redness.

This contrast is deemed problematic by some people, who would like to be able to establish the truth of moral statements in the same 'robust way' as one may establish the truth-value of a statement like 'ripe strawberries are red'.[59] Those people typically worry that Hare's characterisation of moral language as essentially prescriptive rules out the possibility of ethical

[58] 'If moral statements are universalizable in this way, they will inevitably acquire a descriptive function as part of their meaning; for someone who makes such a statement must think that the moral properties of the situation about which it is made supervene on its non-moral properties (the reasons for making it) in accordance with a principle applying to all identically similar situations. Thus he will be taken to hold that there are facts that justify the statement, and it thus acquires a factual, descriptive content or meaning' (RM Hare 1999b, 20).

[59] 'People are attracted by descriptivism because they think it is the only way to achieve a kind of objectivity in moral statements that they want them to have. We may express this by saying that they want to be able to establish some moral principles that no rational person who knew the facts could disagree with'(RM Hare 1999a, 11).

objectivity. This concern is based on a particular, and, according to Hare, mistaken conception of objectivity,[60] assuming that it can only be made possible by a 'robust' kind of factuality, or what Putnam would refer to as the existence of corresponding 'objects'.[61] This particular conception of objectivity, which is still widespread, has contributed to the (mis)characterisation of Hare's theory as a non-cognitivist model excluding the possibility of ethical objectivity (despite his explicit efforts to defend its possibility). As Hart seems to have endorsed this interpretation of Hare (ie non-cognitivism ruling out the possibility of ethical objectivity), and given the importance of the meta-ethical options involved for the rest of the present work, let me introduce some necessary clarifications.

Non-cognitivism is commonly presented as the view that moral judgements are not truth-apt and are not beliefs. According to this position, a moral judgement is more appropriately characterised as a special kind of desire or concern. This non-cognitivist view is often attributed to Hare[62] owing to his characterisation of moral judgements as typically 'not pure statements of facts but *in part*, for example, expressions of attitudes, prescriptions, or something else non-descriptive'.[63] If it does not describe or 'report' anything about the world, if it does not state any 'fact', then there is no element by reference to which one may assess the truth value of a moral judgement, or so runs the kind of reasoning underlying a non-cognitivist understanding of Hare. To counter this kind of understanding, Hare emphasised that the prescriptivist component of moral

---

[60] 'The idea that only some kind of descriptivism — some kind of factuality in moral judgments — can make objectivity possible rests on a very fundamental mistake which nearly everybody commits who studies this question' (RM Hare 1999a, 11).

[61] H Putnam 2004, 51: see n 53 above.

[62] 'Since I myself think both that moral statements can be true or false, and that we can know them to be true or false, I get extremely cross when people classify me as a non-cognitivist' (RM Hare 1999a, 4).

[63] RM Hare 1981, 208 (emphasis added).

judgements does not rule out their having some descriptive content as well.[64] Most importantly, while this prescriptivist element may not itself be truth-apt,[65] it is, according to Hare, what enables moral judgements to claim objectivity, and thus to say what we want to say in ethics.

The purpose of moral language is indeed 'to enable us to discuss with one another how we should behave'.[66] If, when two persons disagree on an issue involving moral values, they are not to merely contradict each other, but actually be able to *argue* and ultimately find a 'rational' solution[67] to their disagreement, then they need a language whose logic allows for a form of universalisation.

> If moral judgements lacked this feature, we could again, if we simply wanted something not to be done, say that it ought not to be done, that is, that it was wrong; and between us and anybody who said it was not wrong, or even that it ought to be done, there would be no way of deciding — no way we could argue with one another to determine which verdict on the act to accept. But moral judgements are different. It is, I think (though some people disagree), a fact of language that if I say that an act ought to be done, I am committed to saying that a similar act ought to be done in all circumstances resembling these, regardless of who is in which position in the situation.[68]

Now, even if one does not deem the universalisability of moral judgements to be a 'fact of language', Hare's understanding of objectivity as essentially linked to the possibility of 'rationally' solving an ethical disagreement has an important consequence: it disentangles the concept of objectivity from the concept of

[64] cf the distinction between 'thick' and 'thin' moral concepts.

[65] It is not truth-apt if one conditions the possibility of truth to its being 'verifiable' by reference to external elements ('truth-conditions'). Someone like Alain Badiou would however probably feel comfortable asserting that a purely prescriptive statement 'produces its own truth' (see A Badiou 1989).

[66] RM Hare 1999a, 9.

[67] According to Onora O'Neill, a 'rational solution' to an ethical disagreement requires that its authority be in principle 'intersubjectively discernible', so that it does not rely on some arbitrary opinion that may not be shared (see O O'Neill 2000, 12).

[68] RM Hare 1999a, 13.

truth.[69] By contrast with the widespread conception of moral objectivism as 'a theory about the truth conditions for moral judgements',[70] Hare's emphasis on what it takes for moral disagreements to be 'solvable' shifts the focus from the truth or falsity of moral judgements to their being susceptible to rational argumentation. For Hare, the possibility of argumentation in ethics requires us to be able to distance ourselves from the principles inculcated by our upbringing or character.[71] This 'critical distancing' should then allow us to isolate only those principles upon which we are ready to act in all comparable circumstances, and which we would wish everybody else to act upon in those circumstances.[72] When a disagreement arises, the possibility of solving it 'rationally'[73] thus lies, according to Hare, in a critical appraisal of the principles underlying each position.

[69] 'Many different things have been discussed as the question of objectivity, but they all tend either to come to nothing, or to come back to one issue: the proper understanding of ethical disagreement. Some philosophers have been very exercised, for instance, with the question whether moral judgments can be true or false. But work has to be done to find what, and how much, that question means. [. . .] I see no way of pursuing that question, which does not lead back to questions such as these: if an ethical disagreement arises, must one party think the other in error? What is the content of that thought? What sorts of discussions or explorations might, given the particular subject matter, lead one or both of them out of error?' (B Williams 1995, 145).

[70] KE Himma 1999, 420.

[71] Hare's distinction between the intuitive and the critical levels of thinking allows him to concede that intuitive judgements may not be objective: they merely reflect one's prima facie principles, which are the result of one's upbringing and character.

[72] The extent and quality of the 'distance' required to achieve the appropriate level of objectivity is a subject of debate. While Hare insists that universalisability requires absolute impartiality on the part of the agent, Simon Blackburn emphasises the unavoidable agent-relativity of moral judgements, which may be universalisable without being impartial: 'Our everyday moralities are firmly rooted in the myriad special relationships that determine the moral status others have for us [. . .] The drive to impartiality inherent in universal prescriptivism is, like our other concerns, the contingent and fragile result of our sentimental natures' (S Blackburn 1998, 226).

[73] This rational solution will, most of the time, lead to identifying one judgement as 'correct' while the other will be deemed mistaken. In some cases, however, one may not be able to compare the two judgements, because they are deemed to rely on incommensurate values.

Now, whether or not one adheres to Hare's specific under-standing of the critical appraisal at stake, what is important for our purposes is that ethical objectivity, on this account, is not dependent upon a moral realist position. If the possibility of 'rationally' solving an ethical disagreement relied upon the exis-tence of some 'intrinsically normative entities' or 'objects' which the parties to the dispute had to accurately track in order to find the *right* answer (thus implying that the 'wrong side' was misled by an inaccurate reading/tracking of the same entities), then indeed ethical objectivism could be said to be a 'theory about the truth conditions of moral judgements', which would need a realist position in order to 'substantiate' these truth con-ditions. Hare and, after him, philosophers from various tradi-tions, such as Habermas on the Kantian side and Blackburn on the Humean side, have provided powerful arguments in support of a constructivist understanding of moral values maintaining the possibility of ethical objectivity. Without venturing further into the respective merits of these positions, the important con-clusion for our purposes is that Hart need not have endorsed the scepticism about ethical objectivity which contributed to his careful exclusion of any 'necessary' reference to moral legitimacy considerations.

While Hart's sceptical position is, in itself, tenable, one may argue that his endeavour to dismiss the issue of ethical objectiv-ity has actually contributed to its problematic status (through its lack of argumentation). Today, given the wide-ranging implications of such a meta-ethical position for legal theory,[74] dismissing such debate as irrelevant to our understanding of law borders on arrogance (or laziness at best). Now, how does the importance of this meta-ethical issue about ethical objectivity relate to my endeavour to trace a genealogy of legal normativi-ty? I will need a few more sections to develop my answer.

---

[74] See section 5.2.2 for a discussion of its implications for the inclusive/exclusive legal positivism debate.

4.3.2 Genealogy made Superfluous

If value is meant to be found in the 'fabric' of the world, if the world offers itself to us with a certain set of fundamental principles which it is our job to discover and intelligently translate into further principles or norms regulating our action, then the endeavour to trace a genealogy of legal normativity seems to rest on a fundamental mistake. This mistake would consist in thinking that normativity somehow *comes about*.[75] Endeavoring to trace the various social and cultural practices explaining how legal normativity, as a social phenomenon, comes about, is pointless because normativity by definition does not come about. On this realist understanding of moral values, a genealogical account of legal normativity would definitely be inappropriate.

Hart did not endorse a realist position, however; that much is clear. One may thus be tempted to think that nothing stood in the way of his developing some kind of genealogical story, had he been interested. The fact is, though, he wasn't interested. One could leave it at that, and argue that yes, Hart could have developed more of a story towards accounting for the context of social interaction that brings law into being, but to try and read some 'further meaning' into his scant concern for law-creating practices can only be misleading. The specificity of Hart's project, his endeavour to analyse the meaning of a normative statement such as 'it is the law that', simply did not require him to look into the various social practices contributing to bringing law into existence. From this perspective, the various conventionalist models which have been developed recently[76] can be seen as a useful follow-up on Hart's theory, seeking to answer a distinct, but complementary question: 'what are the existence conditions of law?'. This distinction between explaining the existence of law, on one hand, and its normativity, on the other

---

[75] A constructivist understanding of moral values, by contrast, denounces the realist assumption that there are 'intrinsically normative entities' out there whose discovery is at the root of our normative practices.

[76] See section 5.2.1.

hand, is most clearly articulated by Jules Coleman: 'As I see it, the fundamental problems of jurisprudence are to explain law's *possibility* and its *normativity*. The Conventionality Thesis speaks for the first of these issues, the Practical Difference Thesis to the second'.[77]

I deem this distinction between law's existence and law's normativity as two distinctive explanatory targets to be a remnant of the positivist trend which I traced back to Montaigne, endeavouring to safeguard law's normativity by somehow isolating it from the contingent social practices enabling law's existence. Hart's scant concern for these social practices could be read as a very English way of dissimulating or 'forgetting' a very actual concern. This actual concern flows from the inability to relate what seems to be the disproportionate 'mess' of the context of social interaction giving rise to law (and, most importantly, its threatening politics) to its purported normative dimension: the fact that law is meant to be obligatory, to impose some non-optional mode of conduct on its subjects. I will come back to this 'shocking disproportion' between the contingency giving rise to law and its purported authority in the next chapter. For now, let me tell you what a genealogy may bring to our understanding of legal normativity, when it is not made superfluous.

[77] J Coleman 2001a, 114.

5
The Story

At first sight, the story I have to tell is commonplace. Law is made by men and women. It has always been so, at least since and to the extent that women's political rights are recognised. Law is also meant to bind us; this normative dimension is an inherent part of what law is. So, given our long-standing practice of creating legal standards that somehow manage to bind us, we should have a pretty good grasp by now of what it is that enables us to do that: what enables us, fallible human beings, to put forward some rules of conduct that are meant to withstand the very whims and desires that may have presided at the creation of those rules.

This is what my story endeavours to explain, in the specific context of legal rules. Yet it is not commonplace. Major legal theorists have devoted considerable effort to circumventing this question by way of various methodological arguments (see Part I). I take this theoretical wariness to be governed by the concern to safeguard the integrity of legal normativity in the face of its potential compromising with the contingency of lawmaking politics.

The effort to conceal the historical variability and contingency of commanding institutions, such as morality, is classically aimed at preserving their claim to authority, which has somehow come to rely on a convenient 'forgetfulness' of their historical genesis. Law, however, seems to differ from other social institutions in this respect, as its 'man-made' character has always been one of its ostensible features. In this context, one may venture to think that law's high exposure to various studies aimed at tracing its historical and anthropological genesis would make it well disposed towards the genealogical endeavour I propose. My genealogical story, however, does not aim at law as such, but rather at its *normative dimension*. While different cultures and times may contribute a wide variety of forms and contents to law, its normative dimension, as a structural element, transcends these cultural variations. As the expression of the need to *bind* ourselves through legal rules, legal normativity is first and foremost a challenge, which revolutionary lawmakers come to experience first-hand.

If they do not count solely on force to establish their authority, revolutionary lawmakers will typically seek to be perceived as legitimate by the bulk of the population. This quest for legitimacy will in turn trigger some reflection as to the status of the values they seek to promote. Are these values merely expressing their own contingent preferences, or can they claim some objective status? There is a range of options available to those who seek to answer this question positively, reflecting different understandings of law and its relationship to both morality and prudence. One recurrent concern underlies each of the options available. This concern proceeds from the eagerness to assert our own place and responsibility as lawmakers, while at the same time insisting that what is created/legislated is not contingent upon 'us', the lawmakers, as we happen to be at the time of lawmaking.[1] The challenge, in other words, is to bridge the apparent gap between the outward contingency of lawmaking

[1] Simon Blackburn describes this dual concern as the 'shaky tightrope' which Kant's account of practical reasoning is trying to walk: based on autonomy on one hand and a priori necessary formal laws structuring our will on the other hand, it would allow Kant to preserve the independence of law from contingent desire while at the same time asserting that 'true freedom demanded self-legislation or "obedience to a law one has prescribed for oneself"' (S Blackburn 1998, 244). While Blackburn formulated this dual concern with Kant's account of practical reasoning in mind, I think it fittingly describes a pervading concern among revolutionary lawmakers or those lawmakers who cannot establish their authority on the basis of a pre-existing set of norms (see section 5.1). The extent to which this structural similarity between the concern underlying Kant's account of practical reasoning and the concern striking revolutionary lawmakers is at all meaningful in terms of Kant's ongoing influence is a question which I would like to consider in due course.

practices and the necessity it is supposed to give rise to: if it is to *bind* us, if it is to survive our future whims and impose some non-optional form of conduct, law had better be able to claim for itself some stronger form of necessity than the contingent preferences of whoever happens to make the law. Or so the argument goes. This challenge is key to understanding the evolution of the concept of legal normativity through the ages: while its available answers have changed, the terms in which the problem is raised have not.

5.1 Taking the Law into our Own Hands

As a genealogy, my story endeavours to trace the various phenomena which contribute or have contributed to bringing about the normative dimension of law. Unlike the endeavour to trace the genealogy of truthfulness or morality for instance, a genealogical account of legal normativity does not require one to posit some fictional 'State of Nature' that would somehow be free of legal normativity. Legal normativity indeed regularly gets 'suspended' in the course of political revolutions, which may be deemed a kind of 'laboratory situation' particularly conducive to analysing the various elements contributing to law's emergence; provided, of course, that legal normativity does indeed get 'suspended' in the course of revolutionary events, an assumption which the 1989 events in Hungary have recently problematised.

5.1.1 Case Study: 'A Revolution without Revolutionaries'

The 1989 events that led to the fall of the communist regime in Hungary had all the apparent features of a revolution. Beyond the economic and social reforms unavoidably accompanying the transition from a communist to a liberal framework, these events 'succeeded in taking power away from the forces in possession of sovereignty [. . .] We can say this much at least: in these countries the new political order is based on equal freedom for all citizens, and this is a revolutionary change of no less significance than the transformation of the *ancien regime* into a civil democracy'.[2] The significance of these changes did not elude the actors who brought them about. Yet a striking feature of the rhetoric accompanying these events was the careful avoidance of the term 'revolution'. The lawyers and politicians involved in setting up the new regime resolutely preferred to speak of a 'restoration' or 'peaceful transition' instead.[3]

This general reluctance to think of their action as a revolution was not only the result of the extent to which the concept of revolution itself had been thoroughly discredited and abused under communist rule. It also conveyed a pervading concern to avoid the kind of rupture normally associated with revolutions, whereby the socio-legal structure in place is overthrown, thus giving rise to the need to bring about a new set of legal norms promoting a new form of society.

In Hungary, despite the radical political overhaul that the 1989 events called for, the lawyers involved in setting up the new regime chose to thoroughly amend the old communist constitution rather than create a new one. This striking concern with preserving legal continuity despite the significance of the political changes triggered various difficulties. Among these was the lack of a directing line for what was hence called a 'patchwork constitution', as it resulted from a variety of popular consultations, roundtable negotiations, etc. Officially dated from 1949[4] (80 per cent of it is new), and still called by some critics the Stalinist constitution, the Hungarian constitution initially gave a tough time to the new constitutional Court, which had to create its own interpretation guidelines rather than find them in the text of the constitution.

[2] UK Preuss 1995, 82.

[3] 'A high-ranking Hungarian jurist who has played an important role in reorganising the government in his country remarked that even enthusiastic supporters of these developments avoid the term "revolution", preferring to speak of a "peaceful transition" instead' (UK Preuss 1995, 91).

[4] This amended 1949 constitution was meant to be only provisory, and the project was to draft a new constitution after the first free elections. They did try to put forward a new draft in 1996, but it was rejected, so today we still have this peculiar situation, with a constitution still officially dated from 1949.

Whether or not Hungary's 1989 political actors were aware of the difficulties that would arise from their endeavour to preserve legal continuity, the interesting question for our purposes is the extent to which this avoidance of any break in legal normativity can be deemed to flow from a reluctance to be confronted with the difficulty underlying the need to (re)construct legal normativity. Had they created a new constitution instead of amending the old one, the Hungarian political actors would indeed have had to face what they took to be the 'unbearable burden' of a *pouvoir constituant*, and all the perplexities traditionally associated with it. But what exactly are these perplexities?

5.1.2 Lending Authority to a Contingent Power: The Call for Meta-referents

Since its emergence in the 18th century, the '*pouvoir constituant*' may be deemed a construct meant to bridge the gap between facticity and validity, between what was a contingent revolutionary force and the normative order it is supposed to give rise to. By being called *pouvoir constituant*, the power in the hands of revolutionaries would cease to be mere force by virtue of its being directed at the creation of a constitutional order. This concept of *pouvoir constituant* doesn't do the trick on its own, however. In Sieyès' theory, it relies on the concept of nation: because it is deemed to represent the nation, the revolutionaries' raw power can claim the authority necessary to its being able to lay down a constitutional order. If, however, one is wary of the fictional homogeneity needed in order to postulate this concept of nation, when the '*demos*' at stake is actually a fractured society united by little more than a common territory, the concept of *pouvoir constituant* (and the facticity/validity bridge it is supposed to enable) may sound like wishful thinking.

The 1989 political actors resolutely rejected any reference to the concept of 'nation'. Rather than relying on a supposedly homogeneous sovereign 'will of the people', the Round Tables formed to negotiate the *transition* to the new democratic regime emphasised the diversity of their composition. According to Ulrich Preuss, their 'understanding of the phrase "we the people" in the plural rather than the classic singular of earlier revolutions means that the sovereignty of the people, the foundation of all democratic rule, can no longer be interpreted as a unified and unlimited *potestas absoluta* in the sense that Abbé Sieyès conceived of the *pouvoir constituant* at the beginning of the democratic era'.[5]

While this plural understanding of 'we the people' may in itself be a welcome evolution, it seems to have contributed to the widespread conviction that the demands associated with the creation of a new normative order could not possibly be met. This conviction was based on the (misguided) belief that if it is to be able to claim the political authority necessary to the *creation* of a new political order, the revolution's 'naked' power must be able to call on some form of meta-referent. If a reference to God's or Providence's patronage is ruled out,[6] and if the revolutionaries' power cannot be deemed to represent some homogeneous entity such as the Nation, then one may be better off avoiding any 'revolutionary break' altogether, for fear of not being able to reconstruct the authority necessary to being able to lay down a new constitutional order.

This is one possible reading of the Hungarian political actors' decision to go through a wave of successive amendments rather than assume the challenge of a new constitution. While it is no doubt a partial account of the multiple factors that have contributed to the 'anti-revolutionary' attitude[7] (and the refusal to enter a new constitution-making process), this explanation nevertheless takes an interesting relief when one confronts it with Preuss's own account of the challenge faced by the 1989 revolutionaries. According to Preuss, these revolutionaries did 'not want to be godlike and to assume the burden of a completely new beginning with all its demanding requirements'.[8]

---

[5] UK Preuss 1995, 95.

[6] See the widespread use of a reference to God, or, alternatively, 'Providence' in constitutional documents. For further development of this idea see K Schmid 2004.

[7] The hypocritical 'revolutionary phraseology' of the preceding 40 years definitely played a major part in this anti-revolutionary spirit.

[8] UK Preuss 1995, 9.

Preuss's analysis of the challenge raised by the creation of a new constitution is actually symptomatic of an old and pervasive misconception of the *kind* of beginning entailed by a constitution-making endeavour. The burden of a godlike beginning indeed only befalls those who think of their lawmaking endeavour as radically unprecedented, arising out of the 'normative nothing and concrete disorder', to use Carl Schmitt's words.[9] Historically speaking, this burden has indeed come upon many, if not most, revolutionaries. The French revolutionaries' decision to create a new calendar can be seen as the epitome of this tendency to deny past experiences and traditions any relevance in the constitution-making process. The peril brought about by the resulting reliance on a reference to God[10] as the ultimate 'countersignature', as the meta-referent enabling *de facto* revolutionaries to acquire that 'supplement of authority' without which bringing about a new constitutional order does not seem viable, has been most notably emphasised by Hannah Arendt. She deplores the French revolutionaries 'lack of faith' in their own capacity to bring about something new.[11]

I deem the 'peril' triggered by this 'lack of faith'[12] to be twofold. On the one hand there is, most importantly, the de-responsibilisation prompted by a sort of 'thinking short-circuit', whereby the revolutionaries would manage to stop reflecting upon what grounds and enables their authority to create a new

[9] See above, ch 4, n 42

[10] Or to the 'Supreme Being', in the French case.

[11] Hannah Arendt deems the French revolutionaries' difficulties to be flowing from a lack of thinking and a concomitant loss of confidence in the human capacity to begin something new and to found a normative order (H Arendt 1990). In *The Human Condition*, she draws an important distinction, based on St Augustine, between 'the beginning which is man (*initium*)' and 'the beginning of the world (*principium*)' (H Arendt 1998, 177). According to Arendt, if the French revolutionaries had not understood their task as an absolute, godlike beginning (*principium*, beginning of the world), which is by definition beyond their capacities, they would probably have been able to avoid many of the perplexities they were confronted with.

[12] It is worth noting here that the faith at stake is a secular, rather than religious one. This concept of 'secular faith' is to be understood as complementary, rather than opposed, to religious faith.

legal order thanks to the 'divine authorisation' embodied in God's countersignature. There is also, on the other hand, the more pragmatic (though related) problem raised by the potential lack of reflection upon what one wants law for, the values and objectives one wants law to promote. The revolutionaries' ability to 'skip' or at least alleviate that fundamental reflection as to what grounds their authority may indeed lessen their concern to establish the legitimacy of their power and thus reflect upon such values and objectives.

Hungary's 1989 (anti)revolutionaries did not seek the comfort of a divine countersignature. Indeed they did not need to, as their refusal to enter a revolutionary process triggering the need to write a new constitution precisely allowed them to avoid the perplexities that a reference to God or Providence can be perceived to alleviate. Their scepticism about a supposedly all-encompassing concept such as 'Nation' ruled out another possible way of bridging the gap between the outward contingency of their power and the authority they needed in order to bring about a new constitutional order.

Now, the unavailability of these two different kinds of meta-referents (divine countersignature, and the 'Nation') need not have led to the conclusion that legal continuity had to be preserved at all costs. If it did, for some people at least, it is in virtue of a long-standing and unfortunate tradition that deems the creation of a new constitution to be 'tantamount to the creation of a new universe'.[13] According to Preuss, 'constitution-making is vested with supreme and unrestrained power [. . .] it is a divine end which has to be accomplished with human means [. . .] it also requires a particular kind of knowledge [. . .] namely, the awareness of the *unbridgeable discrepancy* between a people's power to erect a polity and its intellectual and moral abilities to satisfy the responsibilities which this *unlimited power* involves'.[14]

---

[13] UK Preuss 1995, 6.
[14] UK Preuss 1995, 7 (emphasis added).

5.1.3 Disenchanted Lawmaking

There is no reason to think that our 'intellectual and moral abilities' have lessened dramatically over centuries. Yet recurrent emphasis on the deficiency of these abilities when it comes to lawmaking seems to be a striking feature of modern times. From Montaigne's 'laws are made by fools' to Rousseau's 'it would require Gods to give men laws',[15] all the way to Preuss's account of constitution-making, one may trace an enduring dismay: in view of the 'sanctity' of the task at hand, our moral and intellectual short-sightedness would always fail us, would always place us in want of some 'supplement of authority'.

If this modern dismay cannot be attributed to a gradual decline in our intellectual and moral abilities, could it be that the character of the task at hand has changed? Has the task of lawmaking gradually acquired a 'holy' quality which would have made the gap between it and our pitiful human abilities unbridgeable indeed? The only asset of such a hypothesis is its provocativeness. The very use of the term 'holy' to account for the hypothetical change in the nature of lawmaking is going against the current that associates modernity with a progressive uncoupling of law and theology. In its provocativeness, this hypothesis nevertheless helps unfold a fundamental evolution whose structure does depend on the nature of the contemplated link between God (and the 'natural' order it is deemed to generate) and the possibility of binding ourselves through law.

The Turning Point

If I were to choose a date marking the key transition period between what would be a 'pre-modern' and a modern understanding of legal normativity, I would go for 28 June 1593. On that day, the Paris Parliament upholds the devolution law which designates Henri de Bourbon as the legitimate heir to the throne,

---

[15] J-J Rousseau 1997, II 7, 69.

despite his Protestant denomination.[16] To counter the papal arguments, the *Politiques*[16a] endeavour to show that the *Loi Salique* is
to be understood as the direct expression of God's will which, as
such, cannot be called into question, even by the Pope himself.
The aim of the *Politiques* is indeed to show that the devolution law
must prevail over any other rule: over the '*Loi de catholicité*' introduced by the 1588 Edict of Union, and, most importantly, over
the papal bull which found Henri de Bourbon incapable of reign-
ing. Their strategy, which consists in considering the *Loi Salique*
as the direct expression of God's will (its status being by definition superior to that of any human will), is at the root of a major
upheaval in the conceptualisation of law's normativity.

The consequences of the *Politiques'* strategy are best traced by
reference to their adversaries' powerful but ultimately unsuccess-
ful critical arguments. At a strictly theological level, to claim that
a particular family gets its right to rule out of a particular and
express divine intervention amounts to looking for God in
Nature while one cannot, one should not, find him there. As
Marie-France Renoux-Zagamé brilliantly shows in her detailed
analysis of the debate opposing the *Ligue*[17] to the *Politiques*, 'to
see God's particular will in events which are but the outward
sign of the general order through which he preserves and gov-
erns the world he created — and the births and deaths within the
royal family obviously belong according to them [the *Ligue*] to
that type of events — amounts to confusing two forms of divine
intervention; it amounts to confining God within nature, taking
the risk of confusing the Creator and its creature'.[18] In order to
promote the *Loi Salique* as the expression of a will that cannot
be called into question, the *Politiques* indeed cannot only argue
that the order instituted by this devolution law 'imitates nature's

[16] Shortly after his coronation, Henri IV converted to catholicism.

[16a] Referring to a group of jurists and intellectuals defending, for the most part,
the idea of Gallicanism and, most crucially, arguing for a distiction betweeen the
State and religion, the expression ' Politiques' was mainly used by their critics, the
radical catholic 'Ligue' (which called for the eradication of Protestantism in France).

[17] Suarez was among those whom the Pope entrusted with the task of
defending the 'orthodox' position, faithful to the scholastic tradition.

[18] M-F Renoux-Zagamé 2003, 286 (my translation).

order', which would make it conform to natural law. They must basically present this devolution law as 'positive divine law', and by doing so they abolish the gap between nature and '*surnature*', a contrast that is essential to the scholastic tradition.

It is indeed this gap that allows the scholastic tradition to speak of 'natural and divine law' while maintaining a tension between the two, as natural law expresses divine law while never equating it. Because of this tension, the scholastic tradition was able to construct the power to govern as legitimated by its link to God while nevertheless remaining under human scrutiny: if one discerns a contradiction between the Prince's order and divine commands, one may, with the approval of the Church, resist the Prince's order. The *Politiques'* attempt to bypass any possible discussion as to the 'natural' legitimacy of the *Loi Salique* by rooting it in God's express will thus breaks away from an important and long-lasting model of the relationship between God and Nature. The various problems arising, at a theological level, from the *Politiques'* model have given rise to abundant discussions.[19] Let me concentrate on the legal implications flowing from such a model.

To insist upon the absolute superiority of the *Loi Salique* against any other law, the *Politiques* had to posit this devolution law as the basis and foundation of all the other laws. As such, Professor Renoux-Zagamé argues that it took over what used to be the role of 'natural and divine law', thus substituting a positive, human law for the traditionally transcendent foundation of law: 'The alleged divine will which it [the devolution law] would express may admittedly conceal this substitution. But if, as the *Ligueurs* claim to show, it is only a delusion, then, thanks to this reversal, the *Politiques*, without saying it and maybe without seeing it, trigger a radical break: they detach human law from God, so as to found an autonomous political and legal order'.[20]

---

[19] Cardinal Bellarmin, one of the leading advocates of the *Ligue*, for instance showed that following the *Politiques'* argument would lead one to tie up every aspect of the natural order with God's express and particular will, thus forbidding man to modify anything in that order.

[20] M-F Renoux-Zagamé 2003, 287 (my translation).

The *Politiques'* venture to incorporate a divine foundation *within* the legal corpus (instead of maintaining a distance separating law from its legitimating source) is first and foremost aimed at *guaranteeing* the bindingness of man-made law. The insistence on law's 'inviolability', its characterisation in terms borrowed from a religious vein, referring to the 'sanctity' of the lawmaking task, or law's 'holy' quality,[21] all proceed from the desire to lend man-made laws a normativity that would not have to pale at the invocation of divine authority, and would as such be able to resist assaults from the Church. This process of 'sacralisation' of law may at first sight be perceived as negating the modern spirit, which would have man discover the resources necessary to the construction of binding norms *within himself* and not in some heterogenous source. From such a perspective, the blossoming of the concept of divine right kingship in the 17th century[22] may be perceived as one of these strange detours which history forces upon the development of ideas.

One may, however, see this strengthening of the bond which traditionally ties law to divine authority as a form of radicalisation that actually ends up freeing law's normativity from its dependence upon a theological framework. In their attempt to secure the definitive presence of God at the foundation of law, the *Politiques* abolished the distance that allowed one to question law's bindingness in the name of God's will. The resulting 'perversion' of the traditional relationship between the power to govern and God's authority was the main target of the critique

---

[21] 'A law that is so holy (inviolable) that it is already a crime even to call it in doubt in a practical way, and so to suspend its effect for a moment, is thought *as if it must have arisen not from men but from some highest, flawless lawgiver*; and that is what the saying "all authority is from God" means. This saying is not an assertion about the historical basis of the civil constitution; it instead sets forth an Idea as a practical principle of reason' (I Kant 1991, §49 A, 130, emphasis added).

[22] While the concept of divine right kingship had been developed since the 12th century, the doctrinal battle triggered by Henri de Navarre's succession controversy solidified the idea and disseminated the concept among the population.

developed by the *Ligue*. The eventuality which neither opponent in this controversy seems to have fully anticipated,[23] however, amounts to the fact that, by constructing this 'institutionalised' presence of God at the foundation of law, the *Politiques* may actually have provided for the possibility of its oblivion. Seen from this perspective, the doctrinal controversy preceding the enthronement of Henri IV may be deemed a crucial turning point in the evolution towards a 'modern' understanding of legal normativity, in that it allowed for an independent, 'autonomous' space in which the legal order could develop itself.

Bringing about Legal Normativity: The Scenario

In order to elaborate on this 'modern' understanding of legal normativity, let me recapitulate my 'story of legal normativity' as it stands so far. Unlike mythical stories, it does not have any particular beginning. Normativity, understood generally as all those ideas 'that outstrip the world we experience and seem to call it into question, to render judgement on it, to say that it does not measure up, that it is not what it ought to be',[24] may be deemed a feature concomitant to human nature, which as such would always have pervaded human existence. As 'normative animals', we are prone to questioning the way things are, considering alternative ways of thinking, judging, acting etc. Within that normative framework, the category of *oughts* that is specifically aimed at the way we behave and interact with the rest of society is not the exclusive domain of law. Both morality and, for some people, religion lay a claim on the way we ought to interact with the rest of society. The existence and emergence of these systematised forms of normativity are not necessarily concomitant. As a distinct normative category, the emergence of law is triggered and made possible by a set of factors that are specific to it.

---

[23] Some advocates of the *Ligue* did warily evoke the prospect of God being relegated to 'a corner of the State', but no one seems to have grasped the full potential of the *Politiques'* argument in terms of the possibility of founding an 'autonomous' legal order.

[24] See CM Korsgaard 1996, 1.

Constructing the 'step from the pre-legal to the legal', Hart isolates the needs and deficiencies that a legal system, as a specific form of social control, may be deemed to answer. 'Granted a few of the most obvious truisms about human nature and the world we live in',[25] a pre-legal community is indeed likely to be structured around a set of rules fundamental to the smooth running of society, restricting, among other things, the free use of violence, theft and deception, to refer to the examples mentioned by Hart. Essential as they are to peaceful social interaction, these rules may be deemed to instantiate moral, religious or simply prudential concerns. Whatever their nature, their existence is not conditional upon the emergence of a legal system. Together with other 'normative elements', such as hopes for a better way of living together,[26] they constitute the substratum on the basis and in function of which a legal system may emerge. Hart does not talk about these other 'normative elements', however. His story of the 'pre-legal to the legal' is meant to encapsulate the 'salient features of a municipal legal system' by pointing to the deficiencies[27] that a legal order can remedy *in a primitive structure of social control.* This qualification is easily overlooked, and much depends on what one means by 'social control'.

[25] HLA Hart 1994, 91.

[26] Understood as a wide category, normativity indeed cannot be reduced to rules only and must be taken to include ideals or concepts inducing or demanding a different outlook on the world (here one may think of equality, solidarity, liberty, etc). While these ideas or concepts may not necessarily give rise to positive rules, they may nevertheless be deemed to structure our actions or judgements, and as such be considered as 'normative'.

[27] In a pre-legal society, rules may develop forbidding this or that form of conduct, but there will be no way of 'authoritatively' identifying the body of rules governing that society. Similarly, a pre-legal society will lack the resources necessary to being able to adapt the rules to changing circumstances, and to being able to authoritatively acknowledge and punish the violation of its rules. 'It is plain that only a small community closely knit by ties of kinship, common sentiment, and belief, and placed in a stable environment, could live succesfully by such a regime of unofficial rules. In any other conditions such a simple form of social control must prove defective and will require supplementation in different ways' (HLA Hart 1994, 92).

While it may be understood as a generic term, pointing to all the various mechanisms that contribute to shaping society, the concept of 'social control' does have disciplinary connotations. On a more restrictive understanding, the term 'social control' refers to those social mechanisms specifically aimed at maintaining public order and efficiently coordinating social activities. One would then understand other, non-disciplinary aspirations, such as the endeavour to promote a society based on some form of equality, for instance, as partaking of 'social architecture' as opposed to 'social control'. Hart does not elaborate on his understanding of social control, but his pervading concern to construct a theory of law that is as free as possible from any normative commitment,[28] political or otherwise, points to a restrictive understanding. His endeavour to identify the structural elements that are key to the emergence of a legal system leads him to isolate some sort of 'smallest common denominator' which may be deemed essential to the existence of law.[29] As this 'smallest common denominator' happens to be best understood as the remedy to a series of deficiencies[30] that would characterise a primitive system of social control, Hart would have constructed his pre-legal hypothesis accordingly.

If, however, one comes at it the other way, and seeks to understand the possible factors that may contribute to the emergence of law as a distinct set of norms, Hart's hypothesis seems

[28] See section 3.3.

[29] This 'smallest common denominator' consists in the existence of some 'meta-rules' or 'rules about rules', allowing one to authoritatively identify the rules regulating a society, as well as providing for the possibility of adapting those existing rules to changing circumstances and authoritatively settling disputes. 'The introduction of the remedy for each defect might, in itself, be considered a step from the pre-legal into the legal world; since each remedy brings with it many elements that permeate law: certainly all three remedies together are enough to convert the regime of primary rules into what is indisputably a legal system' (HLA Hart 1994, 94). At the end of his chapter, Hart does include a 'proviso': 'The union of primary and secondary rules is at the centre of a legal system; but it is not the whole, and as we move away from the centre, we shall have to accomodate, in ways indicated in later chapters, elements of a different character' (HLA Hart 1994, 99).

[30] See above n 27.

unnecessarily restrictive. Focusing as it does on the way law may improve a 'disciplinary' structure of social control, it does not mention other possible types of aspirations that law may be called to answer. While any society will have to rely, as a prerequisite, on a structure allowing the peaceful coexistence of divergent interests, the agenda calling for the emergence of a legal order may include further moral ambitions which do not easily fit under the banner of 'social control'. Granted, these further moral ambitions may not be *necessary* to the emergence of law, and their content and form vary greatly from one society to another. Should the variable and aleatory character of these 'further ambitions', however, be a reason to silence their impact upon the normative character of law? It could be, if legal theory was somehow tempted to adhere to a methodology according to which the existence of one invalidating counterexample would be sufficient to dismiss a given model as mistaken. In our case, the possibility of a legal system arising out of purely prudential considerations would be sufficient to rule out an explanation of legal normativity that gives central significance to the political and moral concerns presiding over the creation of a legal system. Needless to say,[31] such a methodology would considerably diminish the explanatory power of legal theory, whose aim is to elucidate the meaning and significance of the concept of law in our past and present experiences, not to treat it as some kind of mathematical object.

A further source of confusion, which may lead one to think that our 'pre-legal hypothesis' should only comprise elements whose necessity to the emergence of law is always verified, amounts to the temptation to look for some distinctly primitive form of society, which would, by an imaginary leap, be postulated as 'the' original scenario. Such a primitive society, it would

[31] In view of some recent debates giving much importance to the conceptual possibility of 'evil' legal regimes, arising and being kept in existence for prudential reasons only, I nevertheless deemed this 'methodological clarification' necessary (see, eg, M Kramer 2004, using this argument to suggest that the ideal of the rule of law need not be connected to any moral aspiration).

be argued, should not be presumed to be structured around anything but the creation and maintenance of the order necessary to the peaceful coexistence of its members. Controversial as it may be, this archaeological claim does not even need to be contested. As a genealogy, my story of legal normativity does not look for its starting point but rather seeks to highlight the various factors that contribute to bringing it about. As such, it is not actually interested in a 'pre-legal hypothesis',[32] but rather in a 'suspension of legal normativity' hypothesis, referring to these intermittent periods of time where the political situation has led to overturning the existing legal order. These — relatively rare — moments provide for a helpful 'laboratory situation' in which the provisional absence of legal order allows the legal theorist to observe, through the lens of history, the various factors deemed to contribute to the (re)construction of legal normativity. These revolutionary situations should not, however, be mistaken as the only possible 'window' for understanding legal normativity and its conditions of possibility. In a healthy legal system, legal normativity is brought about every day, through court cases, popular debates, participation procedures, etc. In the second part of this chapter I will examine the various ways in which legal normativity is, and needs to be, perpetuated on a daily basis. For now, let me set up the scenario that will lie at the centre of my '(very) brief history of legal normativity'.

The interaction of individuals within a community will bring about desires of various sorts. Beyond the obvious physical ones, there will also be desires related to one's self-image (the desire to have a good reputation, for instance) and desires related to the possibility of getting on with one's projects without any interference, as well as the possibility of securing the fruit of these projects. These desires, once coordinated, will give rise to formal and informal rules. Nothing is typically legal in this scenario. What seems to characterise a legal system as a distinct

---

[32] If such a 'pre-legal' point could indeed be found, it would also be, by definition, the 'starting point' of legal normativity.

form of normative order is a certain degree of sophistication, as a set of rules organised around some meta-rules or 'rules about rules'. This formal characterisation, however, does not even begin to account for the reason why we resort to law as a distinct form of social organisation. While it is easy to point at law's formal assets and show the way in which it may greatly improve a 'primitive' disciplinary structure, for instance, the story cannot stop there. One can only start to get an idea of why people adhere to legal standards and treat them as normative if one aims at a broad, all-encompassing picture of the various aspirations which a community may seek to realise through law. Although culturally dependent, these aspirations are not commonly reducible to the mere desire to secure the possibility of non-violent social interaction. Whatever its content, there tends to be a programmatic element meant to encapsulate what that particular society sees as a 'better' way of living together. Relying on the possibility of peaceful coexistence as a presupposition, this programmatic element *typically* combines instrumental concerns and moral values and underpins, as such, the lawmaker's endeavour to be perceived as legitimate. Whether that endeavour underlies the creation of a new legal order or seeks to sustain an existing one, the form it takes is crucial to understanding law's normativity.

Two elements are thus central to understanding the emergence of law as an 'institutionalised', specific form of normativity. First there is the 'fabric' from which law arises: pervaded by both instrumental concerns (such as improving the efficiency of a disciplinary structure) and moral aspirations, other forms of normativity are always already woven into it. These other, pre-existing norms provide the material from which the people involved in bringing about a legal order will have to draw the resources necessary for asserting law's legitimacy. Law's 'transparent positivity'[33] indeed tends to elicit a heightened concern

---

[33] By 'transparent positivity', I mean to refer to law's 'open' characterisation as a social artefact, by contrast with other types of normative phenomena, such as truthfulness or morality.

to construct its legitimacy in terms which will favour its being 'successfully normative'.[34] This is the second point that my 'scenario' seeks to highlight. It is a delicate one, in that asserting a link between law's normativity and its legitimacy exposes one to all sorts of dangerous confusions.

1 Confusing normativity and obedience   First, as a preliminary issue, there is the extent to which the question of law's normativity is distinguishable from the issue of obedience to law. While law's perceived legitimacy will certainly contribute to its being widely obeyed, this legitimacy is neither necessary nor sufficient to secure obedience. Some people will obey the law for motives that are not even remotely connected to legitimacy considerations, and other people may disobey the law even though they deem it legitimate. As for the relationship between obedience and normativity, those same people who decide, for instance, to break the law and steal some food because they are hungry, may acknowledge law's normativity. They may acknowledge legal rules as binding, and these rules may, as such, provide them with a 'special kind' of reason for action. Their impulse to steal some food is likely to have nothing to do with reasons however. Obedience to the law may come down to all sorts of factors that ultimately leave the issue of law's normativity out of the picture. The question of whether law is normative is therefore not just a pompous and complicated way of addressing the issue of obedience.

2 Confusing normativity and legitimacy   Following the above train of thought, there appears to be, on the other hand, a certain parallelism between law's normativity and its legitimacy. In my introduction, I tried to unfold the various levels and ways in which 'normativity' may be understood. In its widest sense, 'normativity' includes all those ideas or propositions 'that outstrip the world we experience and seem to call it

---

[34] For one possible account of the 'test' conditioning law's normative success, see Raz's model below in the text.

into question, to render judgement on it, to say that it does not measure up, that it is not what it ought to be'.[35] From this perspective, my neighbour's judging and stating that the world would be better if I wore a pink hat this morning is normative, in that it lays a claim on how the world (and me in it) ought to be. We are, on a daily basis, confronted with a myriad of such 'normative' claims, and we do not pay attention to most of them. As trivial as it may seem, this understanding of normativity is nevertheless indispensable if we are to make sense of concepts like equality, for instance.[36]

When we speak of law or morality as 'normative', we tend to understand their normativity in a more restrictive or demanding way. Indeed, given the fact that both morality and law are constituted for a large part at least of 'ought statements' enjoining or forbidding this action or that attitude, stating that law and morality are normative in the wide sense mentioned above may otherwise sound like a tautology: if only through their grammatical form, they lay a claim on how the world ought to be by definition. Now, there are various ways in which legal theorists have sought to capture law's specific normativity. As a kind of common ground, most accounts converge in associating law's normativity with a 'claim to provide reasons for action',[37] but

[35] Apologies to the attentive reader who sees this quotation for the third time. I can't find another formulation that is quite so evocative. See CM Korsgaard 1996, 1.

[36] It would be misleading to describe the sense in which the concept of 'equality' is normative for us by asserting that it is 'capable of making a practical difference' in our deliberations. One could, following a Razian approach ('aspects of the world are normative in as much as they or their existence constitute reasons for persons' — J Raz 1999, 67), maintain that the concept of equality is normative in that it 'gives us a reason', say, to consider that these two sticks are not equal. But surely we would not even have conceived of the question, and wondered about the two sticks' putative equality, if the idea of equality had not led us to do so in the first place. To say that the concept of equality 'gave us a reason' to wonder about the equality of the two sticks is equally misleading. I may come to question their equality for all sorts of reasons, but the concept of equality is not among them. If the concept of equality has to be at all related to reasons, one may say that it is, so to speak, their precondition.

[37] J Coleman 2001b, 86.

none of them stops there. As a further specification, Marmor stipulates that 'at least some of these reasons are obligations'.[38] Coleman joins Marmor in referring to the concept of obligation to account for law's normativity, but does so in a more layered fashion, distinguishing between law's capacity to guide behaviour and law's ability to impose 'real'[39] obligations. While law's capacity to guide behaviour is accounted for by the fact that law provides reasons of a particular kind 'that are capable of figuring, in a particular way, in our deliberations about what we ought to do', law's 'obligatory' character depends on those reasons being 'strong enough, or conclusive'.[40] Now, the two 'levels' Coleman introduces by distinguishing between the reasons law may offer and them being 'strong enough' (thus giving rise to an obligation) are particularly interesting for our purposes, as it is in the effort to articulate the gap between these two levels that one's account of legal normativity actually takes shape.

According to Hart, law purports to govern our conduct by giving us *content-independent* and *peremptory* reasons for action. Reasons for action can be deemed content-independent if they derive not from the rule's content, but from the rule's validity, from the fact that this rule has been passed according to the standards set in the Rule of Recognition. Reasons for action may be deemed peremptory, on the other hand, if they are meant to foreclose any deliberation on the merits of the rule they arise from. By giving an absolute, peremptory force to the reasons for

---

[38] 'At the very least [. . .] the idea that law is a normative social practice suggests that law purports to give rise to reasons for action, and that at least some of these reasons are obligations' (A Marmor 2001b, 25).

[39] By introducing this otherwise peculiar qualification, does Coleman mean to oppose 'real' to 'fictional' obligations, as a way of accounting for the possibility of being misguided as to the 'strength' of the reasons a particular law provides? If so, what is the background allowing one to deem an individual to be so misguided? There are different kinds of answers available here, but Coleman carefully avoids any meta-ethical commitment (Coleman also speaks of 'genuine' reasons for action, which he seems to equate with 'moral' reasons for action).

[40] J Coleman 2001b, 123.

action law is meant to create, Hart seeks to ensure that law's normativity is not made to rely on moral considerations at any juncture. One may wonder, however, if in so doing, Hart didn't end up throwing the baby out with the bathwater. His endeavour to assert the specificity of law's normativity indeed leads him to effectively *alienate* law's reasons from the domain of individual reflection: if they are to foreclose any reflection on the merits of the rule they arise from, it is not clear how, if at all, legal reasons are supposed to be part of a global reflection about what one ought to do. '[B]y telling us that we have an obligation to act in a certain way for no reason other than that the law commands it',[41] Hart hopes to build an account of legal normativity that is, in some way, self-sufficient, in that it does not have to rely on any moral consideration to 'bridge the gap' between the two levels presented above, that is, that of making a practical difference in one's deliberation and that of giving rise to an obligation.

Raz's departure from Hart's model on this point is crucial, and it is probably his best contribution to legal theory. While, like Hart, Raz analyses as content-independent the reasons for action law is meant to give us, he does not assume that these reasons are meant to foreclose deliberation on law's merits. Rather, these reasons are supposed to replace or 'pre-empt' another set of reasons, a set that is part of the larger, global scope of reasons or 'claims' that apply to us (including moral, prudential or religious reasons). Now, for those of you who, like me, find this 'reasons talk' messy, let me try to reformulate Raz's account of legal normativity from a different perspective.

Raz's prime question is: what does it take for law to have authority over us? Given 'the intrinsic desirability of people conducting their own life by their own lights'[42], law's claim to govern our conduct (and to do so in a non-facultative way) must appeal to some principle that makes the (partial) relinquishment of one's autonomy desirable as well. The answer, for

---

[41] This is Coleman describing the way in which, in Hart's account, law purports to govern our conduct (J Coleman 2001a, 121).

[42] J Raz 1986, 57.

Raz, lies in what he calls the 'normal justification thesis'. If, when considering all the various requirements that apply to her, the individual concludes that abiding by the law actually enables her to best balance all these demands, thus putting her on the path of 'right reason', then law's authority may be deemed beneficial, rather than detrimental to her autonomy. In this case, law's authority may properly be said to be 'legitimate'. Acting as a kind of shorthand solution to a series of practical problems, law's authority would enable the individual to minimise the consequences of her own moral fallibility and overcome the difficulty inherent in coordinating action between individuals. It is in this sense that law replaces or 'pre-empts' some of the reasons that apply to an individual: it is meant to replace those reasons that a 'reflective individual' would have found to lead her to the course of conduct required by law.

What if, however, in balancing the various requirements that apply to her, the 'reflective individual' found that abiding by the law actually takes her away from the path of 'right reason'? It may be that she is faced with circumstances which the rule-givers did not anticipate, however wise they may be. Or it may be that the individual, in this particular situation, happens to have greater moral expertise or a better perspective on coordination needs than the rule-givers. In these particular circumstances, law's claim to authority fails; it is not deemed legitimate. It need not, however, be devastating to law's overall normative status. The normal justification test, Raz insists, is to be thought of as an ideal guiding the evaluation of law's authority. 'Reality has a way of falling short of the ideal [. . .] naturally not even legitimate authorities always succeed, nor do they always try to live up to the ideal. It is nevertheless through their ideal functioning that they must be understood'.[43]

One question remains. Raz's account of the practical difference law is supposed to make is based on the concept of 'exclusionary', or pre-emptive reasons. When law succeeds in its claim

---

[43] J Raz 1986, 47.

to authority, it is supposed to give us a reason for action that 'replaces' the set of dependent reasons, and thus 'simplifies' our practical reasoning. Freeing the individual from the task of balancing a complex set of reasons (a task for which the individual may lack information or expertise), law is supposed to 'mediate' between its subjects and the reasons that apply to them.[44] Now the problem is: if, in order to assess the legitimacy of law's claim to authority, the individual has to keep peeking back at the underlying reasons which may or may not, on balance, justify law's claim to provide exclusionary reasons, it is not clear when that 'legitimacy assesssment' should stop, and enable the individual to relax and enjoy the benefits of law's 'shorthand solutions' to practical problems. In order to avoid the impracticality (and the possibility of mistakes) inherent in having to reassess the authority of a particular rule or set of rules in every different situation,[45] the individual may rely on an aggregation strategy, granting the law a certain 'credit' based on its overall performance in enabling her to comply with the demands of 'right reason'.[46] For Raz's normal justification test

---

[44] 'The advantage of normally proceeding through the mediation of rules is enormous. It enables a person to consider and form an opinion on the general aspects of recurrent situations in advance of their occurence. It enables a person to achieve results which can be achieved only through an advance commitment to a whole series of actions, rather than by case to case examination' (J Raz 1986, 58).

[45] 'Authority is based on reason and reasons are general, therefore authority is essentially general. On the other hand the thesis allows maximum flexibility in determining the scope of authority. It all depends on the person over whom authority is supposed to be exercised: his knowledge, strength of will, his reliability in various aspects of life, and on the government in question [. . .] The test is as explained before: does following the authority's instructions improve conformity with reason? For every person the question has to be asked afresh, and for every one it has to be asked in a manner which admits of various qualifications' (J Raz 1986, 73–74).

[46] 'In such cases conformity with the underlying reasons is secured by complying with the rule, or rather a better degree of conformity than can otherwise be achieved is so obtained. This can justify complying with the rule even when it requires action which the underlying reasons do not. Such compliance may still be the best strategy to maximise conformity with the underlying reasons' (J Raz 1990, 194).

to be a genuine threshold condition on law's exclusionary force, however, this 'aggregation strategy' cannot last too long, and at some point the individual will have to check that normal justification still holds, that the authority still 'has a sufficiently high normal justification score'.[47] The necessity to keep going back to the dependent reasons that, in Raz's account, law is supposed to replace may lead one to question the benefits of characterising law's normativity in terms of 'exclusionary force'.[48] While this 'exclusionary' account seeks to translate Raz's insight that it is an essential function of law to *mediate* between its subjects and the reasons that apply to them (by simplifying their practical reasoning), ultimately the individual's practical deliberation does come down to *weighing* (rather than excluding) different types of requirements against each other.[49]

Now there are, and there need to be, many instances in which law's binding force is acknowledged 'on credit', on account of law's authority as a social rule. In such cases, the workings of legal normativity may be characterised as 'pre-empting' deliberation on the set of reasons which the individual would otherwise consider, were she to deliberate on the best course of action. This exclusionary force may, however, be deemed a 'surface phenomenon' whose viability is dependent on a recurrent 'check' on the part of those subject to law. Determining the frequency and incidence of this underlying need to deliberate on the merits of law's claim to authority requires balancing practicality considerations with the ideal of individual responsibility.[50]

[47] E Mian 2002, 107.

[48] For an elaborate discussion on this point, suggesting that the practical difference law is supposed to make may be more aptly characterised as a 'contest of weight' between different kinds of reasons, see E Mian 2002.

[49] Raz substantially tempers his account of exclusionary reasons in later publications, notably in J Raz 1989, 1168, where he states: 'One way to put it is to say that even if exclusionary reasons are admitted there is a sense in which nothing is excluded, every valid consideration plays its role (though of course not every reason "wins"). It is merely a matter of *structuring* the reasons, of elucidating their proper interrelations, and this involves the exclusion of some reasons by others.' (emphasis added).

[50] An ideal which even the most paternalistic of democratic states will need to uphold to a minimum degree.

Whatever the verdict on its incidence, individual practical deliberation will always be the unavoidable cornerstone of legal normativity. This will sound like bad news for some, aberration for others: aberration for those for whom normativity by definition 'imposes itself to the deliberating agent', not the other way round; bad news for those who would like to keep legal normativity 'beyond reach', out of the mess of human political affairs and safe from our fallible nature.

Remember Kelsen's striking determination to avoid any account of legal normativity that would make it dependent upon 'subjective recognition', to use his vocabulary: 'the doctrine of the Basic Norm is not a doctrine of recognition as is sometimes erroneously understood. According to the doctrine of recognition, positive law is valid only if it is recognised by the individuals subject to it [. . .] The theory of recognition, consciously or unconsciously, presupposes the ideal of individual liberty as self-determination, that is, the norm that the individual ought to do only what he wants to do'.[51] Besides Kelsen's fundamental mistrust of our political and ethical abilities,[52] this quotation gives voice to the idea that law's requirements are meant to constrain our conduct in a way that does not leave it up to us whether we abide by these requirements or not. An account of legal normativity that gives central stage to practical deliberation would, it seems, fail to grasp the way in which law *demands* a certain conduct of us, whether we like it or not. Characterising the reasons for action that law is supposed to give us as 'peremptory' or 'exclusionary' partakes of this concern to emphasise the way law is supposed to bypass other considerations when imposing its authority over us. If the ideal of civic responsibility is to have any substance, however, this concern needs to be balanced with the need to provide for the possibility of *assessing* the legitimacy of law's claim to authority.

---

[51] H Kelsen 1967, §34 i, 218 note 83. Remember that Kelsen uses the term 'valid' as a synonym of 'binding' or 'normative'.

[52] See section 2.1.2.

One may reformulate Raz's account of legal normativity as one possible way of articulating the two 'levels' suggested by Coleman: law's offering reasons that are capable of figuring in our practical deliberations, on one hand, and those reasons being 'strong enough, or conclusive', on the other. The hinge between these two levels lies, for Raz, in the normal justification test, according to which the reasons law aims to offer may be considered 'conclusive' only if law is deemed to better enable its subject to comply with the various requirements that apply to her. If the individual finds, on a particular instance, that the demands of 'right reason' require her to disregard law's requirements, she will have defeated, in that instance, law's claim to authority. Can one then conclude that law's failure to impose an obligation upon her robs law of its normative force? Answering this question positively would equate the concepts of normativity and obligation and hence forego the possibility (and necessity) of civic responsibility. Answering this question negatively, on the other hand, would imply that law's normativity consists in its making a difference in the subject's practical deliberation, no matter how successful or 'conclusive' law's reasons ultimately are. If law were to systematically fail to give rise to an obligation, being consistently defeated by other types of reasons, there would, however, be a sense of unease in still considering it as 'normative' (and in still considering it as 'law' *tout court*). This is what prompts authors like Marmor to specify that 'at the very least [. . .] the idea that law is a normative social practice suggests that law purports to give rise to reasons for action, and that at least some of these reasons are obligations'.[53]

If one conceives of legal normativity as a *dynamic* concept, whose meaning and substance emerge out of the confrontation with other types of normativity, including morality, one may be able to overcome the dilemma associated with the apparent necessity to 'pitch' one's definition of legal normativity at either one of the two levels presented above (guidance or obligation).

[53] A Marmor 2001b, 25.

This is what my account of legal normativity aims to achieve. Law's normative dimension is not a quality that is somehow mysteriously attributed to law as it arises out of the various social practices that bring it about. Law's power to bind us and impose upon us some non-optional mode of conduct is a property that needs rebuilding on a constant basis. This 'rebuilding' occurs every time a person enters a practical deliberation aimed at balancing law's requirements with other types of demands, such as those of morality or prudence. While it would considerably diminish, and maybe cancel law's efficiency as a social institution if such practical deliberation were to be entered into each time an individual is confronted with law's demands, the total absence of such deliberation would in turn transform legal rules into mere habits devoid of any normative meaning.[54] Once confronted with the demands of morality or prudence, the reasons provided by law may sometimes, on balance, fail to give rise to an obligation. Far from being detrimental to law's normative dimension,[55] these opportunities to challenge law's legitimacy are vital to maintaining legal normativity 'alive' so to speak, in touch with the material that first triggered its emergence: the changing demands of morality and prudence.

[54] One could consider the hypothesis of a totalitarian legal regime whose propaganda is aimed precisely at rendering any kind of practical deliberation on the part of its subjects seemingly irrelevant or pointless. As long as this propaganda still has a point, that is, as long as there are still some individuals out there who will assess law's demands as part of a broader picture including other requirements, one may still speak meaningfully of law's 'normative' dimension. As soon as the possibility of practical deliberation disappears, however, the normative dimension of law becomes illusory, an empty-sounding concept which the totalitarian regime's leaders (themselves indoctrinated, of course) may play with to give an extra '*cachet*' to their discourse. Frightening as this kind of hypothesis is, I do not think it is necessarily to be dismissed as an exotic impossibility.

[55] There is, however, a limit to the extent to which law may 'fail' in its claim to authority while nevertheless remaining normative. Intuitively, one would say that as long as it succeeds in giving rise to an obligation in the majority of cases, law remains normative.

Unlike Coleman, I do not think that one can account for law's 'normative power to create genuine rights and obligations'[56] independently of legitimacy considerations.[57] Expressing the link to the material that contributed to shaping — and still shapes — it, legitimacy considerations cannot be dismissed as 'non-essential' to understanding law's normativity in the name of the fact that one must provide for the possibility of law being normative while deemed illegitimate. The fact that there can be, and indeed often is, a tension between law's normative status and its perceived legitimacy is not only necessary to account for the political pluralism that characterises many legal systems today, it is also the basis upon which we can — and should[58] — continue to exert our responsibility as citizens, judges, legislators, etc. When a legal system becomes unable to integrate expressions of dissent, when the tension between law's perceived legitimacy and its claimed authority becomes too great, a legal system may be brought down by revolution, thus triggering the need to bring about a new normative structure. These revolutionary circumstances should not be mistaken as the only case where one can adequately speak of 'constructing' legal normativity. I will develop the ways in which one can contribute to shaping legal normativity on a daily basis in section 5.2. For now, let me consider the extent to which the 'scenario' I have developed in this section has evolved through the ages: while

[56] J Coleman 2001a, 144.

[57] 'I am not convinced that it is a conceptual feature of law that it necessarily claims *morally* legitimate authority. The fact that law can serve a variety of legitimate human interests may ground the claim that law must be the sort of thing that can possess a normative power to create genuine duties and responsibilities or confer genuine rights and privileges. From this it hardly follows that that normative power represents a moral authority' (J Coleman 2001a, 133). Coleman's position on this point is, I think, made possible by his contention that 'it is not the primary burden of a jurisprudential theory to explain how duties can be created by law. What needs explanation is something else altogether, the possibility of *claiming* to impose such duties as law' (J Coleman 2001a, 160).

[58] The day we stop, law's normative dimension will become an empty, illusory concept devoid of any meaning — see above n 54.

legal normativity is, I think, consistently constituted out of the same normative 'fabric', typically comprising both moral and prudential considerations, it is the status of one of its components — morality[59] — which changes dramatically.

Same Scenario, Different Scenes: Towards a Modern Concept of Legal Normativity

If one were ever seduced by the ludicrous idea of shooting a film tracing the evolution of the concept of legal normativity through the ages, it would be full of rather dramatic scenes: depending on the director's sensibility, it could start with a shot of Hammurabi's code, carved upon a black monument;[60] mythical tales involving gods and heroes would abound; Roman pragmatism would give way to medieval theology; the American and French revolutions would inaugurate an age of exuberant perplexity, progressively deflating until, perhaps, the Hungarian amendment procedure. Among all these events, there would also be, in my version of the film, a rather lengthy and dusty debate about the status of the devolution law which, on 28 June 1593, is upheld by the Paris Parliament against the papal bull declaring Henri de Navarre unfit to reign. It would no doubt take a good deal of cinematographic brilliance to sustain the viewer's attention through the aridity of this politico-theological debate. In the much more ordinary context of this book, a case still needs to be made to explain why I hold this particular episode in the history of the relationship between Church and State to be key to understanding the evolving nature of the concept of legal normativity.

---

[59] As a reminder, my point is not to argue that morality is a necessary component of the social fabric from which law arises, but rather that in *typical cases*, morality will be an important constitutive part of this social fabric, which as such is key to understanding law's normative claim.

[60] Dated c 1780 BCE, Hammurabi's code is deemed to be the first attempt to put in the writing a systematic, publicly available body of law (the monument, set in a public place, was meant to be accessible by all, even though only a tiny fraction of the population could read at the time).

The *Politiques'* endeavour to have the *Loi Salique* recognised as the direct expression of God's will not only turned the traditional relationship between natural and divine law upside down,[61] it also cancelled the distance which traditionally separated positive law from that transcendent order. Having to posit the devolution law as the basis of all the other laws of the system in order to ensure its superiority, the *Politiques* effectively placed a positive, man-made law at the foundation of the legal system. The fact that this devolution law was supposedly the direct expression of God's will may have concealed the magnitude of this change to its contemporaries. This 'institutionalisation' of the presence of God at the legal system's root nevertheless did provide, to use Zagamé's phrase, 'for the possibility of its oblivion'. Once secured in a fundamental, positive law, the link to transcendence traditionally conditioning law's legitimacy does not have to be constantly re-elaborated in a process testing the conformity of positive law to 'natural and divine law'.[62] Fortified by a normative dimension assuring it a new 'inviolability', the legal order can from then on develop itself in an autonomous way, away from the natural and divine order from which it traditionally derived its normativity. This newfound normative autonomy raises a problem which had until then been spared from legal thought: how can law derive from the arbitrariness of social and political practices the binding force necessary to ensure its normativity? While this law-making arbitrariness has always been an integral part of the 'scenario' presiding at the emergence of legal normativity, it had never, until then, been shown under such crude light. As long as human laws were perceived as the mere adaptation of a superior kind of law which, in itself, eluded human ascendancy, the messy character of the practices bringing them about was of little consequence to law's normative force. Once

---

[61] See p 137 above.

[62] In the traditional, scholastic view, there will always be a tension between positive and natural law on one hand, and natural law and divine law on the other hand.

human law is deemed to evolve independently of that superior order, however, its normativity seems somehow to have to arise out of the 'mess' of human affairs, and this perspective proves enough to discourage Montaigne and many authors and politicians after him.

While one may stop at this depressing perspective and content oneself with acknowledging the '*unbridgeable discrepancy* between a people's power to erect a polity and its intellectual and moral abilities to satisfy the responsibilities which this it *unlimited power* involves',[63] one may also choose to look beyond the apparent contingency of lawmaking practices and seek within human resources the material necessary to account for law's normative dimension. One will then find, woven into the social fabric giving rise to legal normativity, the same moral concerns that were once deemed to instantiate a transcendent, natural order. The gradual construction of law's 'normative autonomy' indeed partakes of a wider revolution concerning the way we think of values. For Plato and Aristotle, 'to be guided by value is to be guided by the way things ultimately *are*'.[64] The true, perfect nature of a thing is its form, while matter — the way things appear to us — is the 'potential for form'. When we act according to the way things 'really' are, when we try to actualise 'this potential for form' within ourselves or others around us, we are not bringing about anything new into the world: we are, rather, revealing its true nature. The dramatic change operating in the background of the transition from ancient to modern times consists in reversing the relationship between value and reality: reality, the world as it appears to us, is no longer 'trying to be good' in and of itself. On the contrary, reality, the world of matter, needs to be turned into something good; and this requires our intervention, this requires our *imposing* value upon the world.

---

[63] UK Preuss 1995, 7 (emphasis added).

[64] CM Korsgaard 1996, 2. As a brilliantly short account of this revolution concerning the way we think of values, see Korsgaard's '*very* concise history of Western metaphysics' (CM Korsgaard 1996, 1–5).

Now, how does my story accounting for the evolving nature of legal normativity fit within this broad metaphysical 'revolution'? Answering this question requires a short detour via the role of God — or, rather, the role God was made to play — in the period preceding this revolution. One of the questions nagging ethical thought following Plato and Aristotle consists in asking why, if the true nature of things lies in their perfection, if reality is meant to be good, things 'resist', and don't achieve their natural goodness? According to the doctrine of the Fall, the problem lies with us, human beings. We are at the source of this 'resistance' to goodness. If it wasn't for God inspiring excellence within us and the world around us, we would be hopeless. We would have lost, that is, the capacity to see the way in which the world, and us in it, can be made better. And this is where my story about legal normativity comes in. As a body of rules trying to improve the way we live within this world, the job of human, positive laws was to try to get us closer to the 'natural' order of things. Of course we would never really get there, but at least we could try, and this is what legitimated law's authority. As fallible, short-sighted beings, we had better comply with the demands of positive law if we ever wanted to live a 'good' life, a life closer to the way it is meant to be. Positive law may sometimes misrepresent, or indeed totally fail to grasp, the 'natural' order of things, in which case one may, with the approval of the Church, resist the prince's orders. For the ultimate authority, in this fallen world, is indeed God, and the Church, as its spokesperson, is meant to have the last word when it comes to deciding what does or what does not conform to the natural order of things.

It may be easier to grasp, in this context, the magnitude of the *Politiques'* '*coup*' when, to counter the papal arguments, they maintain that the devolution law designating Henri de Navarre as king is to be deemed the direct expression of God's will. This is introducing a double 'short-circuit', so to speak, for positive law is not only exempted from its traditional confrontation with the 'natural order of things', it is also presuming that God has wanted positive law to be the way it is, and as such positive law is invested with a normative force that warrants Kant's referring to law's 'holiness': 'A law that is so holy (inviolable) that it is already a crime even to call it in doubt in a practical way, and so to suspend its effect for a moment, is thought *as if it must have arisen not from men but from some highest, flawless lawgiver*; and that is what the saying "all authority is from God" means. This saying is not an assertion about the historical basis of the civil constitution; it instead sets forth an Idea as a practical principle of reason'.[65] Notice, however, the 'as if' construction. In Kant's time, what was the institutionalised presence of God at the foundation of law has already become a 'legitimate fiction', to use Montaigne's words.[66] Its 'oblivion' has been 'enacted', so to speak, while the inviolability that was made possible by this divine foundation has nevertheless been preserved. According to some, this leaves us in a terrible conundrum. Robbed of its link to the 'natural order of things' which traditionally conditioned — and enabled — its authority, positive law is still meant to be normative and impose its demands over us, when all it can count on in terms of authority is us, with our fallible, fallen human natures.

As one of the prominent contemporary authors for whom such a prospect demands a revival of the natural law model, thus re-establishing the challenging link between law's normativity and its attempt to conform to the 'natural order of things', John Finnis deserves mention at this stage. In the present context, I will not attempt to do justice to all the aspects of his theory, but rather aim at understanding what motivates his rejection of what he calls the 'positivistic' model. To this end, I will base myself on a fairly dated article, which, however, proves invaluable to grasp Finnis' account of normativity.

[65] I Kant 1991, §49 A, 130 — emphasis added.

[66] '[E]ven our system of Law, they say, bases the truth of its justice upon legal fictions' (M de Montaigne 1991, II 12, 603).

In 'On Positivism and Legal Rational Authority',[67] Finnis endeavours to review the theses developed by Kronman in *Max Weber*. This endeavour is particularly fortunate, as it brings to the fore Finnis's own understanding of normativity or, to use Kronman's words, his particular 'theory of value'. By 'theory of value', Kronman means 'a theory that purports to describe the manner in which norms are established and the kind of reality they possess'.[68] Against the 'positivistic' theory of value which Kronman takes to be underlying Weber's works, Finnis explains why, in his opinion, legal norms cannot be conceived as originating in the human will.

Kronman's dominant thesis in *Max Weber* highlights the link between Weber's according conceptual priority to the legal-rational type of authority (among the other, traditional and charismatic types) and his adopting a 'positivistic' theory of value. Such a theory, Kronman emphasises, 'requires us to think of values as having their foundation not in the world, as Socrates claimed, but in the choosing subject or, more precisely, in the faculty of choice which a person exercises when he commits himself to a norm by adopting it as an evaluative standard'.[69] By contrast with Socrates' model, according to which values are '*discovered* by passive intellectual contemplation',[70] for Weber every value is the product of an act of choice,[71] owing its existence to the 'frightening power we all possess to affirm or disaffirm even those things we understand most clearly'.[72] According to Kronman, this emphasis on the *chosen* — and not *discovered* — character of values is what explains Weber's

---

[67] J Finnis 1985.

[68] AT Kronman 1983, 4.

[69] AT Kronman 1983, 20.

[70] AT Kronman 1983, 21 (emphasis added).

[71] According to Weber's 'positivistic' theory of value, 'the fact that a particular norm happens to be a value for someone, can be accounted for conceptually only if we view the value in question as the product of an act of choice' (AT Kronman 1983, 21).

[72] AT Kronman 1983, 20.

according conceptual priority to the 'legal-rational type of authority', as indeed 'legal-rational authority rests on the assumption that norms are made, not discovered, and on the belief that it is this attribute, and this attribute alone, which confers on them their normative status as standards for the evaluative assessment of human conduct'.[73]

Now, the issue Finnis takes with Kronman's interpretation does not so much concern the construction of this link between the legal-rational type of authority and Weber's positivistic conception of normativity as such, but rather this positivistic conception itself, about which he maintains that 'no good reason has been produced for accepting Weber's "positivist" theory of value, and the new reasons produced by Kronman are no reason at all'.[74]

Among the 'unacceptable' assumptions underlying the legal-rational model of authority is the idea that 'binding social norms have no existence apart from those purposeful acts of human legislation that bring them into being'.[75] By contrast, Finnis emphasises that a system of legal-rational authority cannot rest exclusively on acts of legislation, for the significance of those acts 'must be explained by appeal to *pre-existing, non-posited principles,* binding (on legislator and subject alike) independently of any act of legislation'.[76] In support of this thesis, Finnis refers to the 'great teachers of Western lawyers, say, Aristotle, Cicero [. . .], Aquinas', etc, who would have 'all without exception denied that a system of legal-rational authority rests exclusively

[73] AT Kronman 1983, 52. By contrast, the traditional type of authority rests on a conception of normativity that is exactly the opposite of the legal-rational type: 'From the standpoint of all traditional forms of domination, the binding force of a norm is necessarily lost as soon as it comes to be viewed as a human invention, something deliberately made or created by human beings; traditional norms are uncreated and have a timeless validity that would be fatally compromised if they could either be established or undone by them' (AT Kronman 1983, 52). The charismatic model of authority, for its part, 'is based upon a conception of legitimacy that combines, in a distinctive way, certain elements of each of the other two pure types', and is thus considered by Kronman as 'a logically intermediate position' (AT Kronman 1983, 49).

[74] J Finnis 1985, 91.

[75] AT Kronman 1983, 53.

[76] J Finnis 1985, 80 (emphasis added).

on acts of legislation'.[77] At the core of this argument lies the concept of *purposeful act of human legislation*, which Finnis seems to understand in its most formal sense, as an act of pure decision which no normative meaning can precede. Along this line, Finnis emphasises: 'Someone's directive has normative significance, binding me to act or not to act, *just* because he issued his directive deliberately and wilfully as a directive . . . To say the least, such a principle of legitimation is not invulnerable to questions'.[78]

Whether Weber can actually be said to have endorsed such a purely formal conception of these '*purposeful* human acts of legislation' is open to question. Despite the fact that someone like Leo Strauss supports such a formalist interpretation, underlining the potentially nihilistic undertones of Weber's theory,[79] Weber's emphasis on the *created* character of norms certainly does not imply that these norms must emerge *ex nihilo*[80] or from 'the supposedly will-like sub-rational drives and compulsions of domination, submission, resentment, and so forth',[81] which amounts to the same.[82]

[77] J Finnis 1985, 80. Note the curious anachronism of such a reference (it is difficult to see how philosophers such as Aristotle or Aquinas can be said to have had any view or opinion on Weber's 'legal-rational model of authority').

[78] J Finnis 1985, 81.

[79] 'He [Weber] denied to man any science, empirical or rational, any knowledge, scientific or philosophic, of the *true value system*: the *true value system* does not exist; there is a variety of values which are of the same rank, whose demands conflict with one another, and whose conflict cannot be solved by human reason. [. . .] the solution has to be left to the free, non-rational decision of each individual. I contend that Weber's thesis necessarily leads to nihilism [. . .]' (L Strauss 1953, 41–42).

[80] See what I have called the 'existentialist solitude trap', section 5.2.2.

[81] J Finnis 2002, 8.

[82] Michael Rosen deplores the absence of an alternative interpretation on Kronman's part, emphasising how important such an interpretation would be for the defence of Weber's theory: 'What is more disappointing however, is the fact that Kronman, although evidently highly sympathetic to Weber, restricts himself to the exposition rather that the defence of Weber's views. Although the account he gives is very relevant to the central objections which have been made to Weber's doctrines, Kronman does not meet the arguments of those critics [. . .] who saw in Weber, as de Maistre saw in Locke, the evil genius of his century' (M Rosen 1985, 66).

Finnis's caricatural 'demonisation' of human instincts (when understood apart and detached from those 'pre-existing, non-posited principles' calling for and enabling our 'better selves') lies at the root of his rejection of the positivistic model. It also points at what needs to be mulled over if one is to come to grasp with the challenge raised by the metaphysical revolution I have briefly described. The alternative suggested by Finnis, leaving us a choice between a return to a 'proper' conceptualisation of the link between law and the natural order of things or some form of nihilism, is a way of refusing to tackle precisely this challenge: if the world of matter is not 'trying to be good' in and of itself, if value has to be imposed upon the world, we need to think about what it is about us that enables us to do that. For it would be hard, if not impossible, to conceive of our world without associating with it all sorts of values. If these values are not the result of our *discovering* them in a process revealing the true nature of things, if these values actually *come about* in a process concomitant to human existence, we need to think about what it is that makes us capable of bringing them about, and this may require a second episode to the 'Doctrine of the Fall', a renewed account of our normative nature.

The choice to be made, then, is not between a characterisation of legal normativity that makes it conditional upon its conformity, or at least its attempted conformity, to the 'natural order of things' and some form of nihilism. The choice is between conditioning law's normativity to a 'natural order of things' or conditioning it to a different kind of order, one that we are in the constant process of producing as we learn to live in society, as we try to build a social world that encourages and contributes to what we see as a good way of living together. This order will be built around all sorts of concerns, including moral and prudential ones.[83] It will not provide for any certainty

[83] At one end of the spectrum, one may have a society that is geared towards the maximisation of overall economic growth, even at the cost of slave-like conditions for a large part of the population, while at the other end one may conceive a society whose first and foremost aim is to ensure that every person is provided with the resources necessary to maximise his or her capabilities.

(be it as to the justice of the law or the merits of obeying it). It is, however, the 'fabric' which, as it first called for the emergence of law as a distinct normative phenomenon, constitutes the background conditioning the daily reconstruction of legal normativity. As I suggested before, I think legal normativity is best understood as a dynamic process which feeds itself out of the daily confrontation between legal requirements and other types of demands, including those of morality and prudence. When the individual, confronted with law's requirements, enters a practical reflection which leads her to dismiss law's demands as illegitimate (be it because they infringe upon some moral values she holds particularly dear, or because she considers law's requirements to be counter-productive in relation to some prudential concerns she deems important) she is contributing, however minimally, to changing the fabric from which law arises and against which it is tested. Even if the instances in which a person actually enters a practical reflection assessing law's claims are few, even if moral disobedience cases are relatively rare, these cases contribute, together with court cases and general public debate, to shaping some aspect of the social world we live in: the 'fabric' from which law's normativity continues to arise.[84]

5.2 Shaping the Law

In gathering the elements necessary to constructing my 'story of legal normativity', I have been hovering between functional analysis and history. The importance attributed, in my story, to the 1593 'turning point' — marking legal normativity's progressive detachment from the 'natural and divine order' traditionally grounding it — cannot be understood independently of my

---

[84] When a legal system for some reason loses touch with that social 'fabric', when moral disobedience cases multiply without triggering a change in the law, law's normativity is likely to 'perish' in the course of a political revolution, triggering the need to create a new legal order ' in touch' with this new social fabric.

interpretation of the various factors giving rise to legal normativity (what I have called the 'scenario'). Meant to encapsulate
the functional elements contributing to the emergence of law as
a normative phenomenon, my version of this 'scenario' encompasses not only instrumental concerns (remedying the defects of
a primary structure of social control), but also political and
moral concerns, incarnating what a particular society sees as a
better way of living together. Without this 'programmatic element', the scenario depicting the factors giving rise to legal normativity could do without history: changing attitudes towards
values do not as such affect law's instrumentality in remedying
the defects of a primitive structure of social control.

If the understanding of legal normativity has evolved through
the ages, it is because of the shifting status of the moral values
informing the emergence of a legal system: the values that were
once meant to get us closer to the way things are meant to be,
to the 'natural order of things', become the expression of the
way *we want things to be*. Such is, to put it briefly, the understanding of values that is opened up by the ongoing 'modern
revolution' I have depicted in the previous section. This new
way of thinking of values and our relationship to them presents
legal theory with a challenge: coming to terms with, and making sense of, the social contingency at the root of the values
shaping our concept of law.

5.2.1 What if we don't Care?

The challenge raised by this alternative, constructivist way of
thinking of values may be sidestepped. One may appeal to
some Neo-Kantian ideal of 'methodological purity' *à la* Kelsen,[85]
or one may invoke a 'legitimate fiction' *à la* Montaigne, conveniently rescuing law's normativity from its contingent beginnings thanks to a 'law of pure obedience'.[86] Among recent

[85] See section 2.1.1.
[86] See section 1.2.3.

sidestepping strategies, Coleman's careful avoidance of any meta-ethical issue in his theory is particularly relevant at this stage. As I have briefly mentioned in the previous section,[87] Coleman, unlike Raz, endeavours to account for law's normativity independently of any legitimacy considerations. Among others things, this endeavour leads him to assert the irrelevance of law's 'programmatic element' — the various ideals law may be called to promote — to his account of law. According to Coleman, the fact that 'law can realise some attractive ideals' is not necessarily part of our concept of law, in the same way as the fact that a hammer can bang nails into a wall is not necessarily part of our concept of hammer as 'after all, a hammer is the kind of thing that can be a murder weapon, a paperweight, or a commodity'.[88] Taken literally, Coleman's argument thus consists in invoking the infinite number of potential uses to which an object may be put to dismiss its aim as extraneous to our concept of that object. Now, if I ever had to explain the concept of hammer to a person who has never come across it, I think I would describe it as a tool for applying maximum force at a localised point thanks to the use of high density material. And if, in the process of explaining it, Coleman were to interrupt by pointing to the fact that a hammer can be used as a murder weapon, I would treat this remark as crude provocation. Maybe Coleman has never had to explain the concept of hammer to anybody. But he certainly has had to explain the concept of law. His account is structured around a clear-cut distinction between the project of accounting for what conditions the

---

[87] See above n 57.

[88] 'Let us grant that law does have the inherent potential to realise a variety of moral ideals that other forms of governance cannot realize, and that this distinguishes law from other forms of governance. Is this inherent potential really a part of our concept of law? [. . .] Law is the kind of thing that can realise some attractive ideals. That fact about law is not necessarily part of our concept of it. After all, a hammer is the kind of thing that can be a murder weapon, a paperweight, or a commodity [. . .] However, the fact that a thing, by its nature, has certain capacities or can be used for various projects does not entail that all or any of those capacities, ends, or projects are a part of our concept of that thing' (J Coleman 2001b, 194).

existence of law, on one hand, and that of 'making intelligible law's claim to make a practical difference in the lives of those to whom it applies',[89] on the other hand.

These two explanatory targets set out by Coleman have to connect at some point, and when they do, they form a peculiar story. Given the alleged irrelevance of what we want law for, Coleman's story becomes an account of how a bunch of people, jointly committed to respecting a set of criteria determining what counts as law, manage to create an obligation to respect and apply these criteria. One may of course ask why the officials commit themselves to that particular set of criteria, what their project is in so doing and whether, if at all, the rules that count as law actually have any impact on the 'non-official' part of the population. Significant as they may be, these questions — and the answers they may yield — are not, according to Coleman, a necessary part of our 'concept' of law.

1 The Difference Law Makes

I have briefly developed, in the previous section, Hart's and Raz's respective accounts of the practical difference thesis. Their divergence lies in the kind of impact law is supposed to have on our practical deliberations: while both maintain that law must be capable of providing content-independent reasons, Hart claims that these reasons are also meant to be *peremptory*, while Raz characterises these reasons as merely *pre-emptive* or exclusionary. Raz's account is particularly significant for our purposes, as it requires an account of practical deliberation that explicitly links legal normativity to other forms of normativity, including morality. Unlike Hart, Raz conditions law's obligatory character to its being deemed legitimate, and for him this legitimacy test involves considering whether or not law enables us to better comply with the various demands — including moral ones — that apply to us.

Coleman is uncomfortable with associating legitimacy considerations to the determination of law's normative character. Coleman does acknowledge that law's normative dimension

---

[89] J Coleman 2001a, 114.

involves more than just its capacity to provide reasons for action that 'figure' in our practical deliberation: these reasons for action must also, sometimes, be 'strong enough, or conclusive',[90] thus giving rise to an obligation. He, however, manages to steer away from introducing legitimacy considerations within his account of legal normativity by moderating the scope of the practical difference thesis:[91] while law must, as a whole, be capable of making a practical difference, this is not true of every single rule within the legal system. In order to work, a legal system must be able to impose an obligation on that part of the population entrusted with creating, interpreting and applying its rules. This specific part of the population, the 'officials', must indeed feel under a duty to respect the validity criteria set out in the Rule of Recognition if the legal system is to persist. As for the rest of the population, however, the law need not provide them with reasons for action, conclusive or otherwise: as long as it is capable of *informing* them of their various legal rights and duties, it is 'working'.[92] For Coleman, the task of explaining legal normativity thus comes down to accounting for the obligatory character of the Rule of Recognition for the officials.[93] To grasp the full significance of Coleman's strategy, let me turn to his other 'explanatory target': explaining what conditions the existence of law.

[90] J Coleman 2001b, 123.

[91] For a detailed account, see J Coleman 2001b, 144–148.

[92] Note the implausibility of a situation where the 'non-official' part of the population never even deliberates on law's claim to impose some obligatory form of conduct: a still unlikely, but more plausible, scenario would involve a persistent and generalised failure on the part of law to provide non-officials with reasons for action that are deemed 'strong enough', and thus obligatory. This scenario wouldn't suit Coleman, however, as it would re-introduce the necessity to include legitimacy considerations in one's account of legal normativity.

[93] As for the obligatory character of legal rules for the rest of the population, Coleman seems happy to leave this issue to those who worry about meta-ethics: 'Positivism seeks to show that the way in which law can give rise to duties is no more — *and no less* — mysterious than the way in which promises, pacts, reciprocal expectations, and so on can create duties. The ontology of the duties that inhabit this class of practices is not a *special* problem for legal theory, but is rather in the provenance of meta-ethics' (J Coleman 2001b, 159).

2 What Makes Law Possible

This 'branch' of jurisprudence should be more story-like, for it has to account for a process that is by definition evolutionary, taking one from a pre-legal to a legal society. The imagination of legal theorists tends to be fairly constricted, however, and instead of 'reasons' excluding or pre-empting each other, one hears of 'preferences' confronting and ultimately coordinating each other.

Legal theory owes this vocabulary to Lewis's *Convention: A Philosophical Study*,[94] published a few years after Hart's *Concept of Law*. Far from being initially aimed at legal theorists, Lewis's model was developed as an answer to Quine's argument, according to which one could not possibly talk of a conventional basis of language given that we never agree with one another to abide by these so-called 'language conventions'. Against this view, Lewis maintained that conventions are best understood as solutions to recurrent coordination problems, which emerge not in consequence of an agreement, but as a convenient alternative to such agreement. At the centre of Lewis's account thus lies the concept of a 'coordination problem'. It has been adapted and constructed in many ways, but the leading idea is that there are situations — coordination problems — in which it is instrumentally rational to coordinate one's action with those of others and in which it is more important that we coordinate than how or why we do so.

This idea inspired some legal theorists, who saw in this conventional model an answer to an issue raised by Hart's account of the Rule of Recognition as a 'social rule'. Hart defines the concept of 'social rule' by referring to two elements that, in his opinion, condition its existence: in order to have a social rule, there needs to be both a certain regularity of behaviour and some kind of reflective critical attitude towards that behaviour, which Hart also calls 'acceptance'. Unlike the regularity of behaviour, this reflective attitude need not characterise the whole population, and can be limited to the 'officials' of a legal system.

[94] DK Lewis 1963.

Hart's account was criticised on the ground that it does not explain what gives rise to the reflective attitude supposedly characterising part of the population. As Andrei Marmor puts it: 'There is simply nothing in the practice theory of rules to explain what kind of reasons people have for following a social rule [. . .] Simply pointing to the fact that there *is* a regularity of behaviour, which seems to be suggested by Hart as part of the reason for following a social rule, is clearly the wrong answer. It is only in special and unique circumstances that the reason for following a rule partly consists in the fact that others follow it too: namely in those cases where the rule in question is a social convention'.[95] In his Postscript to *The Concept of Law*, Hart explicitly endorses such a conventionalist interpretation, specifying that the Rule of Recognition is to be understood as a *social convention*: 'The theory remains as a faithful account of conventional social rules which include [. . .] the rule of recognition, which is in effect a form of judicial customary rule existing only if it is accepted and practised in the law-identifying and law-applying operations of the courts'.[96]

Instead of a story, conventionalism provides for the structural elements allowing the passage from a pre-legal to a legal society: remember Hart's emphasis on law's ability to improve a primitive structure of social control, thanks to the introduction of 'rules about rules' including, crucially, the Rule of Recognition. Lewis's account of 'coordination convention' can be taken to provide a clear framework explaining why, and how, a certain group of people — the officials — come to regard a certain set of validity criteria as authoritative, and hence organise their law-making and law-interpreting practices around these standards. Realising that they would be better off with a Rule of Recognition acknowledging one common set of validity criteria, the officials' respective sets of preferences are structured so as to ultimately favour a common solution over no solution at all.

---

[95] A Marmor 2001a, 197.
[96] HLA Hart 1994, 256.

Now, many objections have been raised against this coordination convention model.[97] I will concentrate on two problems raised by Andrei Marmor, as they seem to be at the root of Coleman's recent tack on the subject. First, Marmor emphasises that the concept of a coordination problem implies that, from the agents' own perspective, the choice between the alternative modes of conduct available to them is pretty much arbitrary, as indeed 'they would like to abide by whichever option secures uniformity of action among them'.[98] In the context of legal theory, such a conclusion does not seem easily compatible with the concept of the Rule of Recognition, as indeed 'the rules of recognition define what the law is in a given community, and this is clearly a matter of the utmost political importance. It matters a great deal to all of us who makes the law, and how it is to be enacted. Thinking of such rules of recognition in terms of arbitrariness would certainly strike most jurists and politically conscientious people as a crazy idea'.[99]

The second kind of problem underlined by Marmor raises the fact that the political choices which the fundamental rules of recognition embody 'are far more complex and manifold than the basic structure of a coordination problem'.[100] The meaning and rationale of some fundamental rules, such as those instantiating the federal structure of a state[101] seem to be missed completely if one tries to explain them as the solution to coordination problems. The construction of that kind of rule

---

[97] Underlining the 'thinness' of the concept of preference, Roger Shiner emphasises that, as a formal term, it requires no more than the mere ordinal ranking of states of affairs revealed in conduct. Any kind of consideration can thus theoretically lead to the adoption of a conventional rule of recognition (RA Shiner 1992, 239).

[98] A Marmor 2001a, 201.

[99] A Marmor 2001a, 201.

[100] A Marmor 2001a, 202.

[101] In the case of the United States, Marmor emphasises that indeed 'it was the more pressing political question of whether the emerging states should yield their political independence to a central government at all which generated the famous federalist compromise' (A Marmor 2001a, 202).

indeed relies on a series of political events and debates whose point far exceeds the simple need to coordinate the political power of the states and the federal government.

The strength of these objections is difficult to ignore, and today one would be hard pressed to find a legal theorist still accounting for the emergence of the Rule of Recognition in strict 'Nash equilibrium' terms. The most recent shift comes from Coleman, who now accounts for the context of social interaction allowing the emergence of the Rule of Recognition as a 'shared cooperative activity' ('SCA'). Developed by Michael Bratman,[102] the concept of SCA is supposed to encapsulate three essential features of those practices whose core commitment is to do something *together* (like playing a quartet): mutual responsiveness, commitment to the joint activity and commitment to mutual support. By contrast with those models explaining the emergence of a normative practice by reference to convergent unilateral acceptances of the norms constituting the practice, the SCA model emphasises the multilateral and interdependent character of the commitment at stake. This emphasis on interdependence is key,[103] according to Coleman, as it is what allows us to account for the capacity of conventional rules to impose *duties*.

This capacity has indeed been subject to debate, as some, like Marmor, have pointed out that the existence of a conventional social practice in itself does not provide anyone with an obligation to engage in that practice. While the fact of convergent behaviour coupled with a certain attitude towards it on the part of its participants may provide people with a reason to conform to or take part in a given practice, it cannot in itself be taken to

[102] M Bratman 1992.

[103] 'The notion of an SCA involves more than just a convergence of unilateral acceptances of the rule of recognition. It involves a joint *commitment* on the part of the participants to the activity governed by the rule of recognition [. . .] And there is no mystery (at least not one that a legal theorist is obliged to solve) about how joint commitments can give rise to obligations; in so far as such commitments induce reliance on a justified set of expectations (whether explicitly or not), they can give rise to obligations' (KE Himma 2002, 134).

obligate them. Two issues need to be distinguished here. In the context of accounting for the Rule of Recognition as a conventional rule, what concerns legal theorists is the possibility of characterising the officials' commitment to this Rule of Recognition as an *obligation*. If this commitment is understood as the result of a multitude of independent, unilateral acceptances of the Rule of Recognition's criteria, then the fact that this commitment can be unilaterally extinguished[104] by each official seems to stand in the way of its constituting an 'obligation'. Such is, at least, the kind of reasoning which leads Coleman to favour the SCA interpretation of the Rule of Recognition.

There is also a different, if related, issue raised by Marmor's scepticism: what about the capacity of the Rule of Recognition to be a source of duty for the population at large? As the layman's acknowledgement of the rules validated by the Rule of Recognition as binding is not, strictly speaking, necessary to the existence of a legal system, this question has not bothered legal theorists as much. As a 'meta-rule' setting the criteria determining which rules belong to a legal system, the Rule of Recognition can only be an indirect source of duty for the layman (unlike the official who has to apply and respect these criteria if the legal system is to persist). If, however, our aim is to account for what makes law possible, what conditions its existence as a social practice, one may consider the layman's attitude towards the law, his readiness to acknowledge law's claim to bind him, as an integral and necessary part of the story legal theory is meant to tell.

For law's overall success in giving rise to reasons for action that are deemed 'conclusive' by the non-official part of the population does matter. It matters, probably, to the officials in the process of 'jointly' committing themselves to the criteria

---

[104] 'If I can create a reason by adopting a pattern of behaviour as a norm, then it would seem that I can subsequently *extinguish* the reason that norm provides simply by withdrawing my commitment to it. Yet it is the nature of duties that those bound by them cannot voluntarily extinguish them as reasons' (J Coleman 2001b, 90).

determining what law is or is going to be in a given society. Beyond these criteria, it is a project the officials are committing themselves to, an ambition to structure a given society around a certain set of concerns or ideals.[105] If they do not want to count on sole force to sustain their authority, the officials are likely to want to 'sell' the project behind these criteria, and this marketing ambition is going to influence the criteria's content. Law's overall success in giving rise to obligations matters, also, in that its failure to do so can ultimately 'undo' a legal system: this is the 'efficiency' condition. The merit of this condition, in the present context, is to highlight the 'empty square' left in Coleman's account of what conditions the existence of a legal system.

The main asset of the SCA model, for Coleman, is its strict neutrality: here is a way of accounting for the duty-imposing character of the Rule of Recognition *independently* of its nature or content, by sole reference to the structure of the practice constituted by the officials' behaviour. But this practice does not exist for its own sake. A fundamental premise deserves more attention: 'Suppose it has been agreed that for some reason a legal system is a desirable thing'.[106] Detached from any teleological consideration, the SCA model doesn't do much in the way of accounting for what conditions the existence of law: structural conditions do not, on their own, 'bring about' anything.

Coleman does, of course, mention the various ends law may serve: 'they may include personal security, an efficient cooperative system of production and exchange, or the creation of conditions under which individuals can be responsible for the lives they lead'.[107] But he adds immediately: 'Any

---

[105] Disagreement among officials as to the exact nature and scope of the various ideals law is meant to serve is likely. What matters, however, is not so much substantial agreement as such but the possibility and existence of a continuous discussion and debate among officials (and, ideally, the rest of the population) as to the ideals and concerns law should serve or promote. They have to agree to — and be capable of — continuous discussion.

[106] J Coleman 2001b, 92.

[107] J Coleman 2001b, 101.

or all of these are possible functions of law, but none is necessary to the concept of law'. Formulated this way, one may
take Coleman's argument to merely point at the *diversity* of
the possible aims law may serve. But his argument is more
radical: he works to undermine the claim that there is something about the nature of law that calls for the legal theorist's
reference to 'norms of political morality'. One of the most
promising ways of grounding this claim is to point at law's
'inherent potential' to realise an attractive form of governance. Coleman thus acknowledges this potential, to better
dismiss it: in the same way as a hammer may be used as a
paperweight or as a murder weapon, so can law be used to
realise an attractive ideal of governance. 'However, the fact
that a thing, by its nature, has certain capacities or can be
used for various ends [. . .] does not entail that all or any of
those capacities, ends, or projects are a part of our concept of
that thing [. . .]'. So it would be up to us to demonstrate that
law's capacity to serve moral ideals is indeed part of our concept of it, and according to Coleman, no such demonstration
'appears to be forthcoming'.[108]

You may wonder what would count as a demonstration, in
Coleman's framework. On the basis of his definition of 'conceptual analysis', one may think that what is at stake amounts
to arguing that law's capacity to serve attractive moral ideals is
one of its 'most salient features', one that is 'central to our
understanding and appreciation'[109] of law. If so, then my
demonstration is easily provided: I do argue that law's capacity to promote and serve various ideals, involving both moral
and prudential concerns, is indeed central to our understanding and appreciation of law. As such, this teleological, 'programmatic' element cannot be left out of the picture, and must
be included in an account of what conditions the existence of

[108] J Coleman 2001b, 194.
[109] J Coleman 2001b, 179.

law. Now, I suspect Coleman was expecting something more spectacular or 'robust', when calling for a demonstration that law's capacity to serve moral ideals is part of our concept of law: would he call for such 'demonstration' were we to speak of promises instead of law?

How could we 'prove' that it is part of our concept of promises that they can be used to achieve moral goals, indeed that they often are an essential precondition of these moral goals being 'achievable'? Promises, like law, don't exist for their own sake. What they do — their capacity to bind — is concomitant, and to an extent dependent, on the purpose they serve. The practice of promising is made possible by the capacity we all share, as 'normative animals', to envisage a future structured around some concern or value we or those around us hold dear. When these concerns or values conflict, as they often do, our commitment to them is tested, and the concept of 'promise' gives voice to our capacity to give particular strength to some of our commitments. Similarly, our concept of 'law' also involves giving particular force to some commitments. Only, 'legal' commitments are generally made by a small number of people in the name of and for a much larger proportion of people. This is what calls for the important qualification which Raz introduces under the 'normal justification thesis'. One cannot explain law's normativity, its capacity to *bind* us, without including an account of practical deliberation, without referring to the possibility, and indeed the responsibility we all have, of assessing law's claim to bind us. This assessment, in turn, requires us to consider what we want law for: the values or purposes which are meant to warrant law's claim to impose some non-optional course of conduct upon us.

Coleman claims that he can account for law's normativity independently of legitimacy considerations. Concomitantly, he also claims that the aims law may serve, its capacity to promote important moral ideals, is extraneous to our concept of law. His account of law, his explanation of both its existence conditions and its normative dimension, consequently has to be reduced to a very short and limited story, telling us how a bunch of people, the officials, 'jointly' commit themselves to applying a set of criteria determining what law is. Because of the specific structure of their adherence to these criteria, the officials can effectively be said to be under an 'obligation' to comply with these criteria, and this is all that needs to be established to assert the existence of a legal system. As for the obligatory character of legal rules towards the rest of the population, this is a question which, according to Coleman, is best left to those willing to tackle the more general, 'mysterious' issue of 'the way in which promises, pacts, reciprocal expectations, and so on can create duties'.[110] The duty-imposing capacity of promises or law may, however, only owe this 'mysterious character' to the persevering trend of ignoring what they are for, the ideals or values which preside over their duty-imposing character. Raz puts it this way: '[B]oth [law and promising] are ways of creating obligations by acts intended to do so — a fact often regarded as so mysterious that it has led to most ingenious writings attempting to explain away the mystery. The Thomist type of explanation of authority helps here too. There is a good which binding promises can serve or achieve, and that is why they can be binding.'[111]

Raz's reference to a 'Thomist type of explanation' may look like it could comfort those positivists who see this emphasis on the moral ideal law is capable of promoting as an insidious move towards the natural law model. To avoid this kind of confusion, let me restate what is at stake in the turn towards a 'modern' understanding of legal normativity. The moral aims law and promising may serve are key to accounting for their

---

[110] 'Positivism seeks to show that the way in which law can give rise to duties is no more — *and no less* — mysterious than the way in which promises, pacts, reciprocal expectations, and so on can create duties. The ontology of the duties that inhabit this class of practices is not a *special* problem for legal theory, but is rather in the provenance of meta-ethics' (J Coleman 2001b, 159).

[111] J Raz 2003a, 10.

capacity to *bind* us:[112] this has always been so. What is brought about by the move to a 'modern' understanding of normativity concerns the *status* of the moral ideals law typically seeks to promote: instead of being deemed the instantiation or reflection of a 'natural order of things', these ideals become the expression of a different kind of order, one which *we* are in the constant process of reshaping, according to our evolving conception of what constitutes a good way of living together. From this perspective, emphasising law's capacity to serve moral ideals as one of its central features can be read as a 'natural law move' only if one presupposes that these ideals or values are necessarily the instantiation of a 'natural order of things', one that is 'somehow normative prior to any human choices'.[113] This is the key: this insistence on tracing the source of the values informing law-creating practices 'beyond' human activities, in some metaphysical sphere conveniently 'pre-existing' the mess of human affairs, seems to be one of the fundamental presuppositions underlying natural law theories.[114] If, by contrast, one takes the possibility of a constructivist understanding of values seriously, positivists may build an account of law that gives central stage to the moral ideals law is *capable* of promoting without fearing for the integrity of their position: law's capacity to promote moral ideals does not entail that law always or necessarily does so.

---

[112] The asymmetry between promising and law lies in the fact that, unlike promises, law aims to bind people whose agreement has never been sought. The success of this claim to bind the 'non-official' part of the population thus has to be made dependent on a practical deliberation, empowering the subject to assess law's normative claim in the light of his or her account of what constitutes a 'good' life, and this account will include an idea of what makes law a desirable form of governance.

[113] 'Though it too has a range of meanings, "natural" can be used to signify that some of those criteria or standards are somehow normative prior to any human choices' (J Finnis 2002, 1).

[114] Here I am not arguing that this realist understanding of values is a presupposition exclusive to natural law theories, as there are positivists out there who also defend (or, more likely, presuppose without defending) such a realist position. My aim is not to redefine the positivism/natural law divide, but rather to understand the challenge opened up by a constructivist understanding of values for legal theory, and I haven't so far come across any natural law theory which seems ready to take up that challenge.

Now, the question we need to tackle in order to conclude this section is: does Coleman's 'shrunken' account of what conditions the existence of law as a normative phenomenon work? I have already pointed out his theory's inability to account for the obligatory character of law for the 'non-official' part of the population, an issue which is left to the care of those interested in the more general meta-ethical issue of obligations. While this 'empty square' in Coleman's theory contributes to the general implausibility of his model, it is not, as such, devastating to his argument, which remains consistent on its own terms.[115]

If, however, one takes seriously the positivist ambition to promote moral criticism of the law, an ambition which Coleman's positivism must be assumed to share, one may begin to question the ability of this model to do just that. If the moral ideals law is able to promote are supposed to be 'extraneous' to our concept of law, if one is supposed to account for law's normative character independently of legitimacy considerations, it is not clear where one is supposed to find the basis for such moral evaluation. In the same way as one will evaluate the quality of a knife by reference to its ability to cut (this is what it is for, and part of our concept of it), one cannot evaluate law without reference to what one takes it to be for. If, as Raz puts it, law has a 'moral task', it is to be evaluated in the light of that task.[116] If, by contrast, law's inherent ability to promote some moral

---

[115] By characterising Coleman's model as 'implausible', I mean to point to the fact that it is not able to account for some of the features I take to be central to the existence of a legal system (such as the fact that law's normative character is constantly 'reconstructed' in a process involving the assessment of its legitimacy — see previous discussion). As Coleman defines these features as unessential or 'extraneous' to his concept of law, one can say that his argument remains consistent on its own terms.

[116] 'The claim that law has, by its nature, a specific moral task, is nevertheless an important claim, as it sets the way in which we should think about the law. It sets a critical perspective for judging it. Just as we do not fully understand what chairs are without knowing that they are meant to sit on, and judged (*inter alia*) by how well they serve that function so, the claim is, we do not fully understand what law is unless we understand that it has a certain task, and is to be judged (*inter alia*) by how well it performs it.' (J Raz 2003a, 12).

ideals is taken to be 'accidental' or extraneous to our concept of law, one is left with the only teleological element in Coleman's account: law's ability to improve a primitive structure of social control.

Evaluation of law would have to proceed on the basis of a series of criteria deemed to underlie a 'working' structure of social control, such as those put forward by Raz in his formal analysis of the rule of law. According to that approach, a legal system is 'good' at what it is meant to do — guiding conduct through publicly ascertainable standards — if it complies with a series of principles ensuring that laws are prospective, clear, relatively stable, etc. Compliance with these principles may turn a legal system into a 'better' structure of social control but it cannot on its own warrant a positive evaluation of that legal system. Confronted with a legal system such as that of fascist Italy for instance, a positivist who is committed to dismissing the moral ambitions of law as irrelevant is faced with an equally unattractive alternative: he can either congratulate those Italian officials for their exemplary scrupulousness in making sure that the rules they passed were indeed prospective, clear, publicly available, etc; or he can forego any evaluation attempt and argue that such evaluation is to remain the job of those 'equipped' for it (because moral ambitions are still a central part of their concept of law), that is moral philosophers, sociologists, political theorists and the like.

Avoiding such an 'evaluative impasse' and accounting for the moral ambitions conditioning the evaluation of any legal system demands one fundamental philosophical commitment from positivism: coming to terms with the implications of social contingency for the values informing our law-creating practices. Coleman's theory is clearly not eager to take up this commitment. Having set himself two explanatory targets accounting for our concept of law (the existence conditions of law and the practical difference it makes), Coleman proceeds to show that he can account for these two 'targets' without involving any reference to legitimacy considerations. Considered on its own terms, Coleman's theory 'works', but there is a limit to what one can ask of it: inquire about law's capacity to bind the non-official part of the population or raise the possibility of morally *evaluating* a legal system, and your question will be dismissed as irrelevant or non-essential to our concept of law.

Question the theory's starting point, on the other hand, and dispute the pertinence of dividing one's account of law into two distinct explanatory targets (accounting respectively for law's existence and its normativity), and you get a different story. My genealogy aims at accounting for the context of social interaction conditioning and enabling law's normativity. As such, it does not 'start with the law and ask what room it makes for morality',[117] to take Raz's way of putting it. So far, my story has proved to work the other way round: considering the social 'fabric' underlying and conditioning the emergence of law as a normative phenomenon, it asks what triggers the need for law as a distinct form of governance. Typically, instrumental considerations (such as remedying the defects of a primary structure of social control) are complemented with important moral concerns. The possibility of accounting for these moral values in constructivist terms (opened up by what I have called the 'modern' revolution) allows legal theory to account for law's moral ambitions without endorsing the kind of metaphysical commitment underlying natural law theories. The same moral concerns that were once deemed to instantiate a 'natural' order, an order conveniently removed from human contingency, can be thought to flow from that same contingency without for all that losing any claim to objectivity. For this is what bothers those legal theorists who, like Finnis, point at the 'peril' flowing from a genealogical approach to legal normativity: stripping moral values of their transcendent metaphysical status would leave our legal practices in desperate need of some objective norm presiding over our otherwise arbitrary desires or preferences.

---

[117] J Raz 2004, 2.

This quest for objectivity pervades our legal practices, whether it be in the process of creating a new legal system or in the course of maintaining it: the judge who has to refer to moral values in order to decide a case will worry about their objectivity in the same way as revolutionary lawmakers will worry about the objectivity of the values presiding over their lawmaking endeavour. Among the available answers to this concern for the objectivity of moral values, one can isolate two broad options. Lawmakers may either refer to some metaphysical object or non-natural property (such as Moore's concept of 'the good') that is somehow supposed to guarantee or 'stand behind' the objectivity of their moral values, thus yielding to a form of 'Platonising', to take Putnam's words.[118] Or they may renounce the comfort of realist guarantees and resolve to build an account of objectivity on the basis of their own intersubjective endeavour to formulate a project that is deemed legitimate by a pluralist society.

5.2.2 Why we Care, and How this Changes the Task of Lawmaking

Confronted with Preuss's depressing account of the '*unbridgeable discrepancy* between a people's power to erect a polity and its intellectual and moral abilities to satisfy the responsibilities which this *unlimited power* involves',[119] I asked in section 5.1.3 whether this typically modern wariness towards our lawmaking capacities could be due to a gradual change in the character of the task at hand. Has the task of lawmaking gradually acquired a 'holy' quality which would ultimately have made the gap between it and our pitiful human abilities unbridgeable indeed? This hypothesis was meant to be provocative, and relate the issue of lawmaking to the way we conceive of our relationship to God or some transcendent order.

---

[118] 'What yields to "Platonizing" is yielding to the temptation to find mysterious entities which somehow guarantee or stand behind correct judgements of the reasonable and the unreasonable' (H Putnam 2004, 70).

[119] UK Preuss 1995, 7 (emphasis added).

There was a time when law could not be deemed legitimate, and hence binding, unless it was perceived as a fair approximation of a 'natural order of things', which itself was supposed to be connected to (while remaining distinct from) the 'divine order'. The 1593 coup turned the Thomist account of the relation between positive law and the natural and divine order upside down: by 'institutionalising' the presence of God at the foundation of law, the *Politiques*' strategy actually ended up freeing law's normativity from its traditional dependence upon a theological framework. Fortified by this new-found normative inviolability, law's bindingness was able to be asserted *without* any reference to the 'natural order of things' traditionally conditioning it. This normative autonomy in turn engendered an enduring anxiety: robbed of its link to transcendence, positive law is still meant to be normative and impose its demands over us, when all it can count on in terms of authority is us, with our fallible, fallen human natures. Echoed in Montaigne's 'Laws are often made by fools, [. . .] but always by men, *vain authorities* who can resolve nothing',[120] this anxiety was at the root of Montaigne's reference to a '[divine] law of pure obedience', enjoining men to obey the law 'because it is the law' without asking any further question. Later taken up by Kant and Rousseau,[121] the 'remedy' consists in relying on a 'legitimate fiction' — it is '*as if [law] must have arisen not from men but from some highest, flawless lawgiver*'[122] — to 'patch up' what otherwise looks like the hopelessly deficient (given its contingent beginnings) authority of law.

The need for such remedy, the need to invoke some 'highest, flawless lawgiver' as a surrogate source of legal normativity relies on the presupposition that law's new-found 'inviolability' (its not being conditioned by a 'natural and divine order') must be matched by some infallible source, asking for some flawless, foolproof lawgiver: a requirement which humans, no matter how

---

[120] M de Montaigne 1991, III 13, 1216 (emphasis added).
[121] See section 1.2.3.
[122] I Kant 1991, §49 A, 130 (emphasis added).

virtuous, are not likely to meet. This emphasis on law's 'inviolability' may, however, only be the sign of a perduring difficulty to come to grips with the implications of a new, 'modern' understanding of value. If the 1593 coup allows for the progressive detachment of law's normativity from the 'natural and divine order' traditionally grounding it, it still does not imply that law's normativity is hence supposed to emerge *ex nihilo*. While it used to find its root in a 'natural' order eluding human ascendency, legal normativity may now arise out of a different kind of order, an order which we are in the constant process of reconstructing. Instead of being conditioned by Nature or by God's will, law's normativity is thus conditioned by a different, immanent kind of order, and in this sense is no more 'inviolable' than in pre-Modern times: it is up to us, citizens, judges, or lawmakers, to question or assess law's bindingness, and this requires us to know what *we* want law for (instead of pointing at the way things are meant to be).

Taking up the challenge introduced by a constructivist understanding of morality is demanding and, judging by some legal theorists, 'perilous' as well. In my sense, two broad issues need to be addressed if moral constructivism is to be able to play the role I want it to play in legal theory.

1 Defending the Possibility of Ethical Objectivity

First, to say what we want to say in ethics generally, but also more particularly in legal theory, we need ethical objectivity. Ethical objectivity not only conditions the possibility of assessing a legal system by moral standards, it also underlies the possibility of rationally solving practical dilemmas involving legal standards. Ethical objectivity, in other words, is needed not only to make sense of evaluative statements about the kind of social world we live in (law being part of that social world, a 'piece of furniture' within our social habitation); it also underlies any attempt to answer 'rationally',[123] that is, in a way that is open to

123 See above n 67 in section 4.3.1.

argumentation, the practical dilemma involving legal standards. When an agent asks: 'how should I live, how should I find my way around this social world, with all the various and often conflicting demands it involves?', one needs to be able to think that one's answer is not merely reflecting individual preferences if there is to be any room for argumentation (as opposed to various forms of persuasion).

Doubts about the possibility of ethical objectivity have plagued many legal theorists, including, most prominently, Herbert Hart himself. His scepticism lives on in many contemporary authors including, most recently, Jeremy Waldron. From the perspective of the present work, Waldron's position is particularly interesting, as it explicitly links the 'implausibility' of ethical objectivism to its alleged irrelevance for legal theory, a link which is otherwise left implicit in other theories dismissing the relevance of meta-ethics for law. Briefly put, his argument amounts to a negative answer to the following question: if we were to establish the possibility of ethical objectivity, would it appease the concerns of those opposing 'the contamination of legal decision by moral judgement'?[124] According to Waldron, 'moral decision-making in law is likely to be as arbitrary (in all three senses I mentioned) for a *moral realist* as it is for any opponent of *moral objectivity*'.[125] As this arbitrariness (spelled out as unpredictability, irrationality and democratic illegitimacy) is precisely what fuels the concerns of those wary of ethical reasoning in judicial decision-making, the possibility of ethical objectivity makes no difference to legal thought. Or so the argument goes.

Notice, first, the conflation of moral realism and ethical objectivism, which Waldron treats as interchangeable terms, in a trend typical of 'objectivity sceptics'. For Waldron does not just treat the possibility of ethical objectivity as a putative hypothesis demanding his theoretical neutrality. Waldron's scepticism about ethical

---

[124] J Waldron 1999, 167.
[125] J Waldron 1999, 170 (emphasis added).

objectivity is based on the belief that objectivity presupposes a sort of descriptivism, that the possibility of assessing an ethical judgement as objectively true requires there being some 'object' out there backing up this claim to objective truth. Now, Waldron argues, even if there were such moral 'objects' hanging out there, as the moral realists would have us believe, we do not seem to have any reliable access to them. For if we did, if we had a method allowing us to track these moral 'objects', then surely we would not be faced with the intractable disagreements plaguing contemporary ethical issues (or at least moral realists would be noticeable by their remarkable agreement on such issues).[126] Given the absence of 'an epistemology or a method with which these disagreements might in principle be approached',[127] moral realism cannot alleviate the fears of those wary of the arbitrariness that would flow from any form of 'judicial moralising': 'either we have the arbitrariness of taking one attitude over others equally eligible [moral emotivism/expressivism], or we have the arbitrariness of taking one belief over others equally eligible [the realists' beliefs about moral facts]'.[128] Here, again, notice the slip from moral objectivism to moral realism (which I have allowed for the sake of following Waldron's argument). Waldron's asserted goal was to demonstrate the irrelevance of ethical objectivity to legal thought: he concludes by showing the irrelevance of moral realism instead, without feeling apologetic about it; let me recapitulate why he should be.

---

[126] 'Given what morality is and what it is for (given the sort of fact it must be, if it is a matter of fact), how could there be objective truth and falsity certified by the way the world is, and yet so much disagreement?' (J Waldron 1999, 177).

[127] Here Waldron draws a dubious comparison with scientific enquiry: 'our conception of reality in science is associated with the whole complex apparatus of method, heuristic, observation, and experimentation. We know how to proceed in the face of disagreement. There is nothing equivalent in morals, nothing that even begins to connect the idea of there being a fact of the matter with the idea of there being some way to proceed when people disagree' (J Waldron 1999, 178).

[128] J Waldron 1999, 186.

— Asserting the possibility of ethical objectivity amounts to maintaining that there is a way of rationally solving disagreements in ethics.

— Ethical cognitivism supports the idea that moral propositions are truth-apt.

— Moral realism, for its part, is one way of explaining *why* moral propositions may have truth values: 'moral realism, then, is the view that propositions employing moral concepts may have truth values because moral concepts describe or refer to normative entities or facts that exist independently of those concepts themselves'.[129] Moral realism asks us to believe in the existence of some 'moral facts' or 'intrinsically normative entities' existing independently of our attitude or judgement. It is an ontological thesis which boasts to hold *the* key to accounting for the truth or falsity of moral judgements (and hence, it maintains, conditioning the possibility of ethical objectivity as well). This supposedly necessary link between the possibility of ethical objectivity and there being some 'facts of the matter' backing up this objectivity claim is what keeps moral realism in business. It relies on a 'totally mistaken line of thought' which Hilary Putnam traces all the way back to a common interpretation of Plato: 'As it is very often interpreted, Plato's theory of Ideas represents an early appearance of two persistent philosophical ideas: the idea that if a claim is objectively true, then there have to be *objects* to which the claim "corresponds" — an idea which is built into the very etymology of the word "objective" — and the corollary idea that if there are no obvious natural objects whose properties would make the claim true, then there must be some *non-natural* objects to play the role of "truth-maker". [. . .] Accept these two ideas, and you are likely to accept a third, the idea that if a claim is true, then the claim is a *description* of whatever objects and properties make it true'.[130]

[129] CM Korsgaard 2003b, 100.
[130] H Putnam 2004, 52.

How, then, can there be 'objectivity without objects'? In my view, three elements are essential to developing a constructivist account of ethical objectivity. I can only mention the first one, for it relates to the need to question, and ultimately provide an alternative to, the 'correspondence theory of truth', as it underlies the idea that a statement can be deemed 'objectively true' only if it corresponds to some independent object.[131]

We also need to consider carefully the possibilities opened up by so-called 'discourse ethics'. As one of its most prominent representatives, Habermas seeks to reconcile what he calls 'epistemological realism and moral constructivism',[132] defending the possibility of ethical objectivity while rejecting realist metaphysics. His demonstration (like Hare's[133]) hinges upon the principle of universalisability.[134] Roughly put, his argument runs as follows: when we put forward arguments in the course of a discussion, we cannot help making various validity-claims to truth, normative rightness, etc. These validity-claims in turn call for, or point at, an ideal speech situation freed from all sorts of constraints, guaranteeing that only the force of the better argument prevails. Putting forward the universalisability principle as a test for the 'validity' of normative statements is an attempt to enact this ideal speech situation. Objectivity, from this viewpoint, can be thought

---

[131] For such alternative theory of truth, see notably C Wright's emphasis on 'superassertibility', as 'durable satisfaction of the discourse's internal disciplinary constraints': 'To think of a discourse as dealing with truth-apt contents, accordingly, need involve, when truth is conceived as superassertibility, no work for a type of idea which is absolutely central to traditional realist thinking: the idea of *correspondence*, of representation of real, external states of affairs.' (C Wright 1996, 10–11).

[132] J Habermas 2003, 65 (my translation). For a brilliant analysis of the tension between realist and antirealist elements in Habermas's discourse ethics, see C Lafont 2004.

[133] See section 4.3.1. For those who still consider Hare as a non-cognitivist, see 'Since I myself think both that moral statements can be true or false, and that we can know them to be true or false, I get extremely cross when people classify me as a non-cognitivist' (RM Hare 1999a, 4).

[134] 'Every valid norm must satisfy the condition that all affected can accept the consequences and the side effects its general observance can be anticipated to have for the satisfaction of everyone's interests (and these consequences are preferred to those of known alternative possibilities)' (J Habermas 1990, 65).

of as the result of the effort we all need to make in order to *reach out* to other people in the course of a discussion, and convince them *rationally* (rather than persuade them through force) of the 'validity' of our normative claim, of the merits of our judgement. Objectivity thus conceived comes with no 'guarantee'. But do we want any? Yielding to 'Platonising', as Putnam calls it, positing supposedly independent 'moral facts' backing up our claim to objectivity, can only provide short-lived comfort: when a disagreement arises,[135] these 'moral facts' will be of little help in its resolution. What is more likely to help, by contrast, is the unavoidable background of substantial agreement conditioning and enabling any 'local' disagreement on a particular issue. Rather than a threat or unavoidable nuisance, ethical disagreements provide a healthy reminder of what ethics is really about: instead of a body of statements systematically tracking some independent truths it would be our business to 'discover', ethics is first and foremost a discipline aimed at solving practical problems. 'How should I live?' is the question ethics aims to answer, and the certainties provided by 'ethical knowledge'[136] are not necessarily helpful.

'If ethical conviction is not to be identified with knowledge or certainty, what is it?'[137] If we are to be 'convinced' that this moral judgement, as opposed to another, is correct, what is supposed to be the source of our conviction, if it is not the comforting knowledge of some 'moral fact' existing independently of our beliefs or attitudes?[138] For Williams, 'confidence' is the answer, and it is the third element I deem essential to a constructivist account of ethical objectivity. 'Confidence' is not

---

[135] Whether or not that disagreement involves moral realists only.

[136] As Bernard Williams puts it: 'Ethical knowledge, though there is such a thing, is not necessarily the best ethical state. Here we must remember that, in the process of losing ethical knowledge, we may gain knowledge of other kinds, about human nature, history, what the world is actually like. [. . .] But those traditionalists and those liberals share the error of thinking that what conviction in ethical life has to be is knowledge, that it must be a mode of certainty' (B Williams 1985, 168–9).

[137] B Williams 1985, 169.

[138] We could, of course, talk of knowledge of 'contingent' moral facts, understood as the body of beliefs and attitudes in a given society at a given time. The question can also be raised, then, of whether the knowledge of such 'contingent'

only opposed to knowledge, it is also contrasted with the existentialist account of ethical conviction as emerging out of a radical, unprecedented 'decision' (see below). Confidence is never 'guaranteed'. It can be, and often is, fostered by a whole set of social factors, including a culture that promotes and encourages widespread discussion on ethical issues. In this context, the way we conceive of law, its lawmaking procedures and, crucially, the judges' adjudication task, will have a significant impact on fostering a climate of confidence. The widespread belief that 'judicial moralising' (enabling the judges to sometimes take into account moral values, when their consideration is not excluded by legislation[139]) is necessarily detrimental to the citizens' need for trust in social and legal institutions is misguided. Judicial argumentation can play a key part in relaying and augmenting a public debate about important ethical or societal issues, and to that extent is vital to fostering the 'confidence' needed if a constructivist account of ethical objectivity is to gain in credibility (as such, judicial argumentation could be said to be both conditioned by and conditioning — in the sense of contributing to — the possibility of a constructivist account of objectivity).

2 Avoiding the Existentialist Solitude Trap

Recall the reluctance of Hungarian lawyers and politicians to qualify their endeavour as a 'revolution'. They could not, it was felt, assume the unbearable burden of a 'completely new beginning'. Overthrowing the existing legal order and setting up a new legal system would put these lawyers and politicians in a situation of 'normative break', calling for a project legitimising the rupture with the previous regime in the name of some political or ideological 'vision'. To be perceived as legitimate, this vision would have to appeal to moral values. How could

moral facts can be the source of ethical conviction, to take Williams' words. While it may contribute to forming one's conviction, I do not think such knowledge can or should be the 'sole' source of ethical conviction. A further step has to be taken. It can be called 'confidence'. Whatever it is, it comes from the individual's own critical assessment of the contingent moral facts surrounding her.

[139] See below my discussion of Raz.

these values have the weight they need, and ground the revolutionaries' authority, if they are perceived as the contingent reflection of the lawmakers' fragmented preferences? Hungarian lawmakers needed to believe in the possible objectivity of the moral values presiding over the legitimisation endeavour associated with the creation of a new legal regime. The expedients traditionally used by revolutionary lawmakers — counting on the name of God as the ultimate 'guarantee[or]' or relying on an all-encompassing concept of 'Nation' — lacked credibility. In this context, preserving legal continuity (even if that meant thoroughly amending the old constitution) seemed a convenient and 'lower-cost' alternative to facing the perplexities and, it was feared, the *aporia* concomitant to 'constructing' a new normative order from the ground up.

One proviso: I am not claiming, or even trying, to give an historically and politically accurate picture of the 1989 events in Hungary. I am aware that many other factors (including the wariness towards the concept of revolution and the defiance towards law as a tool for social change induced by the Soviet experience) are likely to account for the decision to proceed with a series of amendments rather than creating a new legal system. My pushing and 'exploiting' one — possibly marginal — reason contributing to the decision to preserve legal continuity is meant to explore the impact of a meta-ethical difficulty in the process of lawmaking. A revolutionary situation is indeed particularly conducive to falling for one of the underlying 'traps' of moral constructivism. In its natural propensity to emphasise the break with the previous regime, the revolutionary rhetoric tends to induce the belief that the revolutionaries' action is radically unprecedented, that the choices and decisions they make emerge out of 'normative nothingness' (to refer, once again, to Schmitt's vocabulary). This belief may be perceived as an amusing form of romanticism reaching its most comic expression in the French decision to create a new calendar. It is not, however, harmless. In encouraging the trend to dismiss any reference to previous moral and political experiences, the romantic emphasis on the unprecedented character of revolutionary lawmaking actually provides for the subsequent need to invoke the name of God or some other form of meta-referent in order to 'stand in' for what otherwise looks like the hopelessly contingent source of legal normativity: what Finnis would refer to as 'the supposedly will-like sub-rational drives and compulsions of domination, submission, resentment, and so forth'.[140]

Finnis is right to emphasise the aporetic character of any conception of normativity that would conceive of legal norms and values in general as emerging '*ex nihilo*', out of the *fiat* of human will. This is what I call 'the existentialist trap'. When Sartre 'remind[s] man that there is no legislator but himself; that he himself, thus *abandoned*, must decide for himself',[141] he gives easy ground to people like Finnis or MacIntyre, eager to reduce moral constructivism to an extreme form of empty voluntarism.[142] Yet one may wonder if even Sartre himself felt comfortable with the implications of this 'extreme voluntarism': if it really meant the possibility of doing whatever one pleases, if it meant choosing among various options from a situation of so-called normative vacuum, where one is bound by nothing but one's own impulses, then it is hard to understand what exactly triggers the overwhelming feeling of anxiety, the *Nausea* which Sartre associates with the discovery of one's freedom. If, on the other hand, the freedom to be discovered is one where the dismissal of the classic meta-referents such as God or Nature actually confronts the individual with the silent demands of her past, then the challenge that is at hand becomes apparent.

The difficulty underlying moral constructivism, from this perspective, does not so much consist in requiring the individual to find heroically within the solitary confines of her own will

---

[140] J Finnis 2002, 8.

[141] J-P Sartre 1973, 55–56 (emphasis added).

[142] 'If the epistemologically justified view were that affirmed by Weber, all human acts and institutions would be afflicted with *radical arbitrariness* [. . .] For if the positive rules of a legal-rational order rest on nothing more that other rules likewise posited by sheer acts of will, the *uncritical arbitrariness* of ascribing authority to all/any of those rules is undisguised' (J Finnis 1985, 90, emphasis added).

the resources necessary to bring about moral values. Instead of heroism, moral constructivism may require both humility and confidence, as what is at stake is the constant (re)building of a moral framework on the basis of and from a prior fabric of social and moral expectations. It requires humility, because the 'construction' of moral values involves an ongoing confrontation with previous moral experiences and other, contemporary moral agents. It also requires confidence, in that the moral agent has to develop the poise necessary to question an existing moral framework and assert her own moral convictions.

Suppose, then, that having succeeded in conceiving of the values presiding over their project as *objective*, and having done so with characteristic humility, trusting to find within their intersubjective experience the resources necessary to building the 'secular faith' needed for these values to be perceived as legitimate, my 'revolutionary lawmakers' proceed to writing a constitution. What difference will it make, you may ask, whether they conceived of this objectivity on the basis of constructivist or realist premisses? Ethical objectivity is what is needed: whether it is 'rooted' in some queer metaphysical objects or in our own intersubjective experiences does not seem, at first sight, to affect the fabric of the law. On this view, the 'modern revolution' I previously described may all sound very dramatic, asking us to introduce value in the world rather than discovering it there 'ready-made', but it does not, as such, affect the nature of law.

This could be true if law's normative dimension only needed to be 'brought about' in revolutionary circumstances. If the lawmakers' concern for the objectivity of moral values was only the product of a temporary and contingent situation, limited to the provisional, transitional process needed to construct a new legal order and *establish* its normativity, one could indeed dismiss the dilemma opened by the constructivist or realist routes to objectivity as irrelevant to legal theory. Law's normativity is never *established* once and for all, however. Emerging out of the confrontation with moral demands, prudential considerations, etc., legal normativity is to be constantly reasserted. Each time an individual is led to assess law's normative claims in the light of morality's demands, each time a judge is led to re-articulate what we want law for: these cases contribute to shaping the 'fabric' enabling law's normativity. These efforts of assessment and articulation depend, in turn, on our conception of normative agency: assert the need to track the truth of ethical judgements to some independent moral 'facts' conditioning their objectivity, and you will get a different understanding of what it is we are doing when we dispute law's authority in the name of moral values. Tracing the truth of moral judgements back to our own social practices rather than conditioning it to their accurately tracking some independent entities not only affects the *nature* of disagreement; it also dramatically increases our responsibility when, as lawmakers, judges, or citizens, we 'take the law into our own hands' and confront it with our moral expectations.

Maybe the task of lawmaking *has* changed then. Maybe the 'modern revolution', introducing a new possible way of thinking of values, has actually contributed to changing our understanding of our role as legislators, judges or citizens. This change is facultative in many ways. For a start, the new, constructivist way of accounting for our moral values may not be embraced. Those lucky enough to 'believe' in the existence of intrinsically normative entities hanging out there may not see the point of renouncing their metaphysical comfort to embrace what is, after all, a 'frustrating' position, offering no remedy to our existential uncertainties but the necessity to discuss them. The 'constructively redefined' task of lawmaking may also be simply *rebuffed*. The endeavour to have one's 'lawmaking project' perceived as legitimate without invoking any 'moral fact' or 'intrinsically normative entity' conveniently backing up its claim to objectivity may sound daunting to efficiency-driven lawmakers. Why embark on a revolutionary project when one can avoid all the perplexities associated with it by merely preserving legal continuity, even if that means extensively amending the previous legal structure? This line of reasoning may have influenced the Hungarian decision to proceed with a series of amendments of the old communist constitution rather than creating a new one.

Is this for all that the 'end of the story'? If it is, it would be rather bad news for the larger story I have to tell. The point of my genealogical story, remember, is to account for the context of social interaction enabling the emergence (and maintenance) of legal normativity. My emphasis on the '1593 turn', highlighting legal normativity's progressive detachment from the 'natural and divine order' traditionally grounding it, was meant to point at a significant change in the understanding of what conditions law's normativity: instead of having to be *derived* from a higher order eluding human ascendency, legal normativity is hence meant to be *brought about* by us, morally short-sighted human beings. From this perspective, the apparent Hungarian refusal to do just that, preferring to maintain legal continuity rather than *bring about* legal normativity, could be read as yet another dramatic 'turn', marking the end of the illusions underlying the 'modern' ambition to assert our responsibility as lawmakers.[143] It could also, more reasonably, be read as the expression of a contingent, historically charged wariness of and lack of confidence towards the task of lawmaking, induced by years of Soviet occupation. Whether in Hungary or elsewhere, legal normativity continues to be 'brought about' on a daily basis: apart from the obvious legislating activities, legal normativity is also shaped and conditioned by the judges' and citizens' daily endeavour to articulate 'what we want law for', the ideals and values conditioning law's legitimacy.

So the story continues: let me relate its contemporary version.

Articulating Values

In my attempt to define the concept of normativity as it applies to law, I was led to pinpoint two different 'levels' at which one

---

[143] This hypothetical turn would mark the victory of those delighting in highlighting the *aporia* constitutive of our existence as social beings, trying to *bind* ourselves through legal rules despite the contingency plaguing our normative choices. In this vein, see J Derrida 1986.

may pitch one's definition of legal normativity.[144] Distinguishing between law's capacity to guide behaviour and law's ability to give rise to obligations, I argued that our account of legal normativity takes shape in the endeavour to articulate the 'gap' between these two levels. When are the reasons provided by law strong enough to give rise to an obligation? If one is to leave any room for the ideal of civic responsibility, the answer has to be framed in terms of moral legitimacy: law's claim to bind us, to impose an obligation upon us, succeeds if it is perceived as legitimate, if it is deemed to promote the ideals or values we want law to foster. Raz's way of articulating this idea lies in the 'normal justification thesis': law is deemed legitimate, and hence binding, if its 'shortcut solution' to the complex balancing of all the reasons that apply to an individual actually enables her to comply with the demands of 'right reason'.

On this view, then, one cannot account for law's normativity just by pointing to its ability to provide reasons that are capable of figuring in one's practical deliberation. For if those reasons were never strong enough to give rise to an obligation, if law's claim to bind us was always defeated by other demands, whether of a moral or prudential kind, there would be a sense of unease in still considering law as normative, and perhaps in still considering it as law *tout court*. It may be tempting, from this perspective, to equate the concepts of obligation and normativity: law is normative if it succeeds in imposing an obligation upon us. The downside of pitching one's definition of legal normativity this high, however, is that either it endangers the possibility and relevance of morally assessing the law, or it presupposes that law may only be intermittently normative (ie that whenever it fails in its claim to impose an obligation over us, it ceases to be normative).

Rather than 'pitching' one's definition of legal normativity at either one of these two levels (guidance or obligation), I suggested in section 5.1.3 that we may be better off conceiving of law's normativity as a *dynamic* concept taking its shape and

---

[144] See section 5.1.3.

meaning out of the confrontation with the concerns that first triggered its emergence, that is, the demands of morality and prudence. Once confronted with these demands, the reasons provided by law may sometimes, on balance, fail to give rise to an obligation. Far from robbing law of its normative force, one may consider every challenge to law's legitimacy as an opportunity to reshape the fabric of moral and social expectations conditioning and defining law's normative dimension (provided, of course, that law's institutional structure remains flexible enough to be able to integrate expressions of dissent).

The classic example here is that of the English doctor deciding to turn off her patient's life-support machine out of what she deems to be her moral duty to respect the dignity of her patient, even if she is aware that in doing so she is acting illegally. Law's claim to bind her fails, in this instance, in the face of a moral value she holds particularly dear. She may be vocal about her conviction that law should help preserve human dignity, even if it sometimes contravenes the sanctity of life, another fundamental value law should preserve. She may voice her concerns publicly, triggering a debate as to which values law should promote, and to what extent. When she appears in court, the jury may be aware of the debate she has triggered. It may decide to charge her symbolically while reducing the sentence to a minimum, calling for the legislative body to introduce new legislation, adapting to the population's changing attitude towards the need to preserve human dignity through death.

This euthanasia example is one way to illustrate how civic disobedience, in challenging law's claim to bind us, can contribute to keeping legal normativity 'alive', so to speak, in touch with the material that first triggered its emergence — the changing demands of morality and prudence. One of the other major forums contributing to renewing and reshaping the 'fabric' enabling law's normativity is provided by the judge's need to sometimes decide cases on the basis of moral principles.

It may be that a question lacks a legal answer. In *Riggs v Palmer*, a murderer was stopped from inheriting under his victim's will, despite the fact that neither statute nor case law contained any provision to that effect. One could argue that this was a situation that had not been foreseen by legislators, which, as such, required the judge to rely on a moral principle — no one should profit from one's own wrong — to avoid what would otherwise have been perceived as an injustice. Now, the question which was famously raised by Dworkin in relation to this case is: can this moral principle be considered 'legally valid', despite the fact that it is neither authorised by a higher norm nor defined as valid by the criteria determining what counts as law?[145] Dworkin's question has given rise to a lengthy debate that is still very much at the centre stage of contemporary jurisprudence.

There are those who, like Hart, reacted by emphasising that 'the rule of recognition may incorporate as criteria of legal validity conformity with moral principles or substantive values'.[146] This position has given rise to what is known as the 'incorporation thesis'. Others, like Raz, preferred to answer Dworkin's challenge by pointing out that, although moral principles can and sometimes should be taken into account by judges, they cannot be deemed 'legally valid' in that they are not made legal by pre-existing validity criteria. Consequently, when courts apply such principles, they 'inevitably break new (legal) ground and their decision develops the law'.[147] Much of this debate thus hinges upon what may be considered a legal technicality: are moral standards susceptible of being 'turned into law' or are they 'standards binding according to law' but not themselves incorporated in the law?[148] This debate does not, in itself, contribute much to the story I have to tell. One of the issues that has arisen in the course of this debate is, however, directly related to one of the central difficulties I have identified in the endeavour to 'construct' legal normativity.

---

[145] R Dworkin 1977, 41.
[146] HLA Hart 1994, 250.
[147] J Raz 1979, 49–50.
[148] J Raz 2004, 12.

If moral principles are to influence judicial decision-making, they have to have an 'objective content'; they have to refer to values which can themselves be deemed objective: 'a nonobjective norm cannot constrain judicial behavior because what that norm means is purely a matter of what the judge believes it means'.[149] Dworkin argues that a commitment to ethical objectivity is problematic for those positivists committed to the 'incorporation thesis'.[150] The basis of his argument is flawed: as Himma has shown, it relies on a distorted interpretation of both the separability thesis and the social fact thesis.[151]

If ethical objectivism is at all problematic for positivism (whether of the 'inclusive' or 'exclusive' kind) it is, I argue, in virtue of the widespread assumption that ethical objectivity presupposes a moral realist position. Keen to avoid the 'unwanted ontological lumber'[152] associated with moral realism, a lot of legal positivists endeavour to dissociate their theory from any commitment to ethical objectivity because of this (mistaken) assumption. From this perspective, Hart famously asserts his readiness to 'drop' his claim that the Rule of Recognition can include moral values were ethical objectivity proven to be impossible: '[I]f it is an open question whether moral principles and values have objective standing, it must also be an open question whether "soft positivists" provisions purporting to include conformity with them among the tests for existing law can have that effect, or instead, can only constitute directions to courts to *make* law in accordance with morality'.[153]

Now, the problem underlying Hart's characteristically uncommitted position is that it assumes that ethical objectivity need only be a concern to those positivists maintaining that moral principles can be part of the criteria determining what law is: drop this 'incorporation thesis' and maintain instead that

---

[149] KE Himma 1999, 416.
[150] See R Dworkin 1977, 348–349.
[151] For further discussion see K Himma 1999, 426.
[152] M Kramer 1999, 194.
[153] HLA Hart 1994, 254.

moral principles are binding standards directing the judge 'to make law in accordance with morality', and you can leave your concerns about objectivity behind. On this view, as long as morality is not potentially 'incorporable' within the legal corpus, the possibility of its claiming an objective status need not bother lawyers. This claim is odd. It could make sense if morality was meant to apply to law if and only if incorporated within the legal corpus. Nobody, however, goes as far as arguing for such a stringent separation of law and morality.

As one of the prominent voices rejecting the incorporation thesis, Joseph Raz actually reverses the way in which the debate is often framed: instead of wondering about 'the room law makes for morality',[154] Raz endeavours to focus instead on 'whether morality, which applies to all humans simply because they are humans, has room for the law. How can morality accommodate the law within it?'.[155] From this perspective, morality applies to judges as a matter of course: 'they would not be subject to the law were they not subject to morality', as indeed 'man-made legal duties bind their subjects only if moral principles of legitimacy make them so binding'.[156] If references to morality are sometimes excluded from the judges' consideration, it is in virtue of law's modulating role: 'the law modifies rather than excludes the way moral considerations apply and, in doing so, advances, all things considered, moral concerns rather than undermines them'.[157] Remember Raz's 'service conception' of legal authority: law may be deemed legitimate, and hence binding, if it provides a good 'shortcut solution' to the balancing of the various moral and prudential demands applying to an individual. Because of the lawmakers' 'moral expertise', or because of their better perspective on the need to secure coordinated conduct, law may contribute to furthering moral aims

[154] J Raz 2004, 2.
[155] J Raz 2004, 7.
[156] J Raz 2004, 6.
[157] J Raz 2004, 9.

by excluding judicial reference to moral considerations. Alternatively, the lawmakers may also sometimes feel the need to delegate consideration of the impact of specific moral values upon legislated standards to the courts. In doing so, they are not, according to Raz, 'incorporating' moral standards into the law, but rather indicating that 'certain considerations are not excluded' from judicial deliberation.[158]

If morality applies *anyway*, if we are all, courts included, 'bound by it even before its incorporation',[159] if we are bound by morality even before law modulates its possible consideration by the courts, then should we not concern ourselves with the possibility of ethical objectivity independently of the side one chooses in the inclusive/exclusive positivism debate? What is at stake is the possibility of *rationally solving* an ethical disagreement. When a judge is made to refer to moral considerations to reach her decision, she will want to think that these considerations do not merely reflect her own preferences; she will need to be confident in her capacity to argue for the relevance of these considerations and rationally convince the parties to the case and the population at large of their merits. Conversely, 'the population at large' will need to be able to take issue with the values invoked in order to argue about the judge's decision and incorporate it within a wider debate about what that particular society wants law for.

For this is, ultimately, the 'fabric' which legal normativity is made of: it arises from, and is made possible by, a society's endeavour to define a certain set of concerns or values which it is committed to promoting through law. In a pluralist society, the task of articulating such a set of values will require a con-

---

[158] 'The courts cannot gainsay the legislation and set it aside because they think that a better standard should be endorsed. The legislation bars them from doing so. It in effect excludes their access to the moral considerations on which the legislator should have relied in passing the act. But they can supplement or modify the standard set by the act in light of the nonexcluded considerations.' (J Raz 2004, 14).

[159] J Raz 2004, 17.

stant process of discussion and re-elaboration. This process in turn can only make sense against the background of ethical objectivity. If we were to lose our confidence in the possibility of solving ethical disagreements through rational argumentation, we had better stop fooling ourselves in believing that law's point is to promote a certain way of living together (a way which, in a democratic society, is meant to be picked *intersubjectively* rather than imposed unilaterally).[160]

Seen from such a disillusioned perspective, law would have to be considered as one set of requirements existing alongside those of morality or prudence, for instance. When these different kinds of requirements conflict, as they often do, the individual would be torn between wholly independent points of view. Take the euthanasia example: in that case, the doctor's decision to turn off the life-supporting machine (to comply with what she deems to be her moral duty) could not have any impact or significance for the future development of law. From this perspective, debating about the conflicting values at stake in the issue of euthanasia would be pointless, as it would be reducible to the expression of conflicting personal preferences not themselves susceptible to rational argumentation.

If, by contrast, one understands law as a set of standards whose aim is to facilitate a way of living together structured around both moral and prudential concerns, accounting for these legal standards as a wholly autonomous and independent set remaining unaffected by expressions of moral dissent seems ludicrous. Those arguing that nothing of importance in their theory turns on the objectivity or non-objectivity of moral norms effectively deny themselves the possibility of accounting for the different ways in which practical dilemmas involving moral and legal standards contribute to 'constructing' legal normativity. The two examples I have developed point at two ways

---

[160] Someone like Jules Coleman may argue that law's capacity to promote moral ideals has never been part of our 'concept of law' anyway. On this basis, the possibility of ethical objectivity may indeed be dismissed as irrelevant, but this comes at a price: forego the possibility of morally assessing a legal system, and confine your explanation of legal normativity to its impact on officials only.

in which such a process of construction can take place: civic disobedience on one hand, and judicial moralising on the other; add to this the activity of legislators, be they revolutionary or otherwise, and more generally any endeavour to critically assess law's authority. All of these 'forums' may be deemed to contribute to shaping the fabric conditioning law's normativity *if* one presupposes the possibility of ethical objectivity.

This objectivity issue has been called back to the attention of legal positivists in the context of the inclusive/exclusive positivism debate thanks to Dworkin. Dworkin's framing his question in terms of validity — 'can this moral principle be considered legally valid?' — however, allowed the debate to be focused upon the problem of the boundaries of the law, thus perpetuating legal positivism's unfortunate trend to 'start with the law and ask what room it makes for morality'.[161] This strategy may have allowed legal positivists to entertain the comforting illusion that they need not tackle the meta-ethical perplexities underlying the possibility of ethical objectivity. It also underlies their enduring difficulty in developing a satisfactory account of legal normativity.

[161] J Raz 2004, 2.

6
Conclusion

Arising out of the ambition to question the normative dimension of law instead of taking it for granted, my story began by considering how Montaigne inaugurated a trend that has pervaded legal positivism ever since. This trend consists in separating, rather than combining, law's social and normative aspects into two distinct explanatory targets. The existence of law is accounted for by reference to some conventional framework of interaction. Law's normativity is explained in terms of the difference it makes in individual practical deliberation: this explanation presupposes the possibility of legal normativity. It proceeds from the assumption that law is indeed normative to then consider how this manifests itself.

Yet law's normative dimension is not a 'property' that is somehow mysteriously attached to law. Law's power to bind us is concomitant to the project we want it to serve. Each time this project is reformulated, confronted with the demands of morality or prudence, law's normativity is concomitantly 'brought about'.

This allows my story to be short. Its historical dimension is meant to emphasise the progressive turn to a new possible way of thinking of moral values. Instead of being discovered 'ready-made' in the world, value may have to be introduced into the world by us, morally short-sighted human beings. This metaphysical revolution in turn confronts legal thinking with an enduring problem: how can law bind us, if all it can count on in terms of authority is us, with our fallible, fallen human natures? This problem, theoretically formulated by Montaigne, was allowed to emerge in the 'real' world of politics thanks, in part, to the Paris Parliament's decision of 28 June 1593. By considering the devolution law as the direct expression of God's will and the foundation of all the other laws, the *Politiques* ended up *incorporating* a divine foundation within the legal corpus. As the divine origin of this fundamental law was gradually 'forgotten', the legal order was allowed to develop its autonomy from the natural and divine order traditionally grounding it. It is from the background of this new-found normative autonomy that the issue of the status of the moral values presiding over our lawmaking endeavours emerged.

Legal normativity is brought about on a daily basis. Whether it be in revolutionary circumstances or in the quotidian need for judges, lawmakers or citizens to confront law's demands with those of morality or prudence, our ability to bind ourselves through law ultimately depends on our capacity to articulate a better way of living together, and to commit ourselves to it. These efforts of assessment and articulation depend, in turn, on our conception of normative agency: assert the need to track the truth of ethical judgements to some independent moral 'facts' conditioning their objectivity, and you will get a different understanding of what it is we are doing when we dispute law's authority in the name of moral values. Tracing the truth of moral judgements back to our own social practices not only affects the *nature* of disagreement; it also dramatically increases our responsibility when, as lawmakers, judges, or citizens, we 'take the law into our own hands' and confront it with our moral expectations.

'Legal philosophers have always been tempted by a crazy dream: to mark the law in force within human societies with the alleviating seal of transcendence and to make it escape the arbitrariness and harrowing loneliness of human volitions. Hence the idea of a law already there independently of us, a law of divine origin present in nature or natural law'.[1] This 'crazy dream' will only truly stop tempting legal philosophers once they accept the need to delve into the status of morality, and trust to find within 'human volitions' the resources necessary to constructing value judgements as objective. Instead of warding off the context of social interaction enabling law's normativity for fear of its 'harrowing arbitrariness', legal philosophers may then rediscover the joys of story-telling.

---

[1] P Amselek 1994, 9 (my translation).

Bibliography

Amselek, P (1994) *Théorie du droit et science* (Paris, PUF).

Arendt, H (1990) *On Revolution* (London, Penguin Books).

—— (1998) *The Human Condition* (Chicago, IL, The University of Chicago Press).

Auroux, S (1990) 'Origine', in S Auroux (ed), *Les notions philosophiques: dictionnaire, Volume 2, 1833–34* (Paris, PUF).

Badiou, A (1989) *Manifeste pour la philosophie* (Paris, Seuil).

Berns, T (2000) *Violence de la loi à la Renaissance: l'originaire du politique chez Machiavel et Montaigne* (Paris, Kimé).

Bindreiter, UU (2001) 'Presupposing the Basic Norm' 14 *Ratio Juris* 143–175.

Blackburn, S (1993) *Essays on Quasi-Realism* (Oxford, Oxford University Press).

—— (1998) *Ruling Passions* (Oxford, Clarendon Press).

Bratman, M (1992) 'Shared Cooperative Activity' 101 *Philosophical Review* 327–341.

Broome, J (2004) 'Reasons', in RJ Wallace (ed), *Reason and Value: Themes from the Moral Philosophy of Joseph Raz* (Oxford, Clarendon Press), 28–55.

Bulygin, E (1998) 'An antinomy in Kelsen's Pure Theory of Law', in SL Paulson and BL. Paulson (eds), *Normativity and Norms, Critical Perspectives on Kelsenian Themes* (Oxford, Clarendon Press), chapter 16, 297–316.

Caldwell, PC (1997) *Popular Sovereignty and the Crisis of German Constitutional Law: the Theory and Practice of Weimar Constitutionalism* (Durham, NC, Duke University Press).

Carrino, A (1998) 'Reflections on Legal Science, Law and Power', in SL Paulson and BL Paulson (eds) *Normativity and Norms, Critical Perspectives on Kelsenian Themes* (Oxford, Clarendon Press), chapter 27, 507–522.

Celano, B (2000) 'Kelsen's Concept of the Authority of Law' 19 *Law and Philosophy* 173–199.

Cohen, GA (1996) 'Reason, Humanity, and the Moral Law', in CM Korsgaard (ed) *The Sources of Normativity* (Cambridge, Cambridge University Press), 167–188.

Coleman, J (2001a) 'Incorporationism, Conventionality, and the Practical Difference Thesis', in J Coleman (ed), *Hart's Postscript, Essays on the Postscript to the Concept of Law* (Oxford, Oxford University Press), 99–147.

—— (2001b) *The Practice of Principle: In Defence of a Pragmatist Approach to Legal Theory* (Oxford, Oxford University Press).

Couzens-Hoy, D (1994) 'Nietzsche, Hume, and the Genealogical Method', in R Schacht (ed), *Nietzsche, Genealogy, Morality: Essays on Nietzsche's Genealogy of Morals* (Berkeley, Los Angeles, London, University of California Press), chapter 14, 251–268.

Dancy, J (2000) *Normativity* (Oxford, Blackwell).

de Certeau (1982) *La Fable Mystique*, volume 1 (Paris: Gallimard).

—— (1992) *The Mystic Fable*, volume 1 (Chicago, IL/London, University of Chicago Press).

de Montaigne, M (1965) *Essais* (Paris, Gallimard).

—— (1991) *The Complete Essays* (trans MA Screech) (London, Penguin).

Delacroix, S (2005) 'Schmitt's Critique of Kelsenian Normativism' 18 *Ratio Juris* 30–45.

Derrida, J (1986) 'Declarations of Independence' 15 *New Political Science* 7–15.

—— (1992) 'Force of Law: The Mystical Foundation of Authority', in D Cornell and M Rosenfeld (eds), *Deconstruction and the Possibility of Justice* (New York, NY/London, Routledge), 3–67.

Dworkin, R (1977) *Taking Rights Seriously* (Cambridge, MA, Harvard University Press).

Dyzenhaus, D (1997) *Legality and Legitimacy* (Oxford, Oxford University Press).

Finnis, J (1973) 'Revolutions and the Continuity of Law', in A Simpson (ed), *Oxford Essays in Jurisprudence*, second series (Oxford, Clarendon Press).

—— (1985) 'On Positivism and Legal Rational Authority' 5 *Oxford Journal of Legal Studies* 74–90.

—— (1996) 'The truth in Legal Positivism', in RP George (ed), *The Autonomy of Law: Essays on Legal Positivism* (Oxford, Oxford

University Press), 195–214.

—— (2002) 'Natural Law: The Classical Tradition', in J Coleman and S Shapiro (eds), *The Oxford Handbook of Jurisprudence and Philosophy of Law* (Oxford, Oxford University Press), 1–60.

Geuss, R (1994) 'Nietzsche and Genealogy' 2 *European Journal of Philosophy* 274–292.

Geuss, R (2002) 'Genealogy as Critique' 10 *European Journal of Philosophy* 211–215.

Gilmore, M (1941) *Argument from Roman Law in Political Thought* (Cambridge, MA, Harvard University Press).

Habermas, J (1990) *Moral Consciousness and Communicative Action* (Cambridge, MA, MIT Press).

—— (2003) *L' éthique de la discussion et la question de la verité* (Paris, Grasset).

Hammer, S (1998) 'A Neo-Kantian Theory of Knowledge in Kelsen's Pure Theory of Law?', in SL Paulson and BL Paulson (eds), *Normativity and Norms, Critical Perspectives on Kelsenian Themes* (Oxford, Clarendon Press), chapter 9, 177–194.

Hare, RM (1981) *Moral Thinking: Its Levels, Method, and Point* (Oxford, Oxford University Press).

—— (1999a) 'Objective Prescriptions', in *Objective Prescriptions and Other Essays* (Oxford, Clarendon Press), chapter 1, 1–18.

—— (1999b) 'Prescriptivism', in *Objective Prescriptions and Other Essays*' (Oxford, Clarendon Press) chapter 2, 20–27.

Hart, HLA (1982) *Essays on Bentham: Studies in Jurisprudence and Political Philosophy* (Oxford, Clarendon Press).

—— (1983) *Essays in Jurisprudence and Philosophy* (Oxford, Clarendon Press).

—— (1994) *The Concept of Law* (2nd edn) (Oxford, Clarendon Press).

Hill, RK (1998) 'Genealogy', in E Craig (ed), *Routledge Encyclopedia of Philosophy*, volume 4 (London/New York, NY, Routledge), 1–5.

Himma, KE (1999) 'Incorporationism and the Objectivity of Moral Norms' 5 *Legal Theory*, 415–434.

—— (2002) 'Inclusive Legal Positivism', in J Coleman and S Shapiro (eds), *The Oxford Handbook of Jurisprudence and Legal Philosophy* (Oxford, Oxford University Press).

Homer (1951) *The Iliad* (Chicago, IL, The Universitiy of Chicago Press).

Jacobson, AJ and Schlink B (2000) *Weimar: A Jurisprudence of Crisis* (Berkeley, Los Angeles, CA/London, University of California

Bibliography

Press).

Jellinek, G (1979) *System der subjektiven öffentlichen Rechte* (2nd edn) (Aalen, Scientia).

Kant, I (1991) *The Methaphysics of Morals* (Cambridge, Cambridge University Press).

—— (1997) *Prolegomena to any Future Metaphysics* (trans G Hatfield) (Cambridge, Cambridge University Press).

Kelley, DR (1984) *History, Law and the Human Sciences: Medieval and Renaissance Perspectives* (London, Variorum Reprints).

Kelsen, H (1911) *Hautprobleme der Staatsrechtslehre* (Tübingen, JCB Mohr).

—— (1914) 'Reichsgesetz und Landesgesetz nach österreichischer Verfassung' 32 *Archiv des öffentlichen Rechts* 202–245.

—— (1925) *Allgemeine Staatslehre* (Berlin, Julius Springer).

—— (1949a) *General Theory of Law and State* (Cambridge, MA, Harvard University Press).

—— (1949b) 'Philosophical Foundations of Natural Law Theory and Legal Positivism', in *General Theory of Law and State* (Cambridge, MA, Harvard University Press), 389–446.

—— (1960) *Das Problem der Souveränität und die Theorie des Völkerrechts* (Aalen, Scientia).

—— (1967) *Pure Theory of Law* (Berkeley, CA, Los Angeles, University of California Press).

—— (1971a) 'Law, State and Justice in the Pure Theory of Law', in *What is Justice?* (Berkeley, Los Angeles, CA/London, University of California Press), 288–352.

—— (1971b) 'Value Judgments in the Science of Law', in *What is Justice? Justice, Law and Politics in the Mirror of Science* (Berkeley, Los Angeles, CA/London, University of California Press), 209–230.

—— (1986) 'The Function of a Constitution', in R Tur and W Twining (eds), *Essays on Kelsen* (Oxford, Clarendon Press), 109–119.

—— (1991) *General Theory of Norms* (Oxford, Clarendon Press).

—— (1992) *Introduction to the Problems of Legal Theory* (trans BL Paulson and SL Paulson) (Oxford, Clarendon Press).

—— (1998a) '"Foreword" to Main Problems in the Theory of Public Law', in SL Paulson and BL Paulson (eds), *Normativity and Norms, Critical Perspectives on Kelsenian Themes* (Oxford, Clarendon), 3–22.

—— (1998b) 'The Pure Theory of Law, "Labandism", and Neo-

Kantianism. A Letter to Renato Treves', in SL Paulson and BL Paulson (eds), *Normativitiy and Norms, Critical Perspectives on Kelsenian Themes* (Oxford, Clarendon Press), 169–175.

Kervégan, JF (1995a) 'La critique schmittienne du normativisme Kelsénien' in CM Herrera (ed), *Le droit, le politique: autour de Max Weber, Hans Kelsen, Carl Schmitt* (Paris, L'Harmattan), 229–241.

—— (1995b) 'L'enjeu d'une "théologie politique": Carl Schmitt' 100 *Revue de Métaphysique et de Morale*, 201–220.

Korsgaard, CM (1996) *The Sources of Normativity* (Cambridge, Cambridge University Press).

—— (2003a) 'Internalism and the Sources of Normativity: An interview with Christine M Korsgaard', in H Pauer-Studer (ed), *Constructions of Practical Reason: Interviews on Moral and Political Philosophy* (Stanford, Stanford University Press), 50–69.

—— (2003b) 'Realism and Constructivism in Twentieth Century Moral Philosophy' in *Philosophy in America at the Turn of the Century* (Charlottsville, The Philosophy Documentation Center), 99–122.

Kramer, M (1999) 'Coming to Grips with the Law: In Defense of Positive Legal Positivism' 5(2) *Legal Theory* 171–200.

—— (2000) 'How Moral Principles Enter into the Law' 6 *Legal Theory* 83–108.

—— (2002) 'Throwing Light on the Role of Moral Principles in the Law: Further Reflections' 8(1) *Legal Theory* 115–143.

—— (2004) 'On the Moral Status of the Rule of Law' 63 *Cambridge Law Journal* 65–97.

Kronman, AT (1983) '*Max Weber* (London, Arnold).

Lafont, C (2004) 'Moral Objectivity and Reasonable Argument: can Realism be Reconciled with Kantian Constructivism?' 17 *Ratio Juris* 27– 51.

Lauterpacht, H (1933) 'Kelsen's Pure Theory of Law' in WI Jennings (ed), *Modern Theories of Law* (London, Oxford University Press), 105–138.

Leiminger, K (1967) *Die Problematik der Reinen Rechtslehre* (Vienna, Springer).

Lewis, DK (1963) *Convention: A Philosophical Study* (Cambridge MA, Harvard University Press).

Marmor, A (2001a) 'Legal Conventionalism' in J Coleman (ed) *Hart's Postscript, Essays on the Postscript to the Concept of Law*, 193–217

(Oxford, Oxford University Press).

—— (2001b) *Positive Law and Objective Values* (Oxford, Oxford University Press).

Mian, E (2002) 'The Curious Case of Exclusionary Reasons' 15 *Canadian Journal of Law and Jurisprudence* 99–124.

Nagel, T (1986) *The View from Nowhere* (Oxford, Oxford University Press).

Nietzsche, F (1994) *On the Genealogy of Morality* (Cambridge, Cambridge University Press).

Nussbaum, M (1995) 'Aristotle on Human Nature and the Foundations of Ethics' in J Altham and R Harrison (eds), *World, Mind, and Ethics* (Cambridge, Cambridge University Press), 86–131.

O'Neill, O (2000) *Bounds of Justice* (Cambridge, Cambridge University Press).

Ost, F and M van de Kerchove (1985) 'La référence à Dieu dans la théorie pure du droit de Hans Kelsen' in *Qu'est-ce que Dieu? Philosophie/théologie. Hommage à l'abbé Daniel Coppieters de Gibson (1929–1983)* (Bruxelles, Publications des Facultés universitaires Saint-Louis), 285–324.

Paulson, SL (1992a) 'Kelsen without Kant', in W Krawietz and G von Wright (eds), *Öffentliche oder private Moral? Vom Geltungsgrunde und der Legitimität des Rechts. Festschrift für Ernesto Garzon Valdés* (Berlin, Duncker Humblot), 153–162.

—— (1992b) 'The neo-Kantian dimension of Kelsen's Pure Theory of Law' 12 *Oxford Journal of Legal Studies* 311–332.

—— (1993) 'Continental Normativism and its British Counterpart: How Different are They?' 6 *Ratio Juris* 227–244.

—— (1998a) 'Four Phases in Hans Kelsen's Legal Theory? Reflections on a Periodization' 18 *Oxford Journal of Legal Studies* 153–166.

—— (1998b) 'Hans Kelsen's Earliest Legal Theory: Critical constructivism', in SL Paulson and BL Paulson (eds), *Normativity and Norms: Critical Perspectives on Kelsenian Themes* (Oxford, Clarendon Press), 23–43.

—— (1998c) 'Introduction' in SL Paulson and BL Paulson (eds), *Normativity and Norms: Critical Perspectives on Kelsenian Themes* (Oxford, Clarendon Press), xxiii–liii.

—— (2000a) 'On the Puzzle Surrounding Hans Kelsen's Basic Norm' 13 *Ratio Juris* 279–293.

—— (2000b) 'On Transcendental Arguments, Their Recasting in Terms of Belief, and the Ensuing Transformation of Kelsen's

Pure Theory of Law' 75 *Notre Dame Law Review* 1775–1796.

Paulson, SL (2001) 'Hans Kelsen's Doctrine of Imputation' 14 *Ratio Iuris* 47–63.

Perry, SR (2001) 'Hart's Methodological Positivism', in J Coleman (ed) *Hart's Postscript, Essays on the Postscript to the Concept of Law* (Oxford, Oxford University Press), 311–354.

Preuss, UK (1995) *Constitutional Revolution: The Link Between Constitutionalism and Progress* (Atlantic Highland, NJ, Humanities Press).

Putnam, H (2004) *Ethics Without Ontology* (Cambridge MA, Harvard University Press).

Raz, J (1979) *The Authority of Law* (Oxford, Clarendon Press).

—— (1980) *The Concept of a Legal System* (2nd ed) (Oxford, Clarendon Press).

—— (1986) *The Morality of Freedom* (Oxford, Clarendon Press).

—— (1989) 'Facing up: A Reply' 62 *Southern California Law Review* 1153.

—— (1990) *Practical Reason and Norms* (rev ed, with postscript) (Princeton, NJ, Princeton University Press).

—— (1998) 'The Purity of the Pure Theory' in SL Paulson and BL Paulson (eds), *Normativity and Norms: Critical Perspectives on Kelsenian Themes* (Oxford, Clarendon Press), chapter 12, 237–252.

—— (1999) *Engaging Reason* (Oxford, Oxford University Press).

—— (2001) 'Two Views of the Nature of the Theory of Law, A Partial Comparison', in J Coleman (ed), *Hart's Postscript, Essays on the Postscript to the Concept of Law* (Oxford, Oxford University Press), 1–37.

—— (2003a) 'About Morality and the Nature of Law,' 48 *American Journal of Jurisprudence* 1–15.

—— (2003b) *The Practice of Value* (Oxford, Clarendon Press).

—— (2004) 'Incorporation By Law' 10 *Legal Theory* 1–17.

Renoux-Zagamé, MF (2003) *Du droit de Dieu au droit de l'homme* (Paris, PUF).

Rosen, M (1985) 'Classical Sociology and the Law,' 5 *Oxford Journal of Legal Studies* 61–73.

Rousseau, JJ (1997) '*The Social Contract and Other Later Political Writings*' (Cambridge, Cambridge University Press).

Saar, M (2002) 'Genealogy and Subjectivity' 10 *European Journal of Philosophy* 231–245.

Bibliography

Sartre, J-P (1973) *Existentialism and Humanism* (London, Methuen).

Schmid, K (2004) 'In the Name of God? The Problem of Religious or Non-Religious Preambles to State Constitutions in Post-Atheistic Contexts' 24 *Religion in Eastern Europe* 19–32.

Schmitt, C (1928) *Verfassungslehre* (Munchen and Leipzig, Duncker Humblot).

—— (1934) *Uber die drei Arten des rechtswissenschaftlichen Denkens* (Hamburg, Hanseatische Verlagsanstalt).

—— (2004) *On the Three Types of Juristic Thought* (trans JW Bendersky) (Westport, CN/London, Praeger).

Shapiro, SJ (2001) 'Hart's Way Out', in J Coleman (ed), *Hart's Postscript, Essays on the Postscript to the Concept of Law* (Oxford, Oxford University Press), 149–191 .

Shiner, RA (1992) *Norm and Nature, the Movements of Legal Thought* (Oxford, Clarendon Press).

Starobinski, J (1985) *Montaigne in Motion* (Chicago, IL/London, The Universitiy of Chicago Press).

Stone, J (1963) 'Mystery and Mystique in the Basic Norm' 26 *Modern Law Review* 34–50.

Strauss, L (1953) *Natural Right and History* (Chicago, IL, The University of Chicago Press).

Tasioulas, J (2002) 'The Legal Relevance of Ethical Objectivity' 47 *American Journal of Jurisprudence* 211–254.

Tournon, A (2000) *Montaigne: la glose et l'essai* (Paris, Champion).

Valdes, EG (1998) 'Two Models of Legal Validity: Hans Kelsen and Francisco Suarez', in SL Paulson and BL Paulson (eds), *Normativity and Norms, Critical Perspectives on Kelsenian Themes* (Oxford, Clarendon Press), chapter 14, 263–272.

VanRoermund, B (2000) 'Authority and Authorisation' 19 *Law and philosophy* 201–222.

Virvidakis, S (1996) *La Robustesse du Bien: Essai sur le réalisme moral* (Nîmes, Editions Jacqueline Chambon).

Waldron, J (1999) *Law and Disagreement* (Oxford, Oxford University Press).

Williams, B (1985) *Ethics and the Limits of Philosophy* (London, Fontana Masterguides).

—— (1995) 'Saint Just's Illusion', in *Making Sense of Humanity and Other Philosophical Papers 1982–1993* (Cambridge, Cambridge University Press).

—— (2000) 'Naturalism and Genealogy' in E Harcourt (ed) *Morality, Reflection and Ideology* (Oxford, Oxford University Press),

148–161.

—— (2002) *Truth and Truthfulness: An Essay in Genealogy* (Princeton, NJ/Oxford, Princeton University Press).

Williams, B (2003) 'Relativism, History, and the Existence of Values' in RJ Wallace (ed), *The Practice of Value*, 106–118 (Oxford, Clarendon Press).

Wilson, A (1982) 'Joseph Raz on Kelsen's Basic Norm' 27 *The American Journal of Jurisprudence* 46–63.

Wittgenstein, L (1981) *Tractatus logico-philosophicus* (trans CK Ogden) (London/New York, NY, Routledge).

Wright, C (1996) 'Truth in Ethics' in B Hooker (ed), *Truth in Ethics*, 1–18 (Oxford, Blackwell).

Index

Index